The Politics of
American Education

Education is fundamentally political in nature. Turning his distinctive analytical lens to the politics of American education, Joel Spring looks at contemporary educational policy issues from theoretical, practical, and historical perspectives. This comprehensive overview documents and explains who influences educational policy and how, bringing to life the realities of schooling in the twenty-first century and revealing the ongoing ideological struggles at play.

Ranging from a theoretical discussion of the political nature of American education to the nitty-gritty practicalities and complexities of political control at all levels—local, district, state, and federal—*The Politics of American Education* is timely and useful for understanding the big picture and the micro-level intricacies of the multiple forces at work in controlling U.S. public schools. Joel Spring's insightful approach to exploring the politics of education is both unique and essential.

Features:

- Analyzes the role of media and politicians in shaping public discussions about education
- Emphasizes the relationship between political parties' agendas and the political structure of American schooling
- Focuses on the political uses of schools
- Demonstrates the influence of business, the educational industry, teachers unions, ideological and religious interest groups and foundations, professional education organizations, and colleges and departments of education on the politics of education
- Examines the influence of global organizations on American school policies
- Reports and analyzes the emergence of open-source and other forms of electronic textbooks vis-à-vis their growing impact on the politics of education

Thought-provoking, lucid, original in its conceptual framework, and rich with engaging examples from the real world, this is the text of choice for any course that covers or addresses the politics of American education.

Companion Website: The interactive Companion Website (www.routledge.com/textbooks/9780415884402) accompanying this text includes relevant data, public domain documents, YouTube links, links to websites representing political organizations and interest groups involved in education, and a forum for discussion of the book's proposed amendment to the U.S. Constitution.

Joel Spring is Professor of Education, Queens College and the Graduate Center of the City University of New York.

Sociocultural, Political, and Historical Studies in Education

Joel Spring, Editor

For additional information on titles in the Sociocultural, Political, and Historical Studies in Education series visit **www.routledge.com/education**

The Politics of
American Education

Joel Spring

Queens College and Graduate Center
City University of New York

Routledge
Taylor & Francis Group

NEW YORK AND LONDON

First published 2011
by Routledge
270 Madison Avenue, New York, NY 10016

Simultaneously published in the UK
by Routledge
2 Park Square, Milton Park, Abingdon, Oxon OX14 4RN

Routledge is an imprint of the Taylor & Francis Group, an informa business

© 2011 Taylor & Francis

The right of Joel Spring to be identified as author of this work has
been asserted by him in accordance with sections 77 and 78 of the
Copyright, Designs and Patents Act 1988.

Typeset in Sabon
by Keystroke, Tettenhall, Wolverhampton
Printed and bound in the United States of America on acid-free paper
by Sheridan Books, Inc.

Library of Congress Cataloging in Publication Data
Spring, Joel H.
The politics of American education / Joel Spring.
     p. cm.
  1. Education—Effect of technological innovations on—United
States.   2. Educational technology—Government policy—United
States.   3. Public schools—United States.   4. Education and
state—United States.   5. Technology and state—United States.
I. Title.
LB1028.3.S64 2011
379.73—dc22   2010024884

ISBN 13: 978–0–415–88439–6 (hbk)
ISBN 13: 978–0–415–88440–2 (pbk)
ISBN 13: 978–0–203–83899–0 (ebk)

Contents

Preface

My intention is to provide a guide to the complex world of U.S. educational politics.

As explained in Chapter 1, the dominant ideology now driving American schools is human capital education, which has the goal of using schools to grow the economy and educate workers for economic competition in global markets. This ideology is focused on business concepts of accountability and seeks to achieve its goals through curriculum standards and testing, and packaged or scripted teaching methods designed as test preparation.

As I describe in Chapter 2, voices heard from civil society groups are often conflicting, ranging from parental satisfaction with local schools to politicians claiming schools are failing.

I use the term "complex" because, as discussed in Chapter 3, the formal structure of school governance encompasses a myriad of politicians and government officials working in federal, state, and local school district offices.

As explained in Chapter 4, this formal organization is inundated by pleas and pressure from a civil society that includes teachers unions, religious groups, administrative organizations, business interests, think tanks and foundations, parents, and other special interest groups.

In Chapter 5 I focus on the role of politicians and education ideologies in influencing and determining education policies. By ideology I mean a particular set of interlinked ideas about what should be the goals, curriculum, and instructional methods of American schools.

Another important influence, which I describe in Chapter 6, is the education business, which encompasses textbook publishers, test producers, tutoring and test preparation companies, charter school management companies, for-profit schools, online schooling, software makers, and a host of other supporting industries. Since education is mainly government funded these companies want to influence the adoption of school policies that will increase their profits. In addition, special interest groups, as illustrated in Chapter 6 by the textbook controversies in Texas, want their pet ideas disseminated through textbooks and other school materials.

Who is going to pay and who is going to benefit from the tax monies raised for education by local, state, and federal governments? In Chapter 7, I look at the political issues surrounding school financing including: Will more money for schools make a difference? Why are there rich and poor school districts? Can court decisions lead to equality of educational opportunity? Who should pay? How should educational monies be distributed? How should money for education be collected? How much money should be spent on education?

Today, as I discuss in Chapter 8, American schools are nested in a global education structure. Currently, the federal government is benchmarking school standards and tests against international tests, such as PISA (Program for International Student Assessment), PIRLS (Progress in International Reading Literacy), and TIMSS (Trends in International Mathematics and Science Study). These tests are often referred to as the Global Academic Olympics, with national scores considered indications of the quality of local schools. These tests are developed and distributed by two global groups: the Organization for Economic Cooperation and Development (OECD) and the International Association for the Evaluation of Educational Achievement (IEA). Also, education associations and government education officials share ideas in global settings. In addition, the education business is global, with test makers, tutorial and test preparation services, for-profit schools, online instruction companies, publishers, and other education services selling their products in a global market.

How does the governance structure of schools affect the workings of a democratic society? In Chapter 9, I consider theoretical issues regarding the control of the dissemination of knowledge through schools and its effect on decisions made by voters in a democratic society. What is the best governance structure for ensuring that schools educate informed and thoughtful voters? In conclusion, I propose an education amendment to the U.S. Constitution. This proposed amendment will raise many questions in the reader's mind about the relationship between schools, freedom of ideas, the role of teachers, and the protection of cultural and linguistic minorities.

Chapter I

Introduction
The Politics of Education
and the Politics of Knowledge

The politics of education explores one aspect of the general field of the politics of knowledge which is concerned with how knowledge is created and disseminated. Schools, along with the media, libraries, and the Internet, are central to the process of disseminating knowledge to the public. All aspects of the politics of education involve knowledge dissemination, including the governance structure of schools; media portrayal of educational issues; politicians; parents and parent organizations; special interest groups; foundations and think tanks; professional organizations; teachers unions; and the education industry.

The politics of education involves power struggles over three important questions:

- What knowledge is most worth teaching?
- What are the best instructional methods and school organization for teaching this knowledge?
- What should it cost to disseminate this knowledge?

The first question deals with the school curriculum and the politics of knowledge. The second question deals with teaching methods and school governance including highly debated topics such as choice, scripted lessons, progressive instructional methods, home schooling, charter schools, and a host of other issues. And the third question deals with how much a society is willing to spend on education; how money should be collected to support schools; and how money should be spent on education. The answers to these three questions elicit differing educational agendas from individuals and groups. These agendas provide the substance for potential political debates. These debates occur within a complex educational governance structure whose parameters are the world.

Educational Governance and Competing Voices

In the United States, the educational governance structure embraces political units ranging from the U.S. Congress and U.S. Department of Education to state governments to local school districts. In addition, there are many professional, business, political, special interest, and other organizations trying to influence what is taught in schools, how it is taught, and how much it will cost. In addition, as I explain in this book, many aspects of schooling are now globalized, including nations having similar educational ladders leading from primary school to post-secondary education; using the same international tests to compare their schools with other nations; and having the same educational goal of economic growth and supplying workers for global economic competition. Educational policies are also globalized through international organizations like the Organization for Economic Cooperation and Development, United Nations, and the World Bank. In general, educational professional organizations are international and provide opportunities for the global exchange of ideas. The educational landscape is dominated by multinational corporations which publish school materials and standardized tests, produce software, and manage for-profit schools and tutoring facilities. The scores from international science and math tests pit country against country as each country tries to win the knowledge race in the global economy.

What Do People Talk About When They Talk About Schools?

In Chapter 2, I will discuss the range of conflicting opinions about public schools, including those of parents, students, teachers, school administrators, foundations, interest groups, politicians, and the media. National media primarily and uncritically report the opinions of politicians who claim schools are failing and want to implement economic goals for education. In contrast, as discussed in Chapter 2, parents feel that their local schools are doing a good job. Also, school administrators stress the importance of outside factors affecting school achievement such as children's poverty and health care, racial and economic segregation between and within schools, and the lack of bilingual teachers. Many teachers and students object to the current emphasis on standardized testing. Students want classes that are interesting and teachers who personalize their teaching methods, and a reduced reliance on standardized testing to measure learning. One question that emerges from Chapter 2 is why some voices are more influential than others in determining school policies.

For decades, politicians have harped on the role of education in preparing students for work or college. However, the media seldom report parental reaction to these statements. Today, a majority of politicians say that the curriculum should be organized to ensure American economic development in a global system and should prepare students to compete in a global labor market. While there are polls showing parental satisfaction with their local schools, I could not find one showing that parents want the public school curriculum designed to advance the United States in global economic competition. Maybe most parents do want the curriculum to be determined by the requirements of global economic competition. The important issue is that most parents and students were never asked and there is no direct way they can express their wishes. They can act indirectly by voting for school board members and state and federal representatives or by joining a politically active special interest group.

What educational ideas are espoused by these conflicting voices? Many politicians talk about educating students so that the U.S. economy can grow and compete globally. These same politicians want a test-driven school system where students, teachers, schools, school systems, states, and even national school systems are judged by the results of standardized testing. As noted in Chapter 2, only politicians, the wealthy, and some educators support assessment as the key to good schooling. Most students, teachers, and school administrators think this is a bad idea and believe other factors are more important. Their voices don't seem to be heard by those making the decisions about schools, or if they are heard they are ignored. Parents, students, teachers, and school administrators espouse a diversity of educational ideas that are often in conflict with economic-oriented school policies.

From the Local to the Global in School Governance

Chapter 3 outlines the political arena in which public voices try to be heard. The chapter describes the complex structure of American schools from local school boards to state governance to federal power, along with a consideration of the political role of civil society and global influences. The chapter stresses the growing nationalization and centralization of decision-making. The growing centralization of educational control has occurred over time, particularly with the advent of federal categorical aid in the 1950s. Federal aid linked school policies to national policy objectives. For instance, No Child Left Behind strengthened the power of state education authorities over local schools. With federal demands in recent times to internationally benchmark standards and tests, the decision over the content of the curriculum has been moved to a global arena.

Civil Society and Schooling

Within the political arena described in Chapter 3, America's civil society tries to influence educational policies. Civil society, as discussed in Chapter 4, is composed of special interest groups, professional organizations, teachers unions, foundations, and think tanks. American civil society has been traditionally organized around the religious principles of community service and a competitive marketplace of self-interested groups. However, some members of civil society have more money and connections than others and, therefore, are more influential. For instance, the funding and policy reports from the world's richest foundation, the Bill and Melinda Gates Foundation, are currently having a significant impact on American school policies.

Politicians and Educational Ideologies*

Civil society organizations and politicians espouse a wide variety of educational ideas that impact school policies. As I describe in Chapter 5, these differing educational ideas encompass human capital economics; liberal and conservative cultural ideals; a belief in American exceptionalism; free market economics; regulated markets; multiculturalism and multilingualism; English-only; liberal and conservative religious values; progressive education; environmentalism; and arts-based schools.

However, the majority of liberal and conservative Democrats and Republican politicians espouse the goals of human capital education, with variations in their educational agendas reflecting differing cultural values. As I explain in more detail in the last sections of this introductory chapter, human capital education is premised on the idea that investment in education will grow the economy and provide educated workers to help the nation compete in the global knowledge economy.

The Education Business: Making Money and Influencing Schools

Education businesses influence school politics in a quest for profits which are in part dependent on government outlays for textbooks, software, equipment, tutoring services, and charter schools. Education is big business! In Chapter 6, I discuss the politics of publishing and political influences on textbooks; for-profit and franchised educational services; testing corporations; educational management companies; and supplementary education services. No Child Left Behind provides funds to hire

---

* I am using the term ideology to mean an integrated set of ideas that guide practice.

for-profit companies to provide supplementary education services to schools identified as needing improvement or restructuring. Supplementary education services provide tutoring and classes for remediation and for test preparation or, in the polite language of industry, achievement enhancement. Globally these services are referred to as the shadow education system, which ranges from cram schools in Japan to Sylvan Learning Centers in the United States.

Human capital ideology supports the educational policies that will maximize profits for education businesses. It supports the testing companies and the shadow education industry because of the ideology's emphasis on high-stakes testing to promote and sort students for careers and higher education and for evaluating teachers and school administrators. Because schools put testing pressure on students, parents are willing to fork out extra money to the shadow education industry. Consequently, the shadow education system and multinational testing corporations are interested in public acceptance of human capital ideology and the legitimization of assessment-driven school systems.

Politics of School Finance and the Economics of Education

In Chapter 7 I explore the politics of school finance, which generally centers on two questions: Who pays? Who benefits? Education policies should be examined according to who pays. The recent pattern is for the wealthy and corporations to pay less for the support of schools, and for middle- and lower-income groups to pay more for the support of public schools. In addition, because of federal and state funding for schools serving low-income students, schools serving families in the top 20 percent of income and those serving families in the lowest 20 percent of income spend the most per pupil. The remaining 60 percent of families, who are classified as middle-income, have the least spent on their schools. In addition, some scholars argue that more money will not improve American schools. Other factors besides money might be more important, such as teacher efficacy and control, teachers' advanced degrees, and teacher development.

The reader should keep in mind these basic financial questions when analyzing the impact of school policies:

- Who should pay?
- How should educational monies be distributed?
- How much money should be spent on education?

Global Education Politics and the United States

U.S. educational policies are nested in a global network that is being used to benchmark U.S. tests and curriculum standards. Global benchmarking tests, as described in Chapter 8, include PISA (Program for International Student Assessment), PIRLS (Progress in International Reading Literacy), and TIMSS (Trends in International Mathematics and Science Study). Comparisons of national scores on these exams can spark praise or criticism of national school systems. In Chapter 8, I explore this issue along with others affecting U.S. school policies. The chapter describes the work of the Organization for Economic Cooperation and Development (OECD) and the World Bank in establishing global education standards for developed and developing countries, respectively. Also analyzed in the chapter is the influence of publishers and producers of textbooks, tests, software, and online education on global education policy including that of the United States. A major issue for all global schools, and particularly in the United States, is the global migration of workers. Chapter 8 treats this issue in the framework of "brain gain" and "brain loss" for nations. American schools must accommodate the growing global circulation of workers. And, of course, American schools press an English acquisition agenda as in the national interest and as part of the global use of English as the language of commerce.

The global nesting of the U.S. school system contributes to arguments that the quality of U.S. schools is the key to international economic competition. Thus, the application of human capital ideology to U.S. school policies is reinforced by the general direction of global schooling, the work of the OECD, and the global benchmarking of U.S. standards and tests to PISA, PIRLS, and TIMSS.

Human Capital: Dominant Global Education Ideology

Today, the dominant educational ideology is human capital economics which defines the primary goal of education as economic growth, in contrast to other ideologies that might emphasize the passing on of culture or the education of students for social justice. Human capital economics contains a vision of school as a business preparing workers for businesses. Consequently, human capital economics values knowledge or curriculum according to how it meets the needs of the economic system. The conceptualization of education as a business includes the use of accounting methods that rely on standardized high-stakes testing to measure productivity. Workers within the education business, particularly administrators and teachers, are made accountable for ensuring productivity as measured by the results of student assessments. The same conceptual framework is used to evaluate how schools and school systems are organized.

The concept of human capital and the knowledge economy can be traced to the work of economists Theodore Schultz and Gary Becker.[1] In 1961, Theodore Schultz pointed out that "economists have long known that people are an important part of the wealth of nations."[2] Schultz argued that people invested in themselves through education to improve their job opportunities. In a similar fashion, nations could invest in schools as a stimulus for economic growth.

In his 1964 book *Human Capital*, Gary Becker asserts that economic growth now depends on the knowledge, information, ideas, skills, and health of the work force. Investments in education, he argued, could improve human capital which would contribute to economic growth.[3] Later, he used the word "knowledge" economy: "An economy like that of the United States is called a capitalist economy, but the more accurate term is human capital or *knowledge* capital economy."[4] Becker claimed that human capital represented three-fourths of the wealth of the United States and that investment in education would be the key to further economic growth.[5] Following a similar line of reasoning, Daniel Bell in 1973 coined the term "post-industrial" and predicted that there would be a shift from blue-collar to white-collar labor, requiring a major increase in educated workers.[6] This notion received support in the 1990s from Peter Drucker who asserted that knowledge rather than ownership of capital generates new wealth and that power was shifting from owners and managers of capital to knowledge workers.[7] During the same decade, Robert Reich claimed that inequality between people and nations was a result of differences in knowledge and skills. Invest in education, he urged, and these inequalities would be reduced.[8]

The knowledge economy was also linked to new forms of communication and networking. Referring to the new economy of the late twentieth century, Manuel Castells wrote in *The Rise of the Network Society*: "I call it informational, global, and networked to identify its fundamental distinctive features and to emphasize their intertwining."[9] By informational, he meant the ability of corporations and governments to "generate, process, and apply efficiently knowledge-based information."[10] It was global because capital, labor, raw materials, management, consumption, and markets were linked through global networks. "It is networked," he contended, because "productivity is generated through and competition is played out in a global network of interaction between business networks."[11] Information or knowledge, he claimed, was now a product that increased productivity.

The human capital and knowledge economy argument became a national issue in 1983 when the federal government's report *A Nation at Risk* blamed the allegedly poor academic quality of American public schools for causing lower rates of economic productivity than those of Japan and West Germany. In addition, it blamed schools for reducing the lead of the United States in technological development. The report states, "If only to keep and improve on the slim competitive edge we still retain in world markets, we must rededicate ourselves to the reform of the educational system for the benefit of all."[12] Not only was this argument almost impossible to prove but some have claimed it was based on false data and assumptions, as captured in the title of David Berliner and Bruce Biddle's *The Manufactured Crisis: Myths, Fraud and the Attack on America's Public Schools*.[13]

In the 1990s, President Bill Clinton used the rhetoric of human capital and the knowledge economy. When Clinton ran for the presidency in 1992, the Democratic platform declared: "A competitive American economy requires the global market's best educated, best trained, most flexible work force."[14] Education and the global economy continued as a theme in President Clinton's 1996 reelection: "Today's Democratic Party knows that education is the key to opportunity. In the new global economy, it is more important than ever before. Today, education is the fault line that separates those who will prosper from those who cannot."[15]

In the twenty-first century, variations on human capital and education for the knowledge economy pervade education discussions by Republicans and Democrats. In Chapter 5 I will discuss the educational ideologies of both parties. To illustrate my point at the beginning of this book I will refer to the 2008 national platforms of both major U.S. political parties, which I will again review in Chapter 5. The very title of the education section of the 2008 Republican national platform captures the economic thrust of the party's education agenda: "Education Means a More Competitive America."

Also included in the 2008 Republican education platform was the idea that American schools should be judged in the context of the world's education systems. The platform states:

> Maintaining America's preeminence requires a world-class system of education, with high standards, in which all students can reach their potential. That requires considerable improvement over our current 70 percent high school graduation rate and six-year graduation rate of only 57 percent for colleges.[16]

Reflecting the shared vision of the role of schooling in society, the 2008 Democratic education agenda sounded a little like that of the Republicans. Under its section titled "A World Class Education for Every Child," the Democratic platform claims:

> In the 21st century, where the most valuable skill is knowledge, countries that out-educate us today will out-compete us tomorrow. In the platform hearings, Americans made it clear that it is morally

and economically unacceptable that our high-schoolers continue to score lower on math and science tests than most other students in the world and continue to drop-out at higher rates than their peers in other industrialized nations.[17]

President Obama in his book *The Audacity of Hope: Thoughts on Reclaiming the American Dream* reflects the language of education for the knowledge economy: "in a knowledge-based economy where eight of the nine fast-growing occupations this decade require scientific or technological skills, most workers are going to need some form of higher education to fill the jobs of the future."[18]

There are criticisms regarding human capital theory and the ability of schools to educate students for occupations in the global economy. One criticism is that there are not enough jobs in the knowledge economy to absorb school graduates into skilled jobs and that the anticipated demand for knowledge workers has not occurred. Also, so-called knowledge work has been routinized, allowing for the hiring of less skilled workers. "It is, therefore," Phillip Brown and Hugh Lauder conclude, "not just a matter of the oversupply of skills that threatens the equation between high skills and high income, where knowledge is 'routinized' it can be substituted with less-skilled and cheaper workers at home or further afield."[19]

Brown and Lauder argue that multinational corporations are able to keep salaries low by encouraging nations to invest in schools that prepare for the knowledge economy. An oversupply of educated workers, it could be argued, depresses wages to the advantage of employers. This could be occurring in the United States, as suggested by Brown and Lauder, through a combination of immigration of educated workers from other countries and the increased emphasis on college education for the work force. In fact, Brown and Lauder argue there has been no real increase in income for college graduates since the 1970s except for those entering "high earner" occupations. However, college graduates still earn more than non-college graduates.[20]

Economist Andrew Hacker criticizes the very foundation of human capital arguments. Human capitalist economists premise their arguments on the fact that growth in school attendance parallels the growth of the economy. But it is a big leap from this fact to say that increased education causes economic growth. Hacker flips the causal relationship around and argues that economic growth provides the financial resources to fund educational expansion and offer youth an entertaining interlude in life. Hacker notes that much of the original funding of higher education came from innovative industrialists who were not college graduates. Today, college dropouts lead the list of innovative developers, such as Larry Ellison (Oracle), Bill Gates (Microsoft), Steve Jobs and Steve Wozniak (Apple), and Michael Dell (Dell).[21]

Hacker's argument does not mean that schooling is not important for jobs. Even high-tech instrument jobs require some high school education. However, human capitalists may have oversold their argument about education causing economic growth and being necessary for global competition. First, the state of the global economy and jobs is uncertain and constantly changing. Secondly, there may be an overeducation of the population causing educational inflation. Inflation refers to employers increasing the educational requirements of jobs when there is an over-abundance of graduates. In this situation, the economic value of a high school or college degree declines when there is an overabundance of well-schooled workers.

Are jobs really tied to getting more schooling? Not according to economist Andrew Hacker.[22] In a review of *The Race Between Education and Technology* by Claudia Goldin and Lawrence Katz, Hacker questions the argument that more schooling, particularly more higher education, is necessary for employment in today's job markets.[23] To check this assertion, Hacker sat down with the U.S. Bureau of Labor Statistics' *Occupational Outlook Handbook, 2008–2009 Edition*.[24] Shockingly, at least for those saying they go to college to get a job, Hacker finds that in the future the number of jobs operating high-tech instruments will outnumber jobs requiring college-trained scientists and engineers. High-tech instrument occupations require only a high school education and the training to use the instrument is usually done at the workplace. For example, and this is only a short listing, these high-tech instrument occupations include gynecologic sonography, avionics equipment mechanics, semiconductor processing, air traffic controlling, endoscopic cameras, and blood bank clinical work. In the United States, engineering occupations will grow by about 10 percent by 2016 which means that the projected number of 2016 engineering graduates will be four times larger than the number of openings. The same small growth is predicted for occupations employing college-graduate physicists and mathematicians.

Ironically even business enterprises seem to disregard the quality of schooling when they can train employees at the work site. Consider the decision by foreign auto manufacturers to locate in states with low wages and no unions but with high dropout rates: Nissan, Coffee County, Tennessee, 26.3 percent dropout rate; BMW, Spartanburg County, South Carolina, 26.9 percent dropout rate; Honda, St. Clair County, Alabama, 28.7 percent dropout rate; and Toyota, Union County, Mississippi, 31.5 percent dropout rate. Hacker argues that these companies didn't care about local school quality because worker training was on the job.[25] Based on the above arguments, more schooling may *not* result in a higher paying job.

The Human Capital Education Paradigm

Human capital arguments contain an educational agenda of standardization of the curriculum; accountability of students and school staff based on standardized test scores; and the deskilling of the teaching profession. What is meant by deskilling is that in some cases teaching has been reduced to following a scripted lesson created by some outside agency, or teachers are forced to teach to the requirements of standardized tests. The deskilling of teaching includes the disappearance of teacher-made tests and lesson plans and the ability of teachers to select the classroom's instructional methodology. What I refer to as the human capital paradigm has made teachers into technicians carrying out predetermined instructional packages.

Below is a list of features of the human capital education paradigm.

Human Capital Education Paradigm
- The value of education is measured by economic growth
- National standardization of the curriculum
- Standardized testing for promotion, entrance, and exiting from different levels of schooling
- Performance evaluation of teaching is based on standardized testing of students
- Mandated textbooks
- Scripted lessons

Why has human capital ideology come to dominate global school systems including that of the United States? What reasons do people have for accepting and/or promoting this particular educational ideology? What other educational ideologies exist and how might an alternative ideology affect educational goals, instructional methods and curricula, the evaluation of students, teachers and administrators, and organization of schools and school systems?

Through the course of American and global history there have been a number of alternative educational goals and plans proposed for defining what knowledge is most worth teaching in schools, including, to name just a few, nationalism and patriotism; active democratic citizenship; progressive education; social justice; environmental education; human rights; arts education; cultural studies; consumer and critical media studies; and the social reconstruction of society. The reality is that most politicians and business people believe that human capital goals should dominate schooling.

Conclusion: Questions

I will end this introductory chapter with a summary of questions about the politics of education. These questions can provide the reader with a guide to analyzing education policies. First there are the major questions dealing with the practice of schooling as they are played out in the political arena.

- What knowledge is most worth teaching?
- What are the best instructional methods for teaching this knowledge?
- What is the best organization of schools and school systems for teaching this knowledge?

Secondly, there are questions related to the financing of education.

- How much money should a nation, state or individual spend on education?
- How should tax money for schools be collected (who should pay and how much)?
- How should tax dollars for schools be distributed (who benefits)?

Thirdly, there are questions about the relationship between U.S. schools and global influences.

- What is the effect on U.S. education policies of international tests like PISA, PIRLS, and TIMSS?
- What is the effect of the global migration of labor on American schools?
- What is the effect of the global education industry on American schools?

And lastly, there are questions related to the dominant ideology of American and global school systems.

- Why has human capital ideology come to dominate global school systems including that of the United States?
- What reasons do governments, organizations, and people have for accepting and/or promoting human capital ideology?
- What other educational ideologies exist and how might an alternative ideology affect educational goals, instructional methods and curricula, the evaluation of students, teachers and administrators, and organization of schools and school systems?

Notes

1 See Brian Keeley, *Human Capital: How What You Know Shapes Your Life* (Paris: OECD Publishing, 2007), pp. 28–35, and Phillip Brown and Hugh Lauder, "Globalization, Knowledge and the Myth of the Magnet Economy," in *Education, Globalization and Social Change*, edited by Hugh Lauder, Phillip Brown, Jo-Anne Dillabough and A. H. Halsey (Oxford: Oxford University Press, 2006), pp. 317–340.
2 As quoted in Keeley, *Human Capital*, p. 29.
3 Gary Becker, *Human Capital* (New York: Columbia University Press, 1964).
4 Gary Becker, "The Age of Human Capital," in *Education, Globalization and Social Change*, edited by Hugh Lauder, Phillip Brown, Jo-Anne Dillabough and A. H. Halsey (Oxford: Oxford University Press, 2006), p. 292.
5 Ibid.
6 Daniel Bell, *The Coming of the Post–industrial Society* (New York: Basic Books, 1973).
7 Peter Drucker, *Post–capitalist Society* (London: Butterworth/Heinemann, 1993).
8 Robert Reich, *The Work of Nations: A Blueprint for the Future* (New York: Vintage, 1991).
9 Manuel Castells, *The Rise of the Network Society* (Oxford: Blackwell, 2000), p. 77.
10 Ibid.
11 Ibid.
12 National Commission on Excellence in Education, *A Nation at Risk* (Washington, DC: U.S. Government Printing Office, 2003).
13 David Berliner and Bruce Biddle, *The Manufactured Crisis: Myths, Fraud and the Attack on America's Public Schools* (New York: Perseus Books, 1995).
14 Democratic Party Platform of 1992: A New Covenant with the American People (July 13, 1992), p. 5. Retrieved from the American Presidency Project Document Archive http://www.presidency.ucsb.edu/ws/index.php?pid=pid 29610 on January 5, 2009.
15 Democratic Party Platform of 1996: Today's Democratic Party: Meeting America's Challenges, Protecting America's Values (August 26, 1996), p. 5. Retrieved from the American Presidency Project Document Archive http://www.presidency.ucsb.edu/ws/print.php?pid=29612 on January 8, 2009.
16 Republican Party Platform of 2008, p. 43. Retrieved from the American Presidency Project Document Archive http://www.presidency.ucsb.edu/papers_pdf/78545.pdf on February 10, 2009.
17 Democratic National Convention Committee, "Report of the Platform Committee: Renewing America's Promise." Presented to the 2008 Democratic National Convention, August 13, 2008, p. 18. Retrieved from the American Presidency Project Document Archive http://www.presidency.ucsb.edu/papers_pdf/78283.pdf on November 13, 2008.
18 Barack Obama, *The Audacity of Hope: Thoughts on Reclaiming the American Dream* (New York: Vintage Books, 2006), p. 194.
19 Brown and Lauder, "Globalization, Knowledge and the Myth of the Magnet Economy," p. 320.
20 Ibid., p. 326.
21 Andrew Hacker, "Can We Make America Smarter?" *The New York Review of Books* (April 30, 2009), p. 38.

22 Ibid., pp. 37–40.
23 Claudia Goldin and Lawrence Katz, *The Race Between Education and Technology* (Cambridge, MA: Harvard University Press, 2008).
24 U.S. Bureau of Labor Statistics, *Occupational Outlook Handbook, 2008–2009 Edition* (Washington, D.C.: U.S. Printing Office, 2008).
25 Hacker, "Can We Make America Smarter?" p. 38.

Chapter 2

What Do People Talk About When They Talk About Schools?

Before doing a systematic analysis of American school politics from the local to the global, I would like the reader to consider the public's deliberation about schools, particularly the existence of a general crisis mentality that doesn't seem to be shared by students and parents. What are the most important issues in this crisis mentality and in the politics of education? Throughout this book I will touch on the three most important questions discussed by the public and which are at the heart of the politics of education:

1. What knowledge is most worth teaching?
2. What are the best methods and school organization for teaching this knowledge?
3. What should be the cost of disseminating this knowledge?
4. What educational ideology is reflected in the responses to the above questions?

The first question deals with the school curriculum and the politics of knowledge. Many public voices can be heard about what students should learn. The second question deals with methods of instruction, teachers and staff, and the organization of education, such as choice, charter schools, school districts, for-profit schools, and a whole host of other possibilities. It is these two questions that engage public discussions and the politics of education. And the third question refers to how much a society is willing to expend on education.

To exemplify conflicting public voices, I am using as an example the 2009 public discussion of the educational requirements of the U.S. Department of Education's Race to the Top. The differing voices about Race to the Top carry over to future political debates. In this context, and as an example of the general crisis mentality of public leaders, consider former Microsoft head, founder of the Gates Foundation and college dropout Bill Gates' sweeping 2009 statement, "It's no secret the U.S. education system is failing?"[1] Or consider U.S. Secretary of Education

Arne Duncan's 2009 declaration, "The fact is that we are not just in an economic crisis; we are in an educational crisis."[2]

The assertions by Gates and Duncan might seem obvious and almost commonsensical to a public receiving a constant stream of negative statements from the media that American schools are failing and costing the country its competitive edge in global markets. But are the statements true? Does the public share this vision of American schools? How do others define current educational problems? Why do some voices have a greater influence than others?

What Do Politicians Talk About When They Talk About Schools?

What do politicians talk about when they talk about schools? They talk about how the schools are in crisis and their plans—usually not based on any research—to fix them. When Gerald Bracey mentioned "Sputnik in 1957" as the beginning of the media's outpouring of criticism about schools, he was referring to politicians and public leaders who blamed public schools for the Soviet Union launching a space satellite before the United States. The result was a national political campaign to make schools tougher in math and science so that the U.S. could win the technological and military race with the Soviet Union. After the launch of the Soviet satellite, President Dwight Eisenhower blamed the American schools for not preparing students as well as Soviet schools to excel in math and science. Standing before a large audience in Oklahoma City, he declared, "My scientific advisors place this problem above all other immediate tasks of producing missiles, of developing new techniques in the armed forces."[3] Other politicians and scientific leaders publicly announced that the schools were failing and, consequently, the Soviets were winning.[4] These events were followed in the 1960s with the schools being blamed for poverty, resulting in the launch of a bundle of educational programs that were part of the so-called War on Poverty program.[5] One of these pieces of legislation contained a section called "Title I" which was renamed in the twenty-first century No Child Left Behind.

But there was no real proof either that American schools had caused the U.S. to fall behind the Soviet Union in the space race, or that schools had failed to solve the problem of poverty or even could solve the problem of poverty. The charge in the 1950s that American schools weakened America's ability to compete in the technological race with the Soviet Union appears absurd when you try to calculate the effect of school graduates on society. For instance, let's assume that people reach the height of their careers and their related effect on society in their forties and fifties. In the 1950s, people who were in their forties and fifties graduated from high school, if they attended, somewhere between roughly

1920 and 1940. So if schools were to be blamed for failure to compete with the Soviet Union it would have to be the schools during the period of the 1920s and 1940s and not the schools of the 1950s.

The schools' ability to end poverty is highly questionable given all the other social and economic factors. In part, the 1960s War on Poverty was based on human capital theory which assumes, and this still remains unproven, that investment in education will grow the economy and cause poverty to disappear. Not only has time proven the argument wrong—poverty has not ended—but the basis of human capital theory is now being challenged by economists like Andrew Hacker.[6]

From the 1980s to the present, politicians, including U.S. Presidents, have charged that public schools are failing, resulting in the U.S. falling behind in global economic competition. This was sparked by the 1983 report *A Nation at Risk* issued by the Republican administration of President Ronald Reagan.[7] In the 1990s, conservative educational critics Chester Finn and Diane Ravitch recalled:

> To put it mildly this bombshell [*A Nation at Risk*] awakened parents, educators, governors, legislators, and the press . . . Its warning of "a rising tide of mediocrity" helped launch what came to be called the excellence movement, which included a mass of other commissions, studies and reports.[8]

A Nation at Risk provided no proof that the quality of schools was causing the U.S. to lag in global economic competition. How could you prove this assertion? For instance, what cohort group of school graduates was the report referring to—the graduates of the 1950s, 1960s, or 1970s? Certainly the report was not referring to the graduates of the late 1970s and early 1980s since a high school student cannot bring down the economy immediately after graduation. In *The Manufactured Crisis: Myths, Fraud, and the Attack on America's Public Schools*, David Berliner and Bruce Biddle called *A Nation at Risk* a hoax for claiming that the American economy was failing because of public schools.[9] Berliner and Biddle provided statistics showing that U.S. students taking courses similar to those of students in other countries, such as Japan and Germany, do as well or, in some cases, better, and that it is the comprehensiveness of the student body in U.S. public schools that tends to lower overall international test scores.

Politicians continue to make the claim that schools are putting the nation at risk in the global economy. For instance, the 2008 Democratic platform called for "A World Class Education for Every Child":

> In the 21st century, where the most valuable skill is knowledge, countries that out-educate us today will out-compete us tomorrow.

In the platform hearings, Americans made it clear that it is morally and economically unacceptable that our high-schoolers continue to score lower on math and science tests than most other students in the world and continue to drop-out at higher rates than their peers in other industrialized nations.[10]

President Obama during and after his election offered a whole host of unproven school reforms—unproven in the sense that there was no evidence they would help the U.S. economically in global competition—including more charter schools, a national data system of student test scores, and expanded preschool education.[11]

Why do politicians primarily talk about crises in public education and offering educational solutions to problems not directly related to education such as poverty, national defense and global economic competition? Why did President Bill Clinton decide to launch his political career in Arkansas in the 1980s by claiming to be the education governor?[12] Blaming schools makes good politics because otherwise politicians might have to blame corporate managers, factory owners for moving their factories offshore, and leaders of financial institutions for economic problems. These are powerful and wealthy interests that can use their influence to thwart political ambitions. It is politically safe to just blame the schools.

What Does the Media Talk About When It Talks About Schools?

A 2009 Brookings Institution study complained that the media were not keeping the public informed about education issues. How can the public know about major changes in education policies such as No Child Left Behind and Race to the Top if they are not reported through the general media. The Brookings Institution study states: "despite the importance of media coverage for public understanding of education, news reporting on schools is scant . . . there is virtually no national coverage of education."[13] The study found that in 2009, "only 1.4 percent of national news coverage from television, newspapers, news Web sites, and radio dealt with education."[14] This was actually more than in 2007 and 2008 when only 1.0 and 0.7 percent, respectively, of national news covered education issues. Most of this reporting has little to do with education policy issues. As the report concludes, "This makes it difficult for the public to follow the issues at stake in our education debates and to understand how to improve school performance."[15]

The Brookings Institution report claims that part of the problem is the difficulty newspapers and television stations face in assigning reporters to cover schools. Consequently, the report recommends that: "Newspapers and other media outlets that have cut back on education reporting should reconsider these decisions both on public interest grounds, and also because there is widespread interest in the issues surrounding education."[16] Also it recommends that: "Foundations and non-profit organizations should focus on developing alternative forms of education coverage both nationally and locally."[17]

However, there are still problems when the media report on education. Cynthia Gerstl-Pepin studied what the media talks about when it talks about schools.[18] Her work focuses on the role of the media in the 2000 presidential elections. She argues that education became a focus of the 2000 campaign when Gallup polls found education to be the major problem concerning the general public. This poll did not escape the attention of politicians. Also, and this is important for theories of democracy, she asserts that, "Because most voters increasingly use the media as their primary source of information, their role in electoral politics is key to the functioning of our democracy."[19]

Gerstl-Pepin found that during the 2000 elections the media focused on reporting the candidates' positions on educational issues. In other words, the media, particularly news broadcasters, did not frame the education issues but simply relied on what politicians had to say. Seldom, if ever, did the media offer any analysis of what politicians said were the education problems and solutions. Gerstl-Pepin wrote:

> They turn to others to make those assessments as a result of the "veil of objectivity". Oftentimes, the candidates or their advisors or supporters are designated to represent their side of the debate . . . Rather than informing the public, the media serve to represent the issues as framed by the candidates of the two main political parties.[20]

One of Gerstl-Pepin's interesting examples of the media's failure to inform the public about education issues was the controversy over the test scores in Texas. Like his predecessor Democratic President Bill Clinton, future Republican President George W. Bush ran for the White House in 2000 on claims of being Texas' "education governor." During the 2000 election, Gerstl-Pepin writes, the national media just accepted Bush's claim of improving Texas schools, creating a public image of Bush as an education expert who could raise test scores. What went unquestioned in media coverage was the issue of whether or not improved test scores were good for the economy and global economic competition and, probably more importantly, for students. In describing the media's presentation of test scores as proof of Bush's educational expertise, Gerstl-Pepin asserts, "There is no substantive proof that higher test scores will improve instruction, address racism and poverty, or lead to a stronger economy. All of these arguments overlook that social inequities are directly linked to school performance."[21] From her perspective real improvement in schools requires addressing: "Long-term, substantive changes such as addressing poverty, racism, and gender discrimination are rendered invisible in shortsighted campaign rhetoric."[22] The media's focus on superficial items like test scores, she claims, was uninformative. A critical media should have examined issues regarding a reliance on reporting test scores as a sign of school improvement.

By merely mouthing the claims of politicians, the media reduce public understanding of complex issues and prepare the public to accept simple remedies and test scores as an indication of quality. The media, as central to democratic deliberation, does a disservice to public understanding of issues. To exemplify the reductionist nature of media and political education discussion, Gerstl-Pepin quotes a letter written by a teacher to the *Los Angeles Times*:

> As I listened to the second debate on Wednesday night and heard George W. Bush's simplistic platitudes like "we won't leave any child behind" and Al Gore's "accountability for students and teachers," I was astounded at what a superficial understanding these "educated" men have of the work I do. There is no two-minute sound-bite answer to the myriad of educational issues facing our communities—so don't give one![23]

What Do Parents Talk About When They Talk About Schools?

Parents do not share politicians' negative views regarding their local schools. Throughout the twenty-first century parents have consistently given their local schools high marks but expressed negative feelings about the nation's schools. In the Phi Delta Kappa/Gallup 2009 poll a sample of the American population was asked the question: "Students are often given the grades A, B, C, D, and Fail to denote the quality of their work. Suppose the public schools themselves in your community were graded in the same way. What grade would you give the public schools here—A, B, C, D or Fail?"[24] Fifty-one percent of those polled gave their local schools an A or B and 32 percent gave them a C. Only 11 percent gave their schools a D and only 3 percent gave them an F (3 percent responded that they didn't know). These results were consistent with the previous four years of polling.[25] Respondents were then asked, "Using the A, B, C, D, and Fail scale again, what grade would you give the school your oldest child attends?"[26] The answers were astonishingly positive compared to the media judgments and fairly consistent with the previous five years: 74 percent gave As and Bs, 17 percent Cs, 6 percent Ds and 2 percent Fs.[27]

There was a contradictory reply from these same respondents when asked, "How about the public schools in the nation as a whole? What grade would you give the public schools, nationally—A, B, C, D, or Fail?"[28] While they gave local schools mainly positive marks, only 19 percent gave the nation's schools As and Bs while 25 percent gave them Ds and Fs. Fifty-five percent gave Cs to the nation's schools.[29]

Why the disparity in perceptions between the local and the national? Most respondents were somewhat familiar with their local schools and probably very familiar with the schools attended by their children. However their source of information about the nation's schools was probably the media. Commenting on these differences between perceptions of local and national public schools, Gerald Bracey stated, "The reasons for this disconnect are simple: Americans never hear anything positive about the nation's schools and haven't since the years just before Sputnik in 1957."[30] And, Bracey continues, "parents use other sources and resources for information about their local schools: teachers, administrators, friends, neighbors, newsletters, PTAs, and their kids themselves; and they're in a much better position to observe what's actually happening in American schools."[31]

Organized parents do not seem to share a crisis mentality about schools. The largest parents organization is the Parent Teacher Association (PTA), founded in 1897. The PTA claims that it is

> the largest volunteer child advocacy association in the country . . . Membership is open to all who support the health and educational achievement of our nation's children, and over 5 million parents, teachers, community members, and other concerned citizens are currently PTA members.[32]

Obviously, the PTA supports greater parental involvement in education which they claim will "lead to improvements in the child's academic achievement, behavior, attendance at school, understanding of diverse viewpoints, planning for the future, and emotional and physical well-being."[33] An important agenda item for the PTA is support and greater funding for the parental involvement requirements of No Child Left Behind. No Child Left Behind states:

SEC. 1118. PARENTAL INVOLVEMENT.

(a) LOCAL EDUCATIONAL AGENCY POLICY.—

(1) IN GENERAL.—A local educational agency may receive funds under this part only if such agency implements programs, activities, and procedures for the involvement of parents in programs assisted under this part consistent with this section. Such programs, activities, and procedures shall be planned and implemented with meaningful consultation with parents of participating children.[34]

In addition to advocating for parental involvement in schools, the PTA, in contrast to many politicians, worries about absenteeism, juvenile delinquency, nutrition, and children's health care. While politicians and others, as I will explain in the next sections, talk about schooling to supply workers to help the U.S. compete in the global economy, the 2009 PTA policy agenda proposes that states adopt a common definition of chronic absenteeism and require: "school-parent compacts to support school and family partnerships in the development of recommendations for student attendance, expectations, and supports for student behavior, and rational disciplinary policies."[35] And, unlike any other voices discussed in this chapter, the PTA worries about protecting the rights of juvenile delinquents in the context of the historic role of the organization: "Protecting the rights of children and youth in trouble has long been at the core of PTA's advocacy work. In 1899, for example, PTA convention delegates passed a resolution supporting the extension of juvenile courts and probation systems."[36]

The 2009 PTA agenda supports better nutrition for children and advocates for the National School Lunch Program and School Breakfast Program. In addition, in its concern for children's health, the 2009 PTA agenda calls for increased funding and expansion of coverage of the State Children's Health Insurance Program.[37]

In summary, parents talk about the fine quality of their local schools but worry about the system as a whole. The major organization claiming to represent parents, the PTA, advocates for more parental involvement in schools, school-parent compacts to reduce chronic absenteeism, protection of juvenile rights, better nutrition and children's health care. When parents talk about schools many seem to not share the negative sentiments of public leaders like Bill Gates and U.S. Secretary of Education Arne Duncan.

What Do the World's Richest Man and Foundation Talk About When They Talk About Schools?

What the world's richest man and foundation say and do about education reveals the complex interrelationship between school policies, private foundations, and personal wealth. Private foundations along with media and politicians influence public dialogue about schools. In later chapters, I will discuss the complex interrelationships between foundations, think tanks, politicians, media, and public.

As previously quoted, Bill Gates, declared the richest man in the world by *Forbes* magazine in 2009, said American schools are failing.[38] The basis of his assertion is unclear. However, the Bill and Melinda Gates Foundation, the world's largest foundation created in 2000 and expanded in 2006 when Warren Buffett pledged $31 billion, has as its stated goals "three broad issues: global health, global development and *programs in the United States that largely have to do with improving education* [author's emphasis]."[39]

Reflecting the role of the world's largest foundation in American education, a 2009 Associated Press article carried the ominous title "The Influence Game: Gates' Sway on Ed Policy."[40] The influence of the Gates Foundation on education became problematic in 2009 when the newly elected President Barack Obama appointed two officials of the Foundation to the Department of Education and the Foundation offered $250,000 to state education departments to prepare applications for education funds —called Race to the Top—that were made available through President Obama's economic stimulus package American Recovery and Reinvestment Act of 2009. One of these officials was Margot Rogers who was appointed Chief of Staff of the Department of Education. Previously she managed the development of the Gates Foundation's five-year education strategy.[41] The other appointee was Jim Shelton who became the assistant deputy secretary for innovation and improvement to manage the Education Department's teacher quality, school choice and learning programs.[42] Both of these appointees signed a "Certification of Public Interest Waiver" which specifically stated that they "*shall not* be restricted from participating in any particular matter involving specific parties that is directly and substantially related to his [her] former employer, the Bill and Melinda Gates Foundation."[43]

There were other connections between President Obama's administration and the Gates Foundation. U.S. Secretary of Education Arne Duncan worked with the Gates Foundation while serving as Chief Executive Officer of the Chicago Public Schools prior to his appointment to the U.S. Department of Education. The Gates Foundation funded Chicago small high schools and charter schools. In 2007, as head of the Chicago school system, Duncan reported in his budget cost-cutting measures related to charter schools: "Approximately 558 net positions were eliminated by the end of FY2007 due to enrollment shifts and expansion of charter- and contract-school providers, resulting in a $28 million reduction in salaries."[44] In the same budget report, Duncan announced that,

> Additionally, the Bill and Melinda Gates Foundation has awarded CPS [Chicago Public Schools] a grant to support a broad effort to improve Chicago public high schools and advance the mayor's school reform program. The grant funds development of a comprehensive strategy to oversee district-wide high school reform, help create new high schools, and support principal development initiatives.[45]

The Gates Foundation's Chicago charter school initiatives were tied to nationally managed charter school designs. Support of nationally managed charter schools became a distinguishing feature of both the Gates Foundation and President Obama's administration. One Chicago charter school, the Mirta Ramirez Computer Science Charter High School, was based on "the educational design of the well-regarded Bill & Melinda Gates Foundation-funded High Tech High learning communities."[46] The nationally marketed High Tech High design, as I explain later, has received special attention and funding from the Gates Foundation. The Gates Foundation also funded two Chicago International Charter schools which were managed by Civitas Schools.[47] Civitas Schools describes itself as "an educational management organization" and claims: "Over the coming years, Civitas Schools will replicate its rigorous college preparatory high school curriculum in three additional small high schools with funding from the Bill & Melinda Gates Foundation."[48] Arne Duncan's commitment to charter schools was recognized in Chicago's 2007–2008 Charter Schools Performance Report, published with "Special thanks to the U.S. Secretary of Education and former CEO of CPS (2001–2008), Mr. Arne Duncan, for his instrumental work on behalf of charter schools in Chicago."[49]

Besides supporting charter schools and national designs for charter schools, the Gates Foundation and President Obama's administration shared an interest in creating a national school data bank to measure schools, teachers, principals, and teacher training institutions. Both the Race to the Top and Bill Gates' pronouncements on education emphasized the importance of collecting student data to evaluate teachers. Consider the similarity between Bill Gates' 2008 education speech and the 2009 statements by U.S. Secretary of Education Arne Duncan. In 2008, Bill Gates, in a speech given at a Foundation-sponsored forum, argued that a data system was necessary for identifying and rewarding good teaching:

> We will also be helping states and districts build data systems that provide teachers timely feedback about student learning . . . Data systems, of course, will tell us which teachers are getting the biggest achievement gains every year. If we're going to retain them, we're going to have to reward them. It's astonishing to me that you could have a system that doesn't allow you to pay more for strong performance, or for teaching in a particular school.[50]

President Obama's 2009 economic stimulus package required the type of data system Gates proposed in his 2008 remarks. Both calls for a national data system emphasized tracking student scores and using them to evaluate teachers. U.S. Secretary of Education Arne Duncan explained the importance of this data system:

We need comprehensive data systems that do three things. One, track students throughout their educational trajectory. Secondly, track students back to teachers so we can really shine a spotlight on those teachers that are doing a phenomenal job of driving student achievement. And third, track teachers back to their schools of education so . . . over time we'll really understand which schools of education are adding value with their graduates.[51]

For the cynical and conspiratorial minded, Bill Gates and his Foundation's emphasis on data systems might be linked to his continued ownership of Microsoft shares and potential sale of software geared to national-common standards. In 2007, *Fortune* magazine reported that he still retained 877,499,336 Microsoft shares valued at $25 billion.[52] In addition, during his previously cited 2008 speech to the Gates Foundation education forum, he placed his hope for improving teaching on better software, with a specific mention of the work done by Microsoft:

> *As states begin to embrace common standards, technology will help us create the next-generation models of teaching and learning.* With interactivity, we can provide software to qualify a student or to bring a subject to life. We need to have the best lectures available online and for free on DVDs. Microsoft did this in India with math courses and saw that it was beneficial in a number of ways [author's emphasis].[53]

It could be argued that after years of building Microsoft this is how Bill Gates and those around him think; data collection is the answer to most problems.

The parallels in language are striking between the Bill Gates and the Gates Foundation and the Obama administration over the creation of a national data system to track student test scores, teachers, and the work of teacher training institutions. And, like many pronouncements on education by public figures, there is no proof that a national data system will improve schools, particularly when one considers all the factors affecting student learning and whether or not standardized test scores are any measure of real learning (whatever that means). However, it is easy for politicians to simply claim that a national data system will improve schools.

After President Obama's inauguration and the appointment of Gates Foundation personnel Margot Rogers and Jim Shelton to the U.S. Department of Education, the Gates Foundation issued a report titled *College Ready* which identified three strategies for increasing high school graduation rates; strategies very close to those of President Obama's administration. Two strategies involved creating curriculum standards that would make high school graduates "college-ready" and developing new technology.[54] The Gates Foundation and the Obama administration also supported charter schools as a source of educational innovation. The third strategy focused on improving the quality of teachers by linking teacher evaluation to student test scores—another part of President Obama's education agenda: "We can make this a reality [better teachers] by establishing clear goals for excellence [standards] and measuring and rewarding [teachers'] achievement of the goals."[55]

Data, in the words of the Gates Foundation's 2009 report *College Ready*, is the priority for all three of the above strategies: "Data : We need better data to tell us if we are making progress. Without better data, educators, students, and the public lack the information needed to make good decisions and midcourse corrections when appropriate."[56] The report calls for more data to identify quality teachers: "We know how crucial effective teaching is for student success, but not enough about how to identify, develop, reward, and retain excellent teachers, especially for the students who need them most. We need evidence, and we need to go where it takes us."[57]

Compare what the world's richest foundation says are educational needs and the education strategy of the Obama administration. On February 17, 2009, the President signed an economic stimulus package which contained within it support for four areas of education reform called "Race to the Top." The Gates Foundation is provided money to help state officials apply for funds under this law. As listed by the U.S. Department of Education, the criteria states had to meet were:

- Adopting internationally-benchmarked standards and assessments that prepare students for success in college and the workplace;
- Recruiting, developing, retaining, and rewarding effective teachers and principals;
- Building data systems that measure student success and inform teachers and principals how they can improve their practices; and
- Turning around our lowest-performing schools.[58]

In an editorial in *The Washington Post*, U.S. Secretary of Education Arne Duncan called the Race to the Top "Education Reform's Moon Shot" and interpreted its goals as:

- To reverse the pervasive dumbing-down of academic standards and assessments . . . [with] common, internationally benchmarked K-12 standards.
- To close the data gap . . . states will need to monitor advances in student achievement and identify effective instructional practices.

- To boost the quality of teachers and principals . . . and have strategies for rewarding and retaining more top-notch teachers and improving or replacing ones who aren't up to the job.
- Finally, to turn around the lowest-performing schools. . . .[59]

Closing the so-called data gap required each state to abandon their own standards for national ones. Duncan proposed "common, internationally benchmarked K-12 standards."[60] With help from the Gates Foundation more than forty-eight states applied for Race to the Top funds to create national common standards.

The effect of the Race to the Top funds was to shape state education policies to meet the requirements of federal guidelines. States rushed to write applications that conformed to federal criteria. For instance, Colorado reported that writing the application "required 5,000 hours of staff and volunteer time."[61] Indicative of the consequences of Race to the Top was a *New York Times* article on the process titled "States Mold School Policies to Win New Federal Money."[62]

In a speech on teacher education on October 22, 2009, Arne Duncan announced,

> For the first time, 48 states have banded together to develop common college and career-ready standards for high school students—and the federal government is providing generous incentives through the Race to the Top Fund to encourage rigorous standards, including setting aside $350 million to fund the competitive development of better assessments for the standards. *Just a year ago, many education experts doubted states would ever agree on common college-ready standards* [author's emphasis].[63]

National standards in contrast to individual state standards would make it possible to link a national data bank of student test scores to individual teachers and eventually to the institutions that trained each teacher. Data could be used to evaluate teacher education programs. Given student and teacher geographic mobility, the analysis of teacher education programs would not be possible without national standards and testing. As Duncan stated in his speech on teacher education, "The draft Race to the Top criteria would also reward states that publicly report and link student achievement data to *the programs where teachers and principals were credentialed* [author's emphasis]."[64] The criteria for selection of state grants under Race to the Top included whether or not states were willing to participate in creating national standards, common tests and a data bank of student scores to be used to evaluate teachers.

Also, the world's wealthiest man and foundation believe charter schools along with data systems will cure whatever ails American schools. Again

Gates' language and that of the Obama administration were very similar. In his 2009 "Annual Letter from Bill Gates," Gates focused on small schools and charter schools. Some of the early grants from the Gates Foundation supported the creation of small high schools. Except for a few schools, most of the small schools did not improve student achievement. However, Gates wrote, those small high schools that did succeed were "charter schools that have significantly longer school days than other schools."[65] Gates specifically named two nationally managed charter school designs, the Knowledge is Power Program (KIPP) in Houston and High Tech High in San Diego, the same school design the Gates Foundation funded in Chicago. Also, in his letter, he mentioned Jay Mathews' book about KIPP called *Work Hard, Be Nice*.[66]

KIPP and High Tech High as nationally managed charter schools represent another form of nationalization of the U.S. school system along with the Race to the Top emphasis on common national standards and data collection. For instance in 2009 KIPP reported that there were eighty-two KIPP public schools in nineteen states and the District of Columbia, enrolling around 20,000 students. This number was close to that given in 2005 by KIPP CEO Richard Barth who "set a goal of expanding KIPP's network to 100 schools serving more than 25,000 students by the year 2011."[67] High Tech High reported operating in 2008 eight schools (five high schools, two middle schools, and one elementary school) with approximately 2,500 students and 300 employees and $57 million in real estate holdings.[68]

In 2009, the Gates Foundation announced that it would stop giving small grants in favor of large ones to support charter schools and new forms of teacher evaluation. Probably the most significant part of the plan was to fund charter school management groups rather than individual charter schools. *The New York Times* reported that "Some $60 million will go to five charter management organizations based in Los Angeles: Alliance for College-Ready Public Schools, Aspire Public Schools, Green Dot Public Schools, Inner City Education Foundation and Partnerships to Uplift Communities Schools."[69]

President Obama's education agenda, like that of the world's wealthiest man and foundation, includes charter schools. In a March 10, 2009 speech to the Hispanic Chamber of Commerce, President Obama called charter schools the fourth part of his education strategy. He told the gathering,

> One of the places where much of that innovation [reinventing the school] occurs is in our most effective charter schools. And these are public schools founded by parents, teachers, and civic or community organizations with broad leeway to innovate—schools I supported as a state legislator and a United States senator.[70]

The criteria for granting aid under Race to the Top required the end of state laws limiting the number of charter schools:

> Increasing the supply of high quality charter schools: (i) The extent to which the State has a charter school law that does not prohibit or effectively inhibit increasing the number of charter schools in the State (as measured by the percentage of total schools in the State that are allowed to be charter schools) or otherwise restrict student enrollment in charter schools.[71]

Given this common talk about charter schools it is not surprising that the KIPP schools received funding from both the Gates Foundation and the Race to the Top stimulus package.

The Gates Foundation newsletters announced funding of KIPP schools:

> (March 18, 2004) SAN FRANCISCO—With 31 college prep public middle schools in operation, KIPP (Knowledge Is Power Program) has received a $7.9 million grant from the Bill & Melinda Gates Foundation to expand its successful, high-performing public middle schools into the high school grades. KIPP will start new high schools linked to its public middle schools, including those in Houston, Texas and Gaston N.C.[72]

Reflecting this interest in KIPP, *Philantopic: A Blog of Opinion and Commentary from Philanthropy News Digest* reported in an August 21, 2009 interview with Richard Barth, CEO of the KIPP Foundation:

> The Obama administration has thrown down the gauntlet to educators and legislators to fix an education system that used to be "the best in the world, and no longer is" . . . The centerpiece of that effort, the Race to the Top Fund, will make available $4.35 billion to identify and replicate effective education reform strategies and classroom innovations, including charter schools. One of the most highly regarded charter school systems in the country, KIPP has grown in fifteen years from two schools, one in Houston and the other in New York City, to a network of eighty-two open-enrollment public schools.[73]

The mutual relationship between the world's wealthiest man and foundation and President Obama's administration resulted in a major influence on national school policies. In reporting work on state applications for Race to the Top funds, the *New York Times* reporter Sam Dillon wrote, "Experts say the process is like watching dozens of states bid for the Olympics."[74] Data, national standards and assessments, teacher evaluations based on test scores, and charter schools are the common language of the Obama administration and the world's wealthiest man.

What Do Teachers Talk About When They Talk About Schools?

In 2009, Scholastic, with support from the Bill and Melinda Gates Foundation, conducted a survey of more than 40,000 public school teachers, and conducted in-depth interviews and held 108 focus groups with K-12 teachers. Unlike politicians, an overwhelming majority of teachers do not think standardized tests are of great importance for measuring student performance. What teachers think are absolutely essential or very important as indicators of student achievement are "Formative, ongoing assessment during class" (92 percent), "Class participation" (89 percent), and "Performance on class assignments" (88 percent). In contrast, only a small percentage of teachers rated as essential or very important "District required-tests" (31 percent) and "State-required tests" (27 percent).[75] The survey summarizes these results:

> Use Multiple Measures to Evaluate Student Performance—From ongoing assessments throughout the year to student participation in individual classes, teachers are clear that these day-to-day assessments are a more reliable way to measure student performance than one-shot standardized tests. Ninety-two percent of teachers say ongoing in-classroom assessment is either very important or absolutely essential in measuring student performance, while only 27% say the same of state-required standardized tests.[76]

On the hot button question of "Pay tied to teachers' performance" only 25 percent thought it was essential or very important for retaining teachers, while 38 percent thought it was somewhat important and 36 percent thought it was not important. On the question 'What did teachers think was essential or very important for retaining teachers in the profession?' at the top of the list was "Supportive leadership" (96 percent) followed by "Access to high-quality curriculum and teaching resources" (90 percent) and "Time for teachers to collaborate" (89 percent).[77]

On the question "What do teachers think will contribute to student achievement?" the overwhelming majority reject a central premise of No Child Left Behind that the achievement gap will be closed by having all students receive the same instruction under the same state standards. This aspect of No Child Left Behind was to overcome the segregation and discrimination that occurred when children were divided into ability groups and received different instruction and assignments. Ninety-five percent of surveyed teachers agreed that "differentiated assignments engage their students in learning" and 90 percent said "having resources to help differentiate instruction is absolutely essential or very important in impacting achievement."[78]

Another 2009 survey conducted by Metlife found that 67 percent of teachers and 89 percent of principals believed that "greater collaboration among teachers and school leaders would have a major impact on improving student achievement."[79] This survey found that teachers (86 percent) and principals (89 percent) believe that high expectations for learning have an impact on student achievement. Also, 92 percent of teachers and 96 percent of principals believed that "having adequate public funding and support for education are very important for improving student achievement."[80]

These surveys show that teachers are not too fond of standardized tests and place their emphasis for student achievement on collaboration, differentiated instruction, teacher-created in-class assessments, and adequate funding. Except for adequate funding, these are not items often called for by politicians.

The two teachers unions represent the public voice of teachers. Of course, individual teachers might not agree with their union. Do teachers believe that public schools are failing? Not all teachers, according to this comment posted on the website of the American Federation of Teachers (AFT): "I feel there is a serious effort to downplay the successes of the public school system in order to promote private charter schools and vouchers. Our schools should be adequately funded and class sizes should be reduced—Connie Goodly, Baltimore Teachers Union."[81]

Some teachers are upset at demands that students follow a single set of standards and assessments. In other words, they seem to reject the idea that data systems will help students and teachers. The National Education Association (NEA), the largest of the two teachers unions, posted this voice from the classroom on its website.

> In our school system, we are working feverishly to develop pacing guides to regulate what is taught every day. We are setting up our children and our teachers for failure. This law [No Child Left Behind] is being used as an excuse to not teach children from where they are; we are discouraged from meeting "Johnny" on his second-grade level and bringing him forward. *Let me show and document progress, and I will be happy to do so. But this law, with its dependency on standardized tests, doesn't accomplish what politicians tell you it does* [author's emphasis]. Michelle Harris, Middle School Teacher, Alabama.[82]

In general, teachers seem to be unhappy with those politicians and public leaders demanding school improvement based on data from student test scores on standardized tests. The AFT posted the following comments from teachers on its website. All of them express frustration at the direction in which politicians are leading the public schools.

- "... to leave the decisions regarding testing to the teachers. We know how to create tests that measure what we have taught, and that are tailored to our students. Uniform testing necessarily targets the lowest common denominator. As an experienced teacher I know that students are not the same from year to year. Even if I teach the same course, and cover the same curriculum, I may have to adjust the pacing or the order of presenting the topics. Let us decide when, how often, and in what format to test our own students." Paula Washington, United Federation of Teachers, New York
- "... to eliminate the use of a single state assessment to determine student proficiency. Measuring student progress throughout the year is a far more effective indicator of student/teacher/school performance." Travis Burns, Cheyenne Federation of Teachers, Wyoming
- "... test less! Students do NOT need to be tested every year to assess their abilities. Millions of dollars could then be better used for smaller class sizes, materials, teachers' salaries. Students get bored with testing ... after a few years many just start guessing on tests. So what is the point?" Tom Liley, AFT Local 604, Illinois[83]

NEA teachers report the same disdain for the emphasis on standardized tests.

- "NCLB [No Child Left Behind] is creating a generation of students who are meeting standards that were set by political considerations rather than those that are necessary for the United States to maintain its technological and scientific edge in the world. Congress needs to allow teachers to set high standards for all students on an individual basis rather than allow political considerations to set the educational agenda." Robert Taylor, High School Teacher, Anchorage, Alaska
- "Teaching is not only my profession, but it is also my life! Be it such, I love to see students' eyes light up when they learn new concepts, or when they are engaged in various activities that allow them to be creative. But in recent years, I have seen bright eyes, that had been full of life and ideas, turn dull with boredom and stress. Why? Where has the curiosity gone? Test prep, test prep, and more test prep! Most of our school days are filled with test-prep activities. If not test prep, then we are reviewing for the test! It saddens me." David Ouch, Elementary School Teacher, Sierra Madre, California

- "These are the symptoms that are being felt even in schools with principals who had not previously made concessions to the testing insanity. Eventually, NCLB will force us all into insanity." John Perry, Elementary School Teacher, Tampa, Florida[84]

What are teachers saying about charter schools as the panacea for education pushed by some political and public leaders? Teachers are wary, according to their comments on the AFT website. Some want the unions to operate charter schools rather than privately managed and nationally marketed plans.

- "We need to start more union charter schools. Let's show the politicians we know how to do it and prove it." Virginia Hill, United Federation of Teachers
- "The public schools do not need more money siphoned away [to charter schools]—you can't fix a problem with less money." Lynn Gustafson, Texas Federation of Teachers[85]

The two teachers unions, of course, are leery of the potential impact of charter schools on the unionization of teachers and the reduction of funds for traditional public schools. The official statement of the NEA on charter schools stresses that local school boards should control charter schools in their districts as opposed to control by state governments. Also, the NEA rejects the operation of public charter schools by for-profit education companies. And, according to the NEA, "Charter schools should be subject to the same public sector labor relations statutes as traditional public schools, and charter school employees should have the same collective bargaining rights as their counterparts in traditional public schools."[86]

How do teachers feel about the Race to the Top requirement that teacher compensation be tied to student test scores? Traditionally, teachers have been paid according to their years of experience and educational attainment. Race to the Top would change this traditional process by paying some teachers more than others based on their student test scores. The position of the teachers unions is clear: all salaries should be determined through collective bargaining at the local level. The unions rejected the idea that any difference in teacher compensation should be based solely on student test scores. The official position of the AFT regarding locally arrived at differentiated pay plans is: "AFT locals have developed schoolwide differentiated pay based on a combination of academic indicators, including standardized test scores, students' classroom work, dropout rates and disciplinary incidents. Teachers reject being evaluated on a single test score."[87]

NEA leaders and teachers have expressed concern about linking teacher pay to student test scores. One teacher commented, "I'd like to see government employees pay be based on how the economy is doing" (11/11/09—Cindy G.).[88] Bill Raabe, the NEA's Director of Collective Bargaining and Member Benefits, warned, "We must be wary of any system that creates a climate where students are viewed as part of the pay equation, rather than young people who deserve a high quality education that prepares them for their future."[89] Most teachers consider it ridiculous to link student test scores to teacher pay according to comments posted on the NEA website.

- "Has anyone really thought about what the effects on the child would be when an adult's pay is based on his/her test scores? I can't think of a worse way to corrupt the relationship between student and teacher than to infuse money into the equation. Imagine the stress on the child, the resentment of students by teachers, the power games older students could play . . . yikes!" (11/11/09—Carol)
- "I was in the private sector—and yes, sometimes increases were based on some things I couldn't control. But, I'd rather have that than trust my pay (and ability to support my own children) to how students decide to perform a few days on one test." (11/11/09—Nicole)
- "I think it's ridiculous to pay teachers based on test scores. There are too many variables in a child's life." (11/11/09—Jenny Brice)[90]

The two teachers unions and their members did not support the regulations for funding in Race to the Top. When the initial stimulus package was being considered, NEA President Dennis Van Roekel wrote to the Senate in support of the American Recovery and Reinvestment Act with the qualification that education funding should be directed toward investing in school infrastructure, such as buildings and grounds, and providing more money for programs serving disadvantaged students and those with special needs. There was no mention in the letter of the need for a national data bank, common national standards, or the use of student tests to evaluate teachers.[91] When the Race to the Top criteria were announced in July 2009, AFT president Randi Weingarten worried about its impact:

> But hopefully we will agree that teacher evaluations must be improved the right way. We need meaningful, fair and multiple measures for supporting and evaluating teachers so that evaluations aren't based on one observation by a principal or one standardized test score.[92]

In summary, teachers provide a countervailing voice to the doom, gloom, and crisis mentality of politicians and the media and to demands for fixing schools with national data systems and standards, student and teacher evaluations that rely on standardized test scores, and charter schools. Similar to parents who give their local schools high marks, many teachers feel positive about their teaching and public schools.

What Do School Administrators Talk About When They Talk About Schools?

In striking contrast to politicians, media, the world's richest man and foundation, and teachers, school administrators talk about the lack of money to fund public schools and blame poverty and welfare conditions for problems faced by students in school. The American Association of School Administrators (AASA) represents the voices of about 13,000 school administrators in the United States and around the world.[93] The reaction of AASA voices to Race to the Top is to say that there is not enough money and it has the wrong emphasis. Typical of the concerns about school funding are the remarks of Charles Maranzano, Jr., Superintendent of Schools, Hopatcong, New Jersey, posted on the AASA blog: "The acronym NCLB, No Child Left Behind, may just become No Country Left Behind, as the federal and state budget shortfalls further erode the quality of public education in America."[94]

AASA places its priority for school improvement on adequate funding and improving the living conditions of students. This organization shifts the blame for underachieving students from schools to conditions outside of school. The organization's main legislative push in 2009 was titled *Educating the Whole Child*.[95] In its proposal to improve schools, AASA highlights the following factors:

- The devastating impact of poverty on our students;
- The lack of universal early childhood education;
- The need for cooperation and collaboration across agencies and organizations.

"The most prevalent and persistent gaps in student achievement," AASA declares, "are a result of the effects of poverty."[96] After summarizing the research on the effect of poverty, its legislative agenda states:

Children of poverty tend to live in low-income neighborhoods and attend schools that have limited resources. They also are more likely to complete fewer years of formal education and face more health issues than do children from higher income families. Poor children may be hindered in their cognitive development by weak social, emotional and behavioral skills and poor nutrition.[97]

Educating the Whole Child cites statistics from the Children's Defense Fund that 1 in 6 children in the United States are poor, 13.3 million children live in poverty, and 5.8 million live in extreme poverty.[98]

In contrast to politicians and others, AASA proposes closing the achievement gap by improving the economic conditions of children instead of a reliance on data systems and charter schools.

> To mitigate the disadvantages poverty brings to the classroom, AASA advocates for local, state and federal funding for human services to address childhood poverty. Focusing education funding where it is needed the most—on schools serving children of poverty— significantly increases the chances that those dollars will actually help close the achievement gap.[99]

Also, AASA thinks that preschools will address some of the school problems faced by children growing up in poverty, children of cultural minorities, and children who are English language learners. The organization advocates universal preschool. *Educating the Whole Child* asserts: "Achievement gaps among students of different socioeconomic, ethnic and linguistic backgrounds are noticeable by age 3 and must be addressed by early childhood education programs that ensure each child begins school prepared to learn."[100] Consequently, the organization supported federal efforts to expand preschool education.

The third legislative proposal is also tied to children's poverty and is based on AASA's assertion that: "Students achieve to higher levels when organizations work with public education to coordinate delivery of health and child development services."[101] Consequently, AASA proposes a coordination of welfare services with schools.

It is important to emphasize the difference between AASA's legislative agenda and the 2001 federal legislation No Child Left Behind. No Child Left Behind sought to close the achievement gap between rich and poor students by creating common curriculum standards, closing failing schools, and the public reporting of student test scores. No Child Left Behind did not address conditions outside of school that could hinder student learning.[102] In contrast, AASA supports remedying negative social conditions existing outside of school as a key to improving the learning of low-achieving students. AASA's legislative agenda supports a health care system serving children from low-income families; federal funding and access to mental health care and dental care; high-quality child care for families in poverty, including the working poor; and compiling research and best practices that will help schools educate the total child.[103]

In summary, school administrators emphasize the welfare function of government over other panaceas for improving American schools, particularly for reducing the achievement gap between high-income and low-income students. Of particular concern is ensuring adequate medical and dental care for low-income families. Also, the organization seeks full funding of public school programs.

What Do Black and Latino Educators Talk About When They Talk About Schools?

The National Alliance of Black School Educators (NABSE) and the Association of Latino Administrators and Superintendents (ALAS) are the two largest organizations representing the voices of African Americans and Latino/Latina educators. NABSE represents approximately 10,000 educators including teachers, administrators, and members of other institutions interested in the welfare of African American children.[104] The stated goals of NABSE are to be advocates for the education of African American children and, "Identify and develop African American professionals who will assume leadership positions in education and influence public policy concerning the education of African Americans."[105]

NABSE is fostering the idea that "Education is a Civil Right" for all children: "NABSE declares that education is not just a privilege, but a birth right, as well as an entitlement."[106] The organization declared February 12, 2009 as Education is a Civil Right Participation Day.

While agreeing with the proposals of the American Association of School Administrators that poverty and social conditions inhibit the learning of some African American children, NABSE emphasizes the necessity of quality schools and the end of racial school segregation, including segregation within schools. In its "Education is a Civil Right Toolkit" special emphasis is placed on quality schools for all children. The "Toolkit" asserts that "Much of the black-white achievement gap can be attributed to substantial differences in quality between the schools that enroll predominantly ethnic minority students and those attended by the white middle class."[107] In addition, the organization continues to worry about the effect of racial segregation, "Race/ethnicity and socioeconomic status are systematically linked within the American society as a whole and, as a result, racial segregation in schools is almost always confounded with concentrated student poverty, and, sometimes accompanied by linguistic segregation as well."[108]

Unlike other voices in education, NABSE has a somewhat critical stance towards immigrant competition for jobs. Post-secondary education is not emphasized because of competition for jobs in the global economy as it is in so much current rhetoric about schools. In contrast, the focus is on immigrant competition:

> Competition for low, medium and high paying jobs will no longer be assured with just a high school or even college education. Even low

wage jobs are no longer available in many cases, as an ever *increasing immigrant population is willing to take lower wages and work longer hours than the traditional low-wage worker* [author's emphasis].[109]

NABSE stresses the importance of providing equal quality schools for all and ending segregation of school facilities, while other voices proclaim that uniform curriculum standards, common testing, and closing failing schools will reduce the achievement gap between oppressed cultural minorities and the rest of the population. From the perspective of NABSE's members: "Since their arrival in this country in 1619, African Americans have been subjected to inferior and disproportionate education and other services. First denied and then suffering an inadequate, underfunded, under resourced and separate education."[110] The organization notes that racial segregation has actually increased from 66 percent of African American students attending majority non-white schools in 1991 to 73 percent in 2003–2004. The organization claims:

> In general, schools in economically depressed, racially segregated communities, are almost always unequal schools, characterized by low teacher morale, strained relationships between teachers and administrators, defiant and oppositional behavior from students, an inordinate number of inexperienced teachers and high turnover in administrative leadership.[111]

One aspect of racial segregation, according to NABSE, is the over-representation and under-representation of African American students in some educational practices and programs. According to the organization there is an over-representation of African American students in:

- special education;
- students receiving suspensions, expulsions, and other disciplinary measures;
- students identified as mentally retarded or emotionally disturbed.

On the other hand, there is an under-representation of African American students in:

- gifted and talented programs;
- advanced placement classes;
- honors classes.[112]

As a result of these conditions, in 2007 NABSE adopted its initiative "Education is a Civil Right." In July 2008, NABSE submitted its Education is a Civil Right initiative to the Committee on Education and Labor, U.S. House of Representatives.[113] The most important parts of

Education is a Civil Right are the elimination of educational inequities and the development of leadership within the African American community to ensure the end of educational disparities and provide help in improving the achievement of African American students.

The Education is a Civil Right initiative has as its goals:

- To foster and develop through dialogue, workshops, political and civil action, and other appropriate means, an awareness of the consequences of educational underachievement in every corner of society;
- To initiate activities that will directly address the educational disparities and inequities faced by African American students and families, and bring about intended and measurable improvements in our public school systems;
- To develop the talents, skills and leadership within our communities that can use its collective expertise and knowledge to continuously monitor, review and effect needed changes relative to the educational civil rights of the students and families in all parts of our society;
- To provide strategies and activities for use in school districts serving a significant population of African American students.[114]

Educational equity problems facing Spanish-speaking students are a central concern of the Association of Latino Administrators and Superintendents (ALAS), as reflected in their choice of an acronym: "ALAS was intentionally selected as a word in the Spanish language that means wings."[115] Organized in 2003, ALAS became an affiliate of the American Association of School Administrators and received support from the California Latino Superintendents Association and the Association of California School Administrators.[116] Since the 1990s there has been a close working relationship between the California Latino Superintendents Association and the Association of California School Administrators.[117] The organization claims to be the voice of Latinos in U.S. education which includes a broad Spanish-speaking population:

> Addressing the needs of the fastest growing minority in the United States—the Latino community is vital to the national interest. Latinos have become the new "America's largest minority." ALAS serves as a voice for Latinos in the United States. This ever growing country is uniquely enriched by large numbers of Latino subgroups, i.e. Mexican-Americans, Puerto Ricans, Cubans, Dominicans, and Latin Americans.[118]

The proposed strategy to help Spanish-speaking youth is to recruit quality bilingual teachers and Latino school administrators. Fernando

Elizondo, Executive Director of the California Latino Superintendents Association, described the plans to reduce the achievement gap between Latino and white students: "More bilingual teachers and administrators and a more inclusive and challenging curriculum. These two basic strategies can positively affect the teaching and learning of Latino children in addressing the linguistic diversity and competencies of English language learners."[119]

Regarding bilingual teachers, Elizondo states that superintendents should contact universities to identify the best candidates for bilingual education teaching positions and give bilingual teachers signing bonuses that would commit them to teaching in the district for a defined number of years. These teachers, besides providing help to English language learners, would also serve as role models for Latino students. The goal of recruiting more Latino school administrators is for them to serve as role models and be attuned to the needs of Latino students. A mentoring program would help bilingual educators become school and district administrators.[120]

Helping Latinos achieve school administrative positions is primary in the relationship between the California Latino Superintendents Association and the Association of California School Administrators. The Executive Director of the Association of California School Administrators described this relationship:

> Over the past 10 years ACSA and CALSA have partnered to close the achievement gap and increase the number of Latino administrators in the state. We've made important progress; for example, we now have more than 1,600 Latino administrators in ACSA, and CALSA has grown from 30 members 10 years ago to more than 300 today.[121]

In summary, the National Alliance of Black School Educators and the Association of Latino Administrators and Superintendents express concerns that are quite different from the voices claiming that schools are the weak link in global economic competition and that school improvement depends on curriculum standards and testing. The National Alliance of Black School Educators advocates desegregation between and within schools, along with providing all children with quality and equal schools, and the Association of Latino Administrators and Superintendents worries about English language learners and providing Latino students with bilingual teachers and administrators who can serve as role models.

What Do Students Talk About When They Talk About Schools?

This is a tough question to answer because of the variety of students and, although the Phi Delta Kappa/Gallup poll reports parental attitudes about schools, there is no national polling of student opinions. Most studies that I've seen are concerned about how student attitudes affect their learning. The international Organization for Economic Cooperation and Development (OECD) has conducted a study of student dislike of school. Of the seventeen countries reported in the study Belgium ranked number one with 42 percent of students found to dislike school, with the United States ranked fifth with 35 percent of students expressing a dislike of school. The countries with the lowest percentages were Sweden and Denmark with 20 percent and 19 percent respectively of students expressing a dislike of school.[122]

Thirty-five percent of students disliking school seems pretty high to me but maybe not to others. In a study of school choice, OECD found students to be fairly satisfied with school, with older students less satisfied than younger students and girls expressing more satisfaction than boys. The major complaint of students was that school is boring. Students stated that the factors making a class boring are poor-quality teaching, the lack of personalization of methods, and their interest in the content.[123]

One attempt to organize student civic action is the Student Voices Project organized by the Annenberg Public Policy Center and funded by the Annenberg Foundation. The project has been adopted by school districts across the United States as part of the study of government. Each school class involved in the project creates a Youth Issues Agenda reflecting local student concerns. Most of these Issues are related to political campaigns as part of an effort to "develop civic engagement in the student body and reinvigorate the civic mission of schools."[124]

While most of the questions students are asked as part of the Student Voices Project deal with specific campaign issues such as gun control, energy policy, global warming, and the qualifications of U.S. Supreme Court Justices, some deal specifically with education policies. One important education question students were asked was, "Is the No Child Left Behind Act helping the education system in the United States?"[125] The overwhelming response to the legislation was negative, primarily because of the mandated use of standardized testing. Typical of these responses in 2008 and 2009 were:

- "The federal government should have a much more limited role in public education practices and teaching method. Students are forced to worry about scores and numbers rather than learning skills that will help them in their lives. With the overall failure of NCLB becoming obvious, the government should be able to take a hint to stop interfering with teaching methods." (Andrew, Trinity High School, Washington, PA)

- "I do not think the No Child Left Behind Act is helping the education system in the United States. It is not an accurate means of testing a student's academic achievement." (Chelsea, Trinity High School, Washington, PA)
- "The NCLB Act is doing nothing but harm [to] the American Educational System. The NCLB is faltering [sic] the very foundations that education was founded upon. Classroom standards are falling, teachers are being put through rigorous military-type training, and class time is being switched to testing time. The federal governments [sic] role in public education must change in favor of a better system." (Jarrett, Trinity High School, Washington, PA)
- "No, I do not think the No Child Left Behind Act is helping the education system. It only focuses on those students in the middle rather than those who are not doing as well and getting very behind or those who are very smart not having people doing soemthing [sic] about it." (Jackie, Trinity High School, Washington, PA)
- "The No Child Left Behind Act does not help the education system in the U.S. because students can do good school work but it can't be reflected when you take so many state wide test because your [sic] a bad test taker." (Monee, Overbrook High School, Philadelphia, PA)[126]

The general feeling of students about No Child Left Behind was expressed by Amanda C. of Trinity High School, Washington, Pennsylvania: "How many times do teachers and students have to say it: standardized tests are not a fair way to judge student success. As a graduating senior I can honestly say that the NCLB act has not helped me in any way."[127]

The above studies and comments do not necessarily reflect the voices of all students. In fact, one wonders how many elementary through secondary school students have even heard of No Child Left Behind. Despite these limitations it is important to note that students responding to the question asked by the Annenberg project on student voices over-whelmingly considered the emphasis on standardized testing as damaging to their education. This is in stark contrast to politicians, foundations, and educational leaders who push an agenda of national assessments as the key to school improvement. And, according to OECD, most students, like parents, are satisfied with their local schools. A small percentage of students find school boring but this has probably always been the case. Not surprisingly, most students appear to want their classes to be interesting with teachers using methods geared to student needs.

Conclusion: So What Do People Talk About When They Talk About Schools?

These are the conflicting voices that were heard in 2009 when the hot topic was the Race to the Top. These multiple voices reflect varying concerns and interests in education policies. However, the national media primarily and uncritically report the voices of national figures, particularly politicians, on school conditions. The overwhelming majority of politicians broadcast human capital ideology through the media to the public. How much the thinking of the public is influenced by these media messages would be difficult to determine. Does the influence of the media shape public thinking to accept that the purpose of schooling should be to make the United States number one in the world economy through common curriculum standards and high-stakes testing?

The human capital ideology is promulgated by the wealthiest Americans including Bill Gates, Warren Buffett, and New York City's billionaire mayor Michael Bloomberg. They support the whole gamut of reforms associated with human capital thinking including charter schools, standardized curricula, and high-stakes testing. The support from these wealthiest Americans is not surprising since human capital ideology reflects their economic interests in using schools to bolster the economy in international trade. In other words, human capital ideology may help increase their bottom lines.

The combination of viewpoints relayed over public media by politicians and some of America's wealthiest has exposed the public to a steady stream of uncritical messages supporting a human capital ideology that claims that saving schools will save the economy and people's jobs. It could be that these messages have been internalized by the public so that they only think about schools as providing jobs and economic growth. As a result of this steady stream of media messages, the public may have internalized human capital ideology to the point of it being the uncritical lens or paradigm that they use in thinking about education.

The media seldom, as far as I can determine, report that parents feel that their local schools are doing a good job and that their major representative organization, the PTA, is focused on children's nutrition and health. It would be difficult to identify a single educational ideology held by all parents. Certainly some parents accept the political message that the development of human capital should be the driving force behind American schools. On the other hand, some parents give little thought to educational goals and policies. In addition, there are some parents who simply reject public school policies and, for reasons of religious, political, or educational beliefs, choose to home school their children or send them to private alternative schools, such as Montessori, Waldorf or Summerhill-type free schools.

The PTA's focus on nutrition and health could reflect a concept of childhood focused on "protected childhood." In *Huck's Raft: A History of American Childhood*, Steven Mintz argues that there are two competing concepts of childhood.[128] One is "protected childhood" where the family focuses on ensuring that children have a carefree life with proper nutrition, shelter, health care, and schooling. Childhood is something to be enjoyed. In this conceptual framework, parents want schools that their children enjoy. The other conceptual framework is "prepared childhood" where the focus is on preparing children to enter work and adulthood. Human capital ideology contains the concept of prepared childhood where the emphasis is not on children enjoying school but on preparation to enter the job market or college. Some parents who are concerned with a protected childhood might be the ones removing their children from public schools and sending them to private alternative schools where they hope their children will enjoy learning.

One might conclude that representative organizations of school administrators conceptualize childhood as a protected period because of their stated beliefs that the primary causes of the achievement gap between children from low- and high-income families are children's poverty and health care, racial and economic segregation between and within schools, and the lack of bilingual teachers. However, the emphasis is on the "achievement gap" which echoes the purposes of No Child Left Behind which attempts to close the achievement gap by adopting state curriculum standards, high-stakes testing, and the closing of failing schools. In this case, organizations representing school administrators are not rejecting the human capital ideology but broadening its scope beyond the school to the child's home environment. It is a broader view of solutions to the achievement gap than that of those who focus exclusively on the school.

What do teachers and students say about the educational crisis imagined by politicians? While there is great diversity in the opinions of teachers and students many do complain about an overemphasis on testing, destroying the quality of school life and classroom instruction. Most teachers, unlike politicians, are generally satisfied with their schools except for the need for increased funding. Many teachers disdain the use of a single test to measure the quality of their teaching and student learning. Contrary to politicians, most students, whose voices are seldom reported by the media, want classes that are interesting, teachers who personalize their teaching methods, and a reduced reliance on standardized testing to measure learning. But who listens to teachers and students? The voices of those most directly affected by the educational system—students, parents, teachers, educational administrators—seem to have little influence over school policies. Because of the diversity of opinions among teachers and students it would be impossible to claim that a single educational ideology reflects all of their viewpoints.

Notes

1 Libby Quaid and Donna Blankinship, "The Influence Game: Gates' sway on Ed. Policy," Associated Press, October 26, 2009. Retrieved from http://www.boston.com/news/education/k_12/articles/2009/10/26/the_influence_game_gates_sways_government_dollars/?s_campaign=8315 on October 27, 2009.

2 Quoted in Gerald Bracey, "Experience Outweighs Rhetoric," *Phi Delta Kappan* (September 2009), p. 11.

3 Quoted in Joel Spring, *The Sorting Machine Revisited: National Educational Policy Since 1945*, updated edn. (New York: Longman, 1989), p. 66.

4 See ibid., pp. 1–76.

5 Ibid., pp. 123–151.

6 See Andrew Hacker, "Can We Make America Smarter?" *The New York Review of Books* (April 30, 2009), pp. 37–40.

7 National Commission on Excellence in Education, *A Nation at Risk: The Imperatives for Educational Reform* (Washington, D.C.: Department of Education, 1983).

8 Chester Finn and Diane Ravitch, "Educational Reform 1995–96 Introduction." Retrieved from ww.edexcellence.net on February 4, 2004.

9 David C. Berliner and Bruce Biddle, *The Manufactured Crisis: Myths, Fraud, and the Attack on America's Public Schools* (New York: Addison-Wesley, 1995).

10 Democratic National Convention Committee, "Report of the Platform Committee: Renewing America's Promise." Presented to the 2008 Democratic National Convention, August 13, 2008, p. 18. Retrieved from the American Presidency Project Document Archive http://www.presidency.ucsb.edu/papers_pdf/78283.pdf on November 13, 2008.

11 See Joel Spring, *Political Agendas for Education: From Change We Can Believe in to Putting America First*, 4th edn. (New York: Routledge, 2010), pp. 1–64.

12 Ibid., pp. 34–36.

13 Darrell M. West, Grover J. Whitehurst, and E.J. Dionne, Jr., *Invisible: 1.4 Percent Coverage for Education is Not Enough* (Washington, D.C.: Brookings Institution, 2009), p. 1.

14 Ibid.

15 Ibid.

16 Ibid., p. 3.

17 Ibid.

18 Cynthia I. Gerstl-Pepin, "Media (Mis)Representations of Education in the 2000 Presidential Election," *Educational Policy* (January and March 2002), pp. 37–55.

19 Ibid., p. 37.

20 Ibid., pp. 49–50.

21 Ibid., p. 50.

22 Ibid.

23 Ibid.

24 "Table 2, Phi Delta Kappa/Gallup Poll," *Phi Delta Kappan* (September 2009), p. 11.

25 Ibid.

26 "Table 3, Phi Delta Kappa/Gallup Poll," *Phi Delta Kappan* (September 2009), p. 11.

27 Ibid.
28 "Table 4, Phi Delta Kappa/Gallup Poll," *Phi Delta Kappan* (September 2009), p. 11.
29 Ibid.
30 Bracey, "Experience Outweighs Rhetoric."
31 Ibid.
32 Parent Teachers Association, "FAQs / PTA Annual Report: PTA Annual Reports." Retrieved from http://www.pta.org/2204.htm on November 25, 2009.
33 Parent Teachers Association, *PTA 2009 Public Policy Agenda: Advocating for the Education, Health, and Overall Well-being of All Children* (Chicago: Parent Teachers Association, 2009), p. 4.
34 Public Law 107–110, 107th Congress, *An Act to Close the Achievement Gap with Accountability, Flexibility, and Choice, so that No Child is Left Behind* (Washington, D.C.: U.S. Printing Office, 2002), p. 1501.
35 Parent Teachers Association, *PTA 2009*, pp. 8–9.
36 Ibid., p. 11.
37 Ibid., pp. 14–17.
38 Luisa Kroll, Mathew Miller, and Tatiana Serafin, "The World's Billionaires," *Forbes* (March 11, 2009). Retrieved from http://www.forbes.com/2009/03/11/worlds-richest-people-billionaires-2009-billionaires_land.html on October 30, 2009.
39 Stephanie Strom, The Bill and Melinda Gates Foundation, *New York Times on the Web* (January 25, 2008). Retrieved from http://topics.nytimes.com/topics/reference/timestopics/organizations/g/gates_bill_and_melinda_foundation/index.html on October 30, 2009.
40 Quaid and Blankinship, "The Influence Game."
41 Press Release, U.S. Department of Education, "Margot M. Rogers—Biography, June 2, 2009." Retrieved from http://www.ed.gov/news/press releases/2009/05/05192009d.html on October 31, 2009.
42 Press Release, U.S. Department of Education, "James H. Shelton III, Assistant Deputy Secretary for Innovation and Improvement—Biography, June 2, 2009." Retrieved from http://www.ed.gov/news/staff/bios/shelton.html.
43 United States Department of Education, Office of the General Counsel, March 23, 2009, "Certification of Public Interest Waiver for Margot Rogers." Retrieved from http://www.usage.gov/directors_corner/pledge_waivers/Rogers_waiver.pdf on October 30, 2009. United States Department of Education, Office of the General Counsel, April 28, 2009, "Certification of Public Interest Waiver for James H. Shelton III." Retrieved from http://www.usage.gov/directors_corner/pledge_waivers/Shelton_waiver.pdf on October 30, 2009.
44 Arne Duncan, "Chicago Public Schools (CPS) Budget Book (August 2007)," p. 6. Retrieved from http://www.cps.edu/About_CPS/Financial_information/Documents/FY08_Online_Budget_Book.pdf on November 9, 2009.
45 Ibid., p. 137.
46 Office of New Schools, Chicago Public Schools, "2007–08 Charter Schools Performance Report (2009)," p. 24. Retrieved from http://www.cps.edu/News/Press_releases/2009/Documents/CPSONSperfreport.pdf on November 9, 2009.
47 Ibid., p. 34.
48 Civitas, "About Us." Retrieved from http://www.civitasschools.org/about/distinguishers/ on November 10, 2009.

49 Office of New Schools, Chicago Public Schools, "2007–08 Charter Schools Performance Report (2009)," p. 2.
50 Prepared remarks by Bill Gates, co-chair and trustee (November 11, 2008). Retrieved from Bill and Melinda Gates Foundation website http://www. gatesfoundation.org/speeches-commentary/Pages/bill-gates-2008-education-forum-speech.aspx on November 1, 2009.
51 "Duncan Underlines Top Federal Education Priorities," *Education Week* (April 1, 2009), p. 21.
52 "Microsoft Without Gates: Bill Gates' Microsoft Stake," *Fortune* (undated). Retrieved from http://money.cnn.com/magazines/fortune/gates/2008/flash/ on November 1, 2009.
53 Prepared remarks by Bill Gates . . .
54 Bill and Melinda Gates Foundation, *College Ready* (2009), p. 5. Retrieved from http://www.gatesfoundation.org/learning/Documents/College-ready-education-plan-brochure.pdf on October 26, 2009.
55 Ibid.
56 Ibid.
57 Ibid.
58 U.S. Department of Education, "Race to the Top Fund—Executive Summary Notice; Notice of Proposed Priorities, Requirements, Definitions, and Selection Criteria (July 29, 2009), p. 1. Retrieved from http://www/ed/gov/programs/racetotop/executive-summary.pdf on September 24, 2009.
59 Arne Duncan, "Education Reform's Moon Shot," *The Washington Post* (July 24, 2009). Retrieved from http://www.washingtonpost.com/wp-dyn/content/article/2009/07/23/AR2009072302634.html on October 12, 2009.
60 Ibid.
61 Sam Dillon, "States Mold School Policies to Win New Federal Money," *The New York Times* (November 11, 2009). Retrieved from http://www.nytimes.com/2009/11/11/education/11educ.html?hp on November 11, 2009.
62 Ibid.
63 Arne Duncan, "Teacher Preparation: Reforming the Uncertain Profession—Remarks of Secretary Arne Duncan at Teachers College, Columbia University" (October 22, 2009). Retrieved from http://www.ed.gov/news/speeches/2009/10/10222009.html on November 1, 2009.
64 Ibid.
65 "2009 Annual Letter from Bill Gates: U.S. Education." Retrieved from http://www.gatesfoundation.org/annual-letter/2009-united-states-education.aspx.
66 Jay Mathews, *Work Hard, Be Nice* (Chapel Hill, NC: Algonquin Books, 2009).
67 "What is the KIPP Foundation." Retrieved from http://www.kipp.org/01/whatisthekippfound.cfm on November 2, 2009.
68 "About High Tech High." Retrieved from http://www.hightechhigh.org/about/ on October 30, 2009.
69 Sam Dillon, "Gateses Give $290 Million for Education" (November 20, 2009). Retrieved from http://www.nytimes.com/2009/11/20/education/20educ.html?_r=1&ref=education on November 20, 2009.
70 "Remarks by the President to the Hispanic Chamber of Commerce on a Complete and Competitive American Education" (March 10, 2009). Retrieved from http://www.whitehouse.gov/the_press_office/Remarks-of-the-President-to-the-Hispanic-Chamber-of-Commerce/ on March 10, 2009.
71 U.S. Department of Education, "Race to the Top Fund," Part III, p. 9.

72 Bill and Melinda Gates Foundation, "KIPP Receives $7.9 Million to Enter World of High School" (March 18, 2004). Retrieved from http://www.gates foundation.org/press-releases/Pages/knowledge-is-power-program-receives-grant-040318.aspx on November 4, 2009.
73 "Newsmaker: Richard Barth, CEO, KIPP Foundation," *Philantopic: A Blog of Opinion and Commentary from Philanthropy News Digest* (August 21, 2009). Retrieved from http://pndblog.typepad.com/pndblog/2009/08/news maker-richard-barth-ceo-kipp-foundation.html on November 4, 2009.
74 Dillon, "Gateses Give $290 Million for Education."
75 Scholastic, *Primary Sources: America's Teachers on America's Schools* (New York: Scholastic, 2010), p. 25
76 Ibid., p. 2.
77 Ibid., p. 39.
78 Ibid., p. 34.
79 2009 MetLife Survey of the American Teacher, Part I, p. 3. Retrieved from http://www.metlife.com on April 8, 2010.
80 Ibid., Part 2, p. 3.
81 American Federation of Teachers, "AFT Voices." Retrieved from http://www.aft.org/voices/views-opinions-1.cfm on November 11, 2009.
82 National Education Association, "NCLB Stories: Highlighted Story." Retrieved from http://www.nea.org/home/18305.htm on November 11, 2009.
83 American Federation of Teachers, "AFT Voices."
84 National Education Association, "Meaningful Accountability." Retrieved from http://www.nea.org/home/12944.htm on November 12, 2009.
85 American Federation of Teachers, "AFT Voices."
86 National Education Association, "Charter Schools." Retrieved from http://www.nea.org/home/16332.htm on November 1, 2009.
87 American Federation of Teachers, "Differentiated Pay." Retrieved from http://www.aft.org/topics/teacher-quality/compensation/performance-pay.htm on November 11, 2009.
88 National Education Association, "Pay Based on Test Scores?" Retrieved from http://www.nea.org/home/36780.htm on November 12, 2009.
89 Ibid.
90 Ibid.
91 Dennis Van Roekel, "Letter to the Senate in Support of The American Recovery and Reinvestment Bill" (February 4, 2009). Retrieved from http://www.nea.org/ home/30426.htm on November 5, 2009.
92 American Federation of Teachers, "AFT to Scrutinize 'Race to the Top' Regulations." Retrieved from http://www.aft.org/news/2009/racetothetop.htm on November 1, 2009.
93 American Association of School Administrators, "About AASA." Retrieved from http://www.aasa.org/About.aspx on November 13, 2009.
94 Ibid.
95 American Association of School Administrators, *Educating the Whole Child: The Total Child Needs Your Attention* (2009). Retrieved from http://www.aasa.org/content.aspx?id=118 on November 9, 2009.
96 Ibid., p. 2.
97 Ibid.
98 Ibid.
99 Ibid.
100 Ibid., p. 3.

101 Ibid.
102 Public Law 107-110—January 8, 2002, "No Child Left Behind Act of 2001." Retrieved from U.S. Department of Education http://www.ed.gov/policy/elsec/leg/esea02/107-110.pdf on February 1, 2009.
103 American Association of School Administrators, *Educating the Whole Child*, p. 4.
104 National Alliance of Black School Educators, "Our Mission." Retrieved from http://www.nabse.org/aboutus.html on November 14, 2009.
105 Ibid.
106 National Alliance of Black School Educators, "Resolution." Retrieved from http://www.nabse.org/CivilRight/ECRResolutionProclamation.pdf. on November 12, 2009.
107 National Alliance of Black School Educators, "Education is a Civil Right Toolkit," p. 7. Retrieved from http://www.nabse.org/CivilRight/ECRToolkit.pdf on November 2, 2009.
108 Ibid.
109 Ibid., p. 2.
110 Ibid.
111 Ibid., p. 3.
112 Ibid.
113 Ibid., p. 4.
114 Ibid., p. 6.
115 Association of Latino Administrators and Superintendents, "Home." Retrieved from http://thealas.net/thealas/site/default.asp on November 14, 2009.
116 Association of Latino Administrators and Superintendents, "About Us." Retrieved from http://thealas.net/10991065145336967/site/default.asp on November 14, 2009.
117 California Association of Latino Superintendents and Administrators, "ACSA, CALSA Grow Relationship." Retrieved from http://www.acsa.org/Functional MenuCategories/Media/EdCalNewspaper/ 2009Archives/June15/ACSACALSA. aspx on November 16, 2009.
118 Association of Latino Administrators and Superintendents, "About Us."
119 Fernando Elizondo, "A Latino Perspective: Better Teachers and Administrators," *The School Administrator* (January 2005). Retrieved from http://www.calso.org/articleupload/fernando%20article.pdf on November 16, 2009.
120 Ibid.
121 California Association of Latino Superintendents and Administrators, "ACSA, CALSA Grow Relationship."
122 "Education Statistics: Student Attitude Dislike of School by Country" (undated). Retrieved from http://www.nationmaster.com/graph/edu_stu_att_wil_not_go_to_sch-education-student-attitude-dislike-school on November 23, 2009.
123 Organization for Economic Cooperation and Development, "Demand-Sensitive Schooling? Evidence and Issues" (2006). Retrieved from http://www.oecd.org/dataoecd/59/5/37655733.pdf on November 21, 2009.
124 Student Voices, "About Student Voices." Retrieved from http://www.student-voices.org/ShowPageInternal.aspx?LocId=1000&Name=About Student Voices on December 1, 2009.
125 Student Voices, "Is the No Child Left Behind Act Helping the Education System in the United States." Retrieved from http://www.student-voices.org/SpeakOutDiscussion.aspx?LocId= 1000&Id=391 on December 1, 2009.

126 Ibid.
127 Ibid.
128 Steven Mintz, *Huck's Raft: A History of American Childhood* (Cambridge, MA: Harvard University Press, 2004).

Chapter 3

From the Local to the Global in School Governance

Understanding the governance structure of U.S. education helps to explain the varying influence of the different public voices described in Chapter 2. However, the actual political structure of education doesn't tell the whole story. Within the governance structure politicians and political parties vie for power. Outside the governance structure, as I will discuss in Chapter 4, civil society attempts to influence the decisions within the educational governance structure. Therefore the governance structure is nested in an arena of political rivalries and ideologies and the competing influences from nongovernment organizations that form civil society. Within this nested governance structure political forces decide what knowledge is most worth teaching and the best conditions and organizational structures for teaching that knowledge.

One trend in America's educational governance structure is greater centralization of control. An important issue is the effect of centralization on which groups have the greatest influence over national school policies. Does centralization of control give more influence to some groups over others? This question leads to the broader question of who should control education.

The above questions generate another set dealing with decisions about what knowledge is most worth teaching:

- How does the political structure of education determine "what knowledge is most worth teaching"?
- How does the political structure determine the instructional methods to impart the knowledge determined to be of most worth for students?
- What educational ideology is most likely to be supported by the governance structure?

Constitutionally state governments have the power to determine the answers to the above questions. In reality the answer is more complicated.

The U.S. Constitution does not mention education and therefore it is a power given to the states. Despite no direct constitutional authority, the federal government today exerts direct power over local schools through requirements and regulations attached to federal spending on schools. States do not have to accept federal money but once they do their schools fall under federal influence. Also, U.S. Supreme Court rulings protect the constitutional rights of parents, students, and school staff. The growing power of the federal government over state education systems allows for greater centralization of control over what should be taught in schools and how it should be taught.

The U.S. school system is also nested in a global system. While other nations have no direct power over U.S. schools there are global competitions between school systems, particularly regarding international test scores in science and math. These international test scores represent a global academic Olympiad and along with other global factors directly impact U.S. schools. When American politicians and those in other countries claim a crisis in education they are sometimes referring to their nation's ranking in math and science according to international tests. Federal officials have called for the benchmarking of national standards and assessments against international standards and assessments.

I will outline this global governance structure by first examining the authority of state governments over schools and their power to create local governance structures such as school boards and mayoral control of schools. I will then turn to the federal government and its mechanisms for influencing state and local systems and then discuss local school boards and mayoral governance of schools. Next I will consider global influence over local schools and the role of civil society. Civil society is composed of nongovernment organizations such as interest groups, foundations, and think tanks. In the U.S. civil society is intimately entangled in power relations in schooling. I will use Chapter 2's focus on the 2009 Race to the Top to illustrate the relationship between federal, state, and local governance in American school politics. Also, I will discuss the role of civil society in these power relationships.

Forms of Representation

There are two forms of representation in the education governance structure, namely trustee and delegate. As I am using these terms, trustee representation refers to an education official who does what he or she thinks is best for you, while delegate representation refers to an official who does what you want. No educational representatives, such as school board members, state boards of education, or federal education officials are purely trustee or delegate representatives. One can think of school officials as being on a spectrum from trustee to delegate with some officials acting closer to a trustee form by doing what they think is good for you, while other officials act closer to what they think people want.

Elections and governance structures can be organized to favor one form of representation over another. The type of representation is affected by the size of the geographical area and population being represented, whether the official is appointed or elected, and the type of election, such as nonpartisan. Trustee forms of representation are supported by elections that are nonpartisan and include a large population and geographical area or involve appointment by another elected official such as a governor or the President of the United States. The more distant the official is from direct influence by citizens the more likely they are to act according to what they think is good for the population. On the other hand, the closer the official is to their constituency the more likely they are to respond to what the constituency wants.

State Governance

Historically, most decisions about curriculum, teaching methods, and recruitment of teachers and other staff were made by local school districts. Over time state governments increased their regulation of local schools and personnel. As states exercised more power over schools the public became less aware of many of the education policies decided upon by state officials. As I discussed in Chapter 2, the media is not very good at informing the public about education issues or at analyzing them.

Symbolic of this increasing state role in education was the 2003 announcement by the National Governors' Association of a standing committee on education. *Education Week* reporter Alan Richard asserts, "The move signals how prominent education has become politically for the nation's governors, and may strengthen the bipartisan group's ability to reach consensus on school related policies and help its lobbying efforts on Capitol Hill."[1] Cooperation between state governments contributes to the nationalization of education policies through the National Governors' Association and the Education Commission of the States. Founded in 1967, the Education Commission of the States was created to:

- Give voice to the diverse interests, needs and traditions of states;
- Enable them to cooperate and communicate with one another;
- Promote their working together to focus national attention on the pressing education issues of the day.[2]

There are many variations in state governance because of differently worded constitutions. Depending on the state, education officials are elected or appointed. An appointed state official is usually less well known by state citizens than one who must campaign for office. As examples of different forms of state governance I will use New York, Mississippi, California, and

Kansas. These states were selected because of differing methods of selecting state education officials, from the indirect process in New York to the more open election process in California and Kansas.

Consider the example of New York, which like other states provides for education in its Constitution. Article XI of the New York Constitution provides for:

[Common schools]
Section 1. The legislature shall provide for the maintenance and support of a system of free common schools, wherein all the children of this state may be educated.

[Regents of the University]
§2. The corporation created in the year one thousand seven hundred eighty-four, under the name of The Regents of the University of the State of New York, is hereby continued under the name of The University of the State of New York. It shall be governed and its corporate powers, which may be increased, modified or diminished by the legislature, shall be exercised by not less than nine regents.[3]

New York has a very indirect method of selecting its chief administrator for education or, as it is called in New York, the Commissioner of Education. The New York Constitution creates an entity called the Regents of the University. The power of Regents is defined in Article V of the state constitution:

The Regents are given the power to appoint the State Commissioner of Education. The head of the department of education shall be The Regents of the University of the State of New York, who shall appoint and at pleasure remove a commissioner of education to be the chief administrative officer of the department.[4]

The Regents, comprised of seventeen members, are elected by the state legislature and in turn its membership selects a Chancellor.

New York's reliance on appointments in contrast to election of the state education officials favors a trustee form of representation. Voters are never directly asked what they want. One important factor ensuring that both the Regents and Chancellor are often elite members of society is the fact that: "Regents are unsalaried and are reimbursed only for travel and related expenses in connection with their official duties."[5] The average worker would be financially pressed to give up paid work for unpaid work as a Regent.

A similar lack of direct voter control is evident in Mississippi. The Mississippi Constitution provides for education:

The Legislature shall, by general law, provide for the establishment, maintenance and support of free public schools upon such conditions and limitations as the Legislature may prescribe.[6]

The Mississippi Constitution creates a gulf between voters and state education officials by specifying that "a State Superintendent of Public Education . . . shall be appointed by the State Board of Education."[7] In turn the members of the State Board of Education are all appointed by a complicated formula involving the Governor, Lieutenant Governor, and Speaker of the House of Representatives. Since all of these education positions are appointed by an elected official it is uncertain how much indirect influence voters have over education policies.

In contrast to New York and Mississippi, California elects the leader of its state educational system. Article 9 of the California Constitution opens:

SECTION 1. A general diffusion of knowledge and intelligence being essential to the preservation of the rights and liberties of the people, the Legislature shall encourage by all suitable means the promotion of intellectual, scientific, moral, and agricultural improvement.[8]

Section 14 of Article 9 gives the state the power to create school districts and local governance structures.

SECTION 14. The Legislature shall have power, by general law, to provide for the incorporation and organization of school districts, high school districts, and community college districts, of every kind and class, and may classify such districts. The Legislature may authorize the governing boards of all school districts to initiate and carry on any programs, activities, or to otherwise act in any manner which is not in conflict with the laws and purposes for which school districts are established.[9]

The State Superintendent of Public Instruction is elected in a nonpartisan election. The nonpartisan requirement makes it difficult for many citizens without the financial means or connections to run for the office. Candidates cannot rely on the funds or organization of an established political party and therefore must seek funds and organization from other groups. It can be argued that this makes it more difficult for a middle- or low-income person to be a candidate for the office. Where would they get the money, organization, and time to campaign? In addition, members of California's State Board of Education are appointed by the governor. While the people elect the governor to represent them it is unclear if the governor appoints members to the State Board of Education who represent the educational interests of those who voted for the governor.

The California governor retains an important role in school governance. For instance, the importance of the governor's position is highlighted by the election of media-bodybuilding idol Republican Arnold Schwarzenegger to replace Democratic Governor Gray Davis. While some questioned the Terminator's movie-star knowledge of education, he was given political control of seven of the eleven members of the State Board of Education which has responsibilities for standards and testing, and the implementation of federally mandated policies. Some, laughingly, wondered if this would give more muscle to state education policies.[10]

In contrast to California, Kansas elects its State Board of Education which in turn appoints the Commissioner of Education. The Kansas Constitution provides for education:

> Schools and related institutions and activities. The legislature shall provide for intellectual, educational, vocational and scientific improvement by establishing and maintaining public schools, educational institutions and related activities which may be organized and changed in such manner as may be provided by law.[11]

The Kansas Constitution stipulates that the State Board of Education will be elected from ten state districts which are composed of four contiguous senatorial districts. Theoretically, the Kansas election process allows for more direct public influence over the state board in contrast to those states where the State Board of Education is appointed by the state legislature. Candidates for the State Board of Education must only campaign within their district, in contrast to campaigning throughout the state where they would need a larger organizational backing and more campaign money.

What happens when electoral politics are introduced in the selection of state education officials? In our examples, this is an issue for California and Kansas but not in New York or Mississippi. In California, the elected State Superintendent of Public Instruction Jack O'Connell was a politician with a track record in the state legislature and dreams of becoming the state's governor. In 2009, State Superintendent of Public Instruction O'Connell thought of running for the governorship but didn't, as headlined in the *Sacramento Bee* newspaper, "Governor's run put aside, California schools chief O'Connell eyes next move," when he found that he lacked public support for the office.[12] O'Connell was elected to his first term as State Superintendent of Public Instruction in 2002 and reelected to the post in 2006. His official state biography highlights his years as a career politician:

> He was elected to the 35th State Assembly District in 1982 and was reelected by wide margins thereafter, once garnering both the

Republican and the Democratic nominations. In 1994, O'Connell was elected to the 18th State Senate District on California's Central Coast and easily won reelection in 1998.[13]

So despite the nonpartisan election, California's most recently elected State Superintendent of Public Instruction comes from the ranks of state politicians who can rely on their past political networking and organizational support. When elected in 2002, O'Connell did not have any controversial education proposals to propel him into office. But he did have the support of state teachers organizations, which backed him because he was the chief author of California's 1996 class-size-reduction legislation which capped elementary school class sizes at twenty. Because of these actions he was endorsed by the California Teachers Association and the California Federation of Teachers.[14]

The issue of what knowledge is of most worth to teach students became a public controversy in Kansas where the electorate selects the State Board of Education by district vote. This method of voting allows for greater influence of voters over the state curriculum. For better or worse, this democratic process created a dispute over the vexing issue of evolution versus creationism in the state curriculum. In 1999 a majority of Kansas' State Board of Education voted to remove the teaching of evolutionary theory and discussion of the origin of the universe from the state's science standards. A political furor resulted from the decision. In the midst of this debate, five seats on the ten-member school board came up for election in November 2000. The major focus of election rhetoric was on evolutionary theory which, of course, allowed for an expression of what voters wanted schools to teach. In 2001, a newly elected Kansas Board of Education voted seven to three to restore evolutionary theory to the state's science standards. In the same year, the Alabama State Board of Education unanimously decided to include in its state's science standards a disclaimer clause declaring evolutionary theory as "controversial." In 2005, the Kansas Board selected Bob L. Corkins as the Commissioner of Education. He was opposed to the inclusion of evolution in the state curriculum. In 2006, political candidates considered moderate on evolution claimed a victory in the state primary election of the Kansas State Board of Education and quickly worked to restore evolutionary theory to the state curriculum.[15]

In Mississippi, the governor and legislature, which appoints the State Board of Education, dominate education policy discussions. Consequently, controversy over evolutionary theory occurred in the state legislature. In 2006, Mississippi state Senator Edwin Ross introduced legislation to support teachers who questioned evolutionary theory which required students to be exposed to criticism of the theory. *Education Week* reporter Sean Cavanagh wrote, "Mr. Ross' measure said that schools cannot bar a teacher from discussing 'flaws or problems' in evolutionary theory, or from talking about intelligent design."[16] His effort didn't make it out of a Senate Committee but similar legislation was being proposed in Mississippi. What is important to note for our purposes is that the legislature, in contrast to Kansas, was the focal point of the controversy.

An example of the workings of a more centralized system of control like the New York Board of Regents will be discussed in the next section on the power of the federal government over educational policy.

Patterns of State Educational Politics

The increasing centralization of state control of local schools is reflected in differing patterns of state educational politics. Joseph McGivney provides categories of state educational politics that help explain centralization of power.[17] His theoretical framework assumes that as social organizations develop, they become more centralized and bureaucratized.

McGivney's categories are based on Lawrence Iannaccone's pioneering work *Politics in Education*.[18] Iannaccone used four categories to describe state educational politics. In the first category, *type I (local-disparate)*, political decisions are primarily the result of linkages between state politicians and local school board members and superintendents. In other words, power is found at the local level. In the second category, *type II (monolithic)*, state educational politics are dominated by a coalition of statewide educational interest groups, including teachers unions and school administrators associations. In this category a coalition of educational interest groups applies pressure to members of the state legislature. In the third category, *type III (fragmented)*, political decisions are a product of conflict between educational interest groups and between educational interest groups and state agencies. The cooperation of type II politics is replaced with competition. Iannaccone modeled the last category, *type IV (syndical)*, on the Illinois School Problems Commission, which tried to establish a cooperative effort among government officials, education groups, and private citizens for the development of state educational policy.

Iannaccone assumes that state educational systems evolve from the local-based type I to the statewide syndical model of type IV. In this evolutionary process, different states are at different levels of development. McGivney accepts the idea of stages of development but recasts Iannaccone's categories, using new research on state politics.

In McGivney's categories, state educational politics evolve to a centralized, bureaucratic form. McGivney's stage I is similar to Iannaccone's type I, in which educators represent primarily a local constituency, and state educational agencies and legislatures work to maintain local control. Like

Iannaccone, McGivney labels stage II "monolithic" and describes a state-wide coalition of educational interest groups working with key members of the legislature. For development, the concerns of stage II are broader than the local concerns of stage I. In stage III, the monolithic structure is replaced with competition among educational interest groups, and new interest groups such as parochial schools become active.

For McGivney, stage III is an important step in centralization because individual interest groups direct their attention to specific state agencies. In the monolithic stage II, interest groups primarily interact with one another and, as a group, with members of the state legislature. In stage III, interaction among interest groups decreases as individual interest groups interact with specific state agencies. McGivney argues that stage III is a product of increasing bureaucracy and centralization. At this stage, competition among interest groups results from a desire to protect their respective share of advantages won from government. In other words, as the role of state government in education increases, each educational interest group becomes dependent on a continuation of a particular state program or funds. In stage III, interest groups begin to compete for more state support of their particular programs. This competition causes the coalition of stage II to disintegrate.

McGivney replaces Iannaccone's type IV or stage IV with a model of statewide bureaucracy in which iron triangles form among members of education lobbies, members of the state legislature, and representatives of the chief executive. In McGivney's words, "Over time . . . increasing influence is gained by or is delegated to the bureaucracy as the former lobby becomes more the bureaucracy . . . Conflict is adapted to through an impersonal, rational, and legalistic process that becomes dominated by the bureaucracy."[19]

McGivney matches his stages of development with Frederick Wirt's national study of state centralization. After closely examining the laws, constitutions, and court decisions in each of the fifty states, Wirt constructed a *school centralization scale* to rate the degree of centralized state control as opposed to local control. Although Wirt found varying degrees of centralization among states, the major gate-keeping functions of teacher certification, accreditation, and attendance were under rigid control even in the most decentralized state.

Overall, Wirt concluded, state politics controls local school policies. Any reform movement that attempts change at the local level will have only a marginal impact. "If the locus of reform is the district or school site," says Wirt, "efforts at reform, even if successful, win only a skirmish; the massive structure beyond it remains unengaged or unaffected."[20] Therefore, Wirt argues, state politics of education is the key to understanding the organization and operation of local schools. "Too often, then," Wirt writes, "local politics is a marginal politics, a struggle over things at the fringe, with the major decisions about how children will be taught having already been made elsewhere and therefore almost untouchable locally."[21]

Accepting Wirt's argument about the power of state educational politics over local schools, McGivney matches Wirt's scale to his political stages. States that rate low on the school centralization scale are in stage I of state educational politics, and states that rate high on Wirt's scale are in stages II and III. Only one state, Hawaii, with complete state control over schools, ranks at the top of Wirt's scale and is placed in McGivney's stage IV. Examples of states in stage I that rank low on the centralization scale are Connecticut, Massachusetts, Maine, and New Hampshire. Missouri, Texas, Rhode Island, Georgia, Illinois, and Tennessee are in stage II; Wisconsin, New York, California, Colorado, New Mexico, Nebraska, Michigan, New Jersey, Minnesota, and Florida are in stage III.[22]

The general patterns in state educational politics found by Iannaccone, Wirt, and McGivney create a picture of increasing centralization and control by state governments over local education.

During the late twentieth and early twenty-first centuries, with the growing concentration of educational policy-making at the state level, governors made education a focus of their political campaigns. As politicians, governors tried to please teachers' organizations and the business community. To the business community, governors promised an improved economic system through better schooling. To teachers, they promised improved salaries and a restructured profession. Sometimes governors were forced to choose one group over another; most often, the choice was the business community.

Catherine Marshall, Douglas Mitchell, and Frederick Wirt conducted an important study of political influence in state education politics. They synthesized previous studies and identified by order of influence the major political actors in Arizona, West Virginia, California, Wisconsin, Pennsylvania, and Illinois. Their study is useful for discussing general patterns of influence in state politics.[23]

For the six states in their study, Marshall, Mitchell, and Wirt established the following list, in descending order of influence, of policy actors at the state level. Since the time of their study No Child Left Behind has put federal mandates at the top of their original list:

1. federal policy mandates;
2. members of the state legislature specializing in educational issues;
3. legislature as a whole;
4. chief state school officer and senior state officials in state departments of education;
5. coalitions of educational interest groups (teachers, administrators, school boards, and other educational groups);
6. teachers unions;

7. governor and executive staff;
8. legislative staff;
9. state board of education;
10. school board associations;
11. associations of school administrators;
12. courts;
13. non-education interest groups (business leaders, taxpayers' groups);
14. lay groups (PTAs, school advisory groups);
15. educational research organizations;
16. education businesses.

Focusing on influences within state governments, Marshall, Mitchell, and Wirt found that certain legislators specialized in educational issues and guided the votes of others, while most legislators gave educational issues only occasional attention. Obviously, the lawmaking power of a legislature would give it the greatest control over educational policy.

Next in order of influence within state government, the power of chief state school officers varied significantly within the six states. Overall, they functioned as long-term bureaucrats who worked patiently to establish educational policies. An earlier study of chief state school officers found them to be primarily white males in their middle fifties with rural backgrounds. Most chief state school officers come from the ranks of public school administrators and teachers. They exert their greatest influence within state departments of education and in their leadership of state boards of education. Elected chief state school officers, as opposed to appointed, tend to exert more influence among legislators.[11]

As Marshall, Mitchell, and Wirt note, governors increased their involvement in educational policy in the early 1980s. Before that time, governors were concerned mainly with school finance issues. Members of legislative staffs gain their influence by acting as links between interest groups and members of the state legislature. Both legislators and interest groups depend on staff expertise. The most influential staff members work for legislators who specialize in educational legislation.

At the bottom of the scale in influence are the state boards of education. Usually, state boards of education are strongly influenced by the chief state school officer, who often sets the agenda for their meetings. State legislators and educational interest groups consider state boards of education as having only a minor role in policy-making. In fact, very few board members believe they have any meaningful influence on legislative actions.[13]

Of course, all of these state functionaries are now pressured to fulfill federal education mandates. As I discuss in the next section, the federal government has significantly decreased the power of state governance over schools.

Federal Government

Symbolic of the expanding educational role of the federal government were the 1979 creation of the U.S. Department of Education and creation of the cabinet post of Secretary of Education. In 1976, Democratic Presidential candidate Jimmy Carter promised the National Education Association, the largest teachers union, in exchange for its support, to establish a Department of Education and the post of Secretary of Education. After his election, Carter fulfilled his promise to the NEA. The establishment of the U.S. Department of Education ensured a strong federal role in national education policy.[24]

With the creation of the U.S. Department of Education there developed a new federal bureaucratic structure as illustrated in Table 3.1 by the 2010 list of the department's offices. Some of these offices are tied to federal programs. Some reflect ideological battles. For instance, the list in Table 3.1 includes, as part of the Office of the Deputy Secretary, the Office of English Language Acquisition, Language Enhancement and Academic Achievement for Limited English Proficient Students. This office was created in the 2001 No Child Left Behind legislation to replace the previous one devoted to bilingual education. Opponents of bilingual education demanded an English-only approach and worried that the United States would become multilingual. The supporters of English-only triumphed over those supporting maintenance of home languages.

How does this federal bureaucracy influence state and local schools? The answer is money. Since the U.S. Constitution does not directly mention education and schools, the federal government must use indirect methods. In the 1950s when local schools were financially strapped by the baby boom and needed more classrooms and teachers, educators asked for federal money that could be used at the discretion of local authorities. For a variety of reasons, including an anti-educator feeling in the U.S. Congress, Washington authorities were reluctant to give local school officials the power to determine how federal money would be spent. During the 1950s, school critics accused local educators of making the schools anti-intellectual, and, because of this, of putting the country at a disadvantage in the Cold War with the Soviet Union. School critics opposed general aid to public schools because they believed local educators would misuse the funds. Consequently, the federal government adopted a policy of categorical aid, to force local schools to abide by federal educational policies.

Simply stated, federal categorical aid comes with strings attached to federal policies and regulations. If local schools and state governments accept federal aid then they must abide by federal requirements. The major precedent for federal funding with categorical aid was the 1958 National Defense Education Act (NDEA). The legislation was in response to the

Table 3.1 Structure of United States Department of Education

OFFICES

Office of the Secretary	Office of the Deputy Secretary	Office of the Under Secretary
Office of Communications and Outreach	Office of Safe and Drug-Free Schools	Federal Student Aid
Office of the General Counsel	Office of Innovation and Improvement	Office of Vocational and Adult Education
Office of Inspector General	Office of Special Education and Rehabilitative Services	Office of Postsecondary Education
Institute of Education Sciences	Office of English Language Acquisition, Language Enhancement and Academic Achievement for Limited English Proficient Students	White House Initiative on Historically Black Colleges and Universities
Office for Civil Rights	Office of Elementary and Secondary Education	White House Initiative on Tribal Colleges and Universities
Office of Legislation and Congressional Affairs	White House Initiative on Educational Excellence for Hispanic Americans	
Office of the Chief Financial Officer		
Office of Management		
Office of the Chief Information Officer		
Office of Planning, Evaluation and Policy Development		
Budget Service		
Risk Management Service		
Faith-Based and Community Initiatives		
International Affairs Office		

Source: U.S. Department of Education, "ED Staff Organization," Retrieved from http://www.ed.gov/about/offices/list/index.html on January 4, 2010.

Soviet Union's launch of the spacecraft Sputnik I. This tied federal education programs to national policy agendas, in this case the Cold War. Later federal education policies would be linked to national policies regarding poverty and global economic competition.

The NDEA required local schools that accepted federal money to implement, among other things, science, math, and foreign language programs, which were considered essential in helping the U.S. win the technological and military race with the Soviet Union.[25] The use of categorical aid was expanded in the 1960s with the so-called War on Poverty and the passage of the 1965 Elementary and Secondary Education Act (ESEA). The most important section of the ESEA was Title I, which provided funds for improved educational programs for children considered as educationally deprived. Title I specifically states:

> The Congress hereby declares it to be the policy of the United States to provide financial assistance . . . to expand and improve . . . educational programs by various means . . . which contribute particularly to meeting the special educational needs of educationally deprived children.[26]

Title I of the 1965 ESEA was reauthorized as the No Child Left Behind Act of 2001 (signed into law in 2002). This legislation became a powerful instrument for federal control of state education systems. By the twenty-first century, state governments were dependent on federal categorical grants, resulting in No Child Left Behind forcing states to standardize school curricula, test students and close failing schools. The stated purpose of this legislation, one that would shape the direction of schooling in the twenty-first century, is:

TITLE I—IMPROVING THE ACADEMIC ACHIEVEMENT OF THE DISADVANTAGED

SEC. 1001. STATEMENT OF PURPOSE.

The purpose of this title is to ensure that all children have a fair, equal, and significant opportunity to obtain a high-quality education and reach, at a minimum, proficiency on challenging State academic achievement standards and State academic assessments.

This purpose can be accomplished by—

(1) ensuring that high-quality academic assessments, accountability systems, teacher preparation and training, curriculum, and instructional materials are aligned with challenging State academic standards so that students, teachers, parents, and administrators can measure progress against common expectations for student academic achievement;

(2) meeting the educational needs of low-achieving children in our Nation's highest-poverty schools, limited English proficient children, migratory children, children with disabilities, Indian children, neglected or delinquent children, and young children in need of reading assistance;

(3) closing the achievement gap between high- and low-performing children, especially the achievement gaps between minority and nonminority students, and between disadvantaged children and their more advantaged peers.[27]

No Child Left Behind pushed the country closer to a nationalized school system with state and local school authorities becoming conduits for federal policies. Originally, Title I of the 1965 Elementary and Secondary Education Act targeted programs for children from low-income families. With the expansion of Title I into No Child Left Behind all children were included and subjected to state standardization of the curriculum and state testing programs in an effort to close the achievement gap between low-income and minority groups and high-income and nonminority students.

Federal Influence and the Race to the Top

The funds offered under the 2009–2010 Race to the Top exemplify the power of the federal purse to influence local schools. The Obama administration's Race to the Top called for a national consortium of states to develop common curriculum standards and tests to be utilized by a centralized data system that would track the performance of students and teachers. While most states rushed to meet the criteria for funding under Race to the Top, Alaska and Texas refused to participate because of the threat to state control of schools.

New York State exemplifies the effect of federal money on state education agencies. With the announcement of funds under Race to the Top, New York set in motion a plan for applying for the money that included the following timeline determined by its State Education Department and supported by its Board of Regents. The timeline illustrates how the offer of federal money can cause a flurry of activity among state officials:

- Phase I: Preplanning May through August, 2009
- Phase II: Early Draft of Proposal Released in July, 2009
- Phase III: Stakeholder Engagement and Development and Refinement of Conceptual Framework from August to November, 2009
- Phase 4: Stakeholder Feedback from September to October, 2009
- Phase 5: Application Development and Commitment of Support from August to November, 2009
- Phase 6: Submission in December 2009.[28]

In announcing the timeline, New York's State Department of Education unquestioningly accepted federal goals for schools without any debate about their worth. In other words, when the federal government offers money with strings attached, states often quickly fall in line to collect. The announcement simply acknowledged the availability of funds:

> On February 17, 2009 President Obama signed into law the American Recovery and Reinvestment Act (ARRA) of 2009, which is intended to stimulate the economy, support job creation, and invest in critical sectors, including education. The ARRA provides $4.35 billion for the Race to the Top Fund, a competitive grant program designed to encourage and reward states that are creating the conditions for education innovation, achieving significant improvement in student outcomes and implementing ambitious plans in four core education reform areas:
>
> - Adopting internationally benchmarked standards and assessments that prepare students for success in college and the workplace;
> - Recruiting, developing, training, and rewarding effective teachers and principals;
> - Building data systems that measure student success and inform teachers and principals how they can improve their practices; and
> - Turning around the state's lowest performing schools.[29]

It should be emphasized that the New York state education officials never debated the worth of "internationally benchmarked standards and assessments" or "data systems that measure student success." Officials just rushed to get the money. The New York State Department of Education simply announced that,

> The Regents will be asked to take action on New York's application at their November meeting. Following Regents action, the application will be signed by the Commissioner and the Chancellor and then submitted to the Governor for his approval and transmittal to the USED [United States Education Department]. Prior to the Regents action and as required by RTTT [Race to the Top], the State Attorney General will be asked to certify that the application's description of, and statements and conclusions concerning State law are complete, accurate and a reasonable interpretation of State law.[30]

With money, the influence of the U.S. Secretary of Education, Congressional legislation, regulations and categorical aid, the federal government has gained the power to steer the direction of American schools. By the twenty-first century, local school policies were tied to national education objectives. For example, Race to the Top, which was suppose to aid the United States in global economic competition by increasing the supply of educated workers, grabbed front page headlines in the January 6, 2010 edition of *Education Week*: "Stimulus Is Spurring Legislation: States Position Themselves To Win Competitive Grants." The article opened with an example of federal power and influence:

> As governors and state legislators gear up for a new year of budget action . . . the federal Race to the Top competition is helping drive a flurry of measures nationwide aimed, at least in part, at making states stronger candidates for a slice of the $4 billion in education grants.[31]

In contrast to the states that hurried to apply for Race to the Top funds, Texas announced in January, 2010 that it would withdraw from the competition for funding because it represented "an unacceptable intrusion on states' control over education."[32] Governor Rick Perry commented about the withdrawal, "We would be foolish and irresponsible to place our children's future in the hands of unelected bureaucrats and special-interest groups thousands of miles away in Washington."[33] Texas' education commissioner, Robert Scott, believed that the state could probably get money from the Race to the Top funds but that the amount was too small to justify giving up state control: "Even if we won the full amount, it would only run our schools for two days, so for that we weren't going to cede control over our curriculum standards."[34] Even Houston Federation of Teachers backed the withdrawal from Race to the Top. Gayle Fallon, president of the Houston Federation of Teachers, announced support of the governor's decision because she feared that it was leading to the adoption of a national test: "I'm relieved because we've got enough problems with high-stakes tests already."[35]

The New York Times also reported that "Thousands of school districts in California, Ohio and other states have declined to participate [in Race to the Top], and teachers' unions in Michigan, Minnesota and Florida have recommended that their local units not sign on to their state's application."[36] Montana also refused to participate. The reasons for these local districts and Montana refusing to participate were criteria requiring teacher evaluations based on test scores and expansion of the number of charter schools.

Despite these dropouts from Race to the Top over forty states joined the effort to get federal money. The indirect power of the federal government over local and state education policies is reflected in a comment regarding Race to the Top by Grover Whitehurst, former director of the U.S. Department of Education's research division: "The administration hasn't spent a dollar yet, and they've already gotten a lot of states to make important legislative changes that are a positive for school reform."[37]

Local Control: School Boards

The common school ideal of the mid-nineteenth century included state governments creating school districts that were governed by locally-elected school boards. Before state licensure of teachers, local school boards determined the qualifications of the teachers they hired and fired. While states had basic outlines of curricula it was the local school board that filled in the blanks and, consequently, had a major influence over what was taught in local schools. Often school boards conducted student examinations, in contrast to the present reliance on nationally and state standardized tests. By the twenty-first century, local control was mainly replaced by federal and state government control.

From the mid-nineteenth century to the present, local school districts underwent significant change. First was the development of a local bureaucratic structure. David Tyack, in *The One Best System*, argues that "the pressure of numbers was a main reason for the bureaucratization that gradually replaced the older decentralized village pattern of schooling."[38]

The bureaucratic organization of these new school systems was made up of the following elements:

1. A hierarchy with a superintendent at the top and orders flowing from the top to the bottom of the organization.
2. Clearly defined differences in roles of superintendent, principals, assistant principals, and teachers.
3. Graded schools in which students progressively moved from one grade to another.
4. A graded course of study for the entire school system to assure uniformity in teaching in all grades in the system.
5. An emphasis on rational planning, order, regularity, and punctuality.

In the late nineteenth and early twentieth century changes designed to remove education from politics reduced public influence on school boards and increased the power of local administrators. There was a reduction in the size of school boards, depending on the locality, to about seven members. Small school boards increased the duties of elected officials, resulting in many of their duties being passed on to school administrators.

Changes in local school board elections illustrate how elections can favor one form of representation over another. School board elections were dramatically transformed in the late nineteenth and early twentieth century to favor trustee forms of representation. Removing schools from politics meant getting political parties out of school board elections. School board elections were made nonpartisan. The ability of citizens to run for school boards was reduced by making elections at-large or city-wide. Voter participation was limited by scheduling school board elections at times different from that of the general election.

The question asked by election reformers was whether or not the average citizen such as a bartender or factory worker should be on school boards. Their answer was "No!" By removing political parties from the election process, candidates had to seek other sources of financial and organizational support. Usually, these other sources were community business, professional, or special interest organizations. Studies of nonpartisan elections reveal that there is a bias in favor of business and conservative groups because they usually have the organization and money to conduct campaigns.[39] In *Nonpartisan Elections and the Case for Party Politics*, Willis Hawley studied nonpartisan elections in eighty-eight cities and concluded that they definitely favored the business community.[40] This was particularly true in cities with populations of more than 50,000 that included many unemployed persons with low incomes and levels of education. Hawley argues that nonpartisan elections result in candidates relying on informal business ties and business and civic organizations that favor elite community members who have connections to these organizations.

The favoring of elite community members who do not represent the general population is aided by at-large elections because candidates must have the organization and money to campaign throughout the city or community. Unlike elections where the candidate is elected by a small district and campaigns simply by going door to door, at-large elections require the candidate to campaign throughout the entire city, requiring more money and organization. Again this favors elites who can rely on connections made in business, professional, and civic organizations. Hawley emphasizes that there is a positive association between high socioeconomic status and participation in community organizations. It is difficult for a poor person to be part of an informal business network or join the local chamber of commerce.

It is important to remember that these changes in school board elections were introduced to decrease general public involvement in schools. The changes in election processes favored trustee forms of representation which allowed school boards to act according to what they thought was best for the community. Of course, as I describe later, some school board elections remain heated affairs with a great deal of community participation. However, most school board elections go unnoticed by the local population.

In addition, local civic elites composed of bankers, industrialists, and heads of local businesses and utilities, newspaper people, civic association executives, clergy, university administrators, and professionals (lawyers, doctors, and the like) wanted to ensure that their group was primarily represented on school boards.[41]

These electoral changes continued into the twenty-first century, with school board elections having the following characteristics:

- At-large elections
- Nonpartisan
- School board elections held on a different date than general elections
- Small school boards

What are the political conditions of local school boards in the twenty-first century given the above election procedures and the incursion of state and federal power? Ann Allen and David N. Plank argue, "that democratic participation in school board elections is generally quite limited and that the voters who come to the polls are not representative of the population at large."[42] According to their survey of current literature on school boards:

> In many school board elections, 5% or fewer of voters cast ballots, which mean that outcomes often turn on a small handful of votes. One possible reason for the relatively low level of participation in school board elections is that these elections are often run by the school districts themselves at times different than general elections. In Michigan, for example, school board elections are commonly held in June, with no other candidates or issues on the ballot. The separation of school board elections from general elections was a deliberate attempt by Progressive-era reformers to reduce partisan influence in the school election process. According to some contemporary critics, however, the institution of separate elections has also served to reduce democratic participation in school governance.[43]

Local Control: Mayoral Governance

Since the 1990s, mayors have played an increasing role in school governance. According to the United States Conference of Mayors school governance is now under the control of mayors in Boston, Chicago, Cleveland, Harrisburg, and New York; while in other cities mayors have become more active in schools without changing the existing governance structure, such as in Louisville, Indianapolis, Long Beach, Nashville, San Jose, Akron, Columbus, St. Louis, St. Petersburg, and Denver.[44]

Mayoral control of schools is seldom defended as allowing more public influence on educational policy. Voters may select a mayor for a variety of reasons such as transportation, sanitation, safety, clean government or other issues besides education. Do voters select mayors purely on their stances on education?

Mayoral control is defended because it is autocratic and provides centralized management of educational resources. However, as Joseph Viteritti suggests, good management is not necessarily supportive of democratic control. He writes regarding the advantage of mayoral management of schools, "Whereas democracy is based on a commitment to wide participation and deliberation in decision-making, management is energized by a determination to get things done efficiently and effectively."[45]

Also, mayoral control promises greater elite control of schools particularly by the business community. Viteritti argues, "Whenever and wherever mayoral control of the schools was implemented, it was usually done with the strong support of business leaders. The latter have a clear stake in education. Good schools are a prerequisite for a business-friendly environment."[46]

However, mayoral elections can be defended because they receive more scrutiny than school board elections with lower voter turnouts. Mayors receive more coverage by the media compared with neighborhood school leaders.

New York City's Commission on School Governance released its 2008 report on whether or not there should be continued mayoral control of New York City schools. The report provided the following advantages for mayoral control:

1. There is a general consensus that putting one elected official in charge of education is preferable to the former governance arrangement that dispersed authority and responsibility.
2. Putting the Mayor in charge of schools has made education a higher priority in the city as is evident from a significant increase in education spending since 2002 ($11.9 billion to $16.9 billion). (Local spending increased from $4.8 billion to $7.1 billion.)
3. Mayoral control improves the process of collective bargaining by better balancing incentives for fostering school improvement while controlling costs.
4. Since 2002, the school system has undergone more change than in any similar period in its history. While it is not the function of this Commission to assess the desirability of these changes, the amount of change that has occurred in a once immovable school system may be the most significant measurable impact of mayoral control. While change is not synonymous with progress, it is a prerequisite for progress.[47]

The recommendation of the Commission on School Governance was:

Mayoral control of the schools should be maintained so that the mayor can remain the principal public official who charts the direction of the school system and through the chancellor is ultimately responsible for operating the schools on a day-to-day basis.[48]

Even though mayoral control allows for centralized management of schools, mayors still must abide by state curricula and testing requirements. In other words, mayors have limited influence over the most important question in education: What knowledge is most worth teaching? As managers, mayors primarily deal with the allocation of resources and the structure of schools in carrying out the requirements of federal and state legislation. Mayoral control is another step in reducing citizen control of schooling while ensuring more efficient operation of a school system.

Patterns in Local Politics of Education

This discussion of local school politics is based on the work of Donald McCarty and Charles Ramsey.[49] Their analysis can serve as a useful guide to school and community relations. Their work is based on the relationship between community structures and the nature of the school board and the superintendent's administrative style. The types of community power structures they identify are:

1. Dominated
2. Factional
3. Pluralistic
4. Inert

Dominated Communities

In a dominated community, a single person or small group of people exercise the major influence on community affairs. Usually, they are part of the community's economic elite though sometimes they are leaders of ethnic, religious, or political groups. Dominated power structures exist primarily in small towns or urban areas. A major characteristic of a dominated power structure is the lack of a strong opposition. The local elite often operate through informal business networks.

The school board in a dominated community shares the beliefs and values of the local elite. Often, the local elite exercises some form of economic influence over board members. There is usually no organized opposition for positions on the school board, and the community elite may be represented on the school board by a majority or by several powerful individuals.

The superintendent in a dominated community will reflect the values of the elite power structure and act in its interests. Usually, the superintendent carries our board policies but does not initiate new policies. For example, in a dominated community studied by McCarty and Ramsey, the elite power structure acted in private, and direct control of the school system was exercised by a superintendent who reflected its values.[50] In this community, the school board was composed of seven members who were not major players in the local power structure and who were not troublemakers. The superintendent looked like a strong decision maker. The event that riled the dominant power structure was a decision by four members to inform the superintendent that he should look for another job, because they felt he was overly involved in educational research and publication and was neglecting the school system. At first, the superintendent ignored the decision and did nothing about finding other employment. At a later board meeting, members asked if he had found another job, and when informed that he hadn't, they voted four to three to fire him. Immediately, the superintendent called the vice president of one of the two largest banks and the general manager of the largest company in the community. The firing surprised both, and the company manager got in contact with the presidents of two other banks, the local newspaper editor, and a lawyer from a highly prestigious family in town. First, this group of community leaders met in the office of the bank vice president and decided to meet as a group with the superintendent before making a decision. At the next meeting, also held at the bank, the superintendent demanded a new contract and a salary increase. After lengthy discussion, the town leaders decided to avoid community conflict and let the superintendent be fired.

The power of this elite group was evidenced in the plans that followed their decision. First, the group felt that the school board had gotten out of control. The most respected member of this elite group was made chairperson of the board's nominating committee, and its members were selected to ensure elite control. The nominating committee recommended candidates for the school board who were either members of the power structure or loyal followers. Traditionally, those recommended by the nomination committee were elected without opposition. After the election to the school board of those recommended by the nominating committee, community leaders kept a close watch on the nominating committee to ensure the selection of candidates they favored. A new superintendent was selected who, it was believed, would act in the interests of the community elite.

McCarty and Ramsey argue that in this situation the superintendent made several mistakes. His major error was not recognizing that he was a servant of the power structure. He should have immediately gone to the elite group about the possible firing. Instead, the superintendent tried to be a political strategist by asking for a new contract and increased pay. The superintendent's demands alienated the elite and resulted in them letting the school board fire him.

Factional Communities

Factional communities, as described by McCarty and Ramsey, usually have two factions that compete for influence. Often these factions reflect differing values, particularly religious values. In these communities, concerns with the needs of the labor market are often secondary to other issues. In factional communities, elections to the school board are often disputed, with board members representing the beliefs and values of particular factions. Power between factions can shift with the election of new members.

In contrast to the calm appearance shown by dominated school boards, factional boards display a great deal of conflict. Unlike the superintendent in the dominated community, the superintendent in a factional community must be a political strategist who can balance competing groups. In a factional community studied by McCarty and Ramsey, the major competition occurred between a somewhat liberal Jewish group and a conservative Catholic group.[51] With almost equal populations in the school district, the control of the school board shifted between groups in highly contested elections. The election campaigns were highly emotional, with each group accusing the other of undermining education. When McCarty and Ramsey arrived in the community, the liberals on the school board had lost their majority to the conservatives, who immediately fired the superintendent. The superintendent, according to McCarty and Ramsey, failed as a political strategist because he appeared to favor the liberal majority. Interviews with community members revealed that they clearly recognized the existence of the two factions; each side admitted to holding secret meetings.

Divided communities usually involve the following types of factions:

1. Religious groups
2. Racial or ethnic groups
3. Taxpayers groups
4. Groups reflecting differing values, such as liberal versus conservative
5. Town people versus a local college community

Religious divisions are one of the most frequent causes of community factionalism. In recent years these divisions have frequently been over sex education and gay and lesbian rights. Racial factions are another source of school board divisions with one group advancing their interests over those of others. Sometimes communities will divide over school taxes. McCarty and Ramsey assert that the true leadership of taxpayers' associations is often unknown; such groups count on the support of a silent majority.[52] "Town and gown" conflicts often plague college towns, with faculty members wanting a more liberal and academic schooling than town people. Town people often disdain the ivory tower demeanor of professors who in turn view the town people as culturally backward.

Pluralistic Communities

In pluralistic power structures, there is competition among several community interest groups, with no single group dominating school policies. Often, a pluralistic power structure is indicative of a high degree of community interest in the schools, with many groups active in school affairs. McCarty and Ramsey found pluralistic power structures to be characteristic of suburban school systems in which there is a high interest in students going to college.

In a pluralistic power structure, board members represent many community groups. Board meetings emphasize discussion and consensus, with no particular group having the majority of influence. The superintendent acts more as a professional advisor to the school board, in contrast to being a political strategist or following the dictates of local elite groups.

McCarty and Ramsey are full of praise for what they consider to be the ideal community power structure: pluralistic. In these communities they found model school boards and superintendents. The problem with their praise, as William Boyd discusses in an insightful review of their study, is that these model boards and superintendents seem to primarily exist in stable, and often upper-middle-class, suburbs.[53]

McCarty and Ramsey argue that pluralistic communities are typically open-minded and rely on facts. On most major issues, community-wide investigative committees are created to report to the board of education and administration. Boards of education in these communities do not meddle in school administration, but are very active in the formulation of policy.

Inert Communities

Inert communities are without any visible power structure. McCarty and Ramsey claim that this situation most often occurs in rural communities in which power is dependent on maintaining the status quo. In inert communities, there is little competition for positions on the school boards. School board membership usually belongs to anyone willing to take the job. In these communities, most students do not intend to enter occupations for which education is a major factor. The primary concern is with a solid general or college preparatory curriculum for a select few.

School boards in inert communities tend to follow the leadership and approve the recommendations of the school administrative staff. In these types of communities it is difficult to get anyone to run for the school board. McCarty and Ramsey report that in some cases superintendents claim that board members accept 99 percent of their recommendations. Very seldom in inert communities does the school board turn to leaders outside the school system for educational advice. In most situations, the superintendent indirectly controls the composition of the school board.

In an inert community studied by McCarty and Ramsey, the superintendent held his position for twenty-nine years and maintained firm control over the selection process for board elections. School board members reported that the superintendent always recommended names of candidates to them. In turn, board members would urge those whom the superintendent had selected to run for office. These candidates usually ran without any opposition. When nominating committees were used, the superintendent would recommend the names for membership. The superintendent's activities were conducted in private by contacting board members about issues to be discussed before future meetings. Therefore, the superintendent knew how each member was planning to vote on a particular issue when it came up at board meetings.

While these different styles of communities, school boards, and superintendents still continue to exercise local control, much of their power is now being taken over by the state and federal government. The following summary of educational governance will show how local education politics is nested in a complex structure involving state, federal, and global education policies.

Summary: Educational Governance in the United States

The center of activity in Figure 3.1 is the state government which constitutionally has responsibility for education. As I have discussed, the structure of governance varies between states. Through a variety of methods, mainly involving money, the federal government wields strong influence over state and local school policies. Local school districts are caught in a web between state and federal control and influence. Federal, state, and local school governance structures and policies are influenced by global organizations and civil society. I will discuss the influence of global organizations and civil society in the next two sections.

It should be noted that in Figure 3.1 most of the connecting lines are two-way, indicating the mutual influence of different parts of the governance structure. However, the two-way lines do not indicate equal influence. For instance, federal officials have more influence over local school districts than local school officials have over federal policies. Also, it is difficult to determine the degree of mutual influence between civil society and global organizations and differing parts of the American educational governance structure. In the next section I will discuss the influence of global testing which can send politicians into a panic if their nation's science and math scores decline compared to other nations. But how do we measure the impact of this panic?

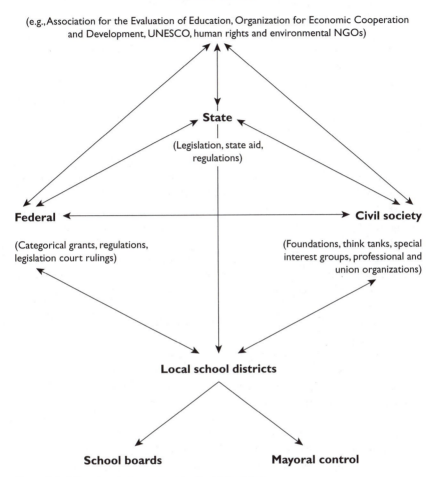

Figure 3.1 Educational governance in the United States

Global Influences

Global testing and curriculum standards were specifically mentioned in the 2009 U.S. Office of Education's criteria for federal money under Race to the Top. The language of the criteria was somewhat vague since no specific standards or tests were mentioned. The reference in the criteria was to a "common set of K–12 standards that are *internationally benchmarked*" and "a consortium of States that is working toward jointly developing and implementing common, high-quality assessments aligned with the consortium's common set of K–12 standards that are *internationally benchmarked* [author's emphasis]."[54]

One can assume that "internationally benchmarked" refers to global testing, which has caused politicians and educators to worry about how their school systems compare to those of other nations, particularly regarding test scores in science and mathematics. International test scores are political fodder when a rise or fall in test scores can lead to self-congratulations or pointing fingers of blame.

The two key organizations (which I will discuss in Chapter 8) in providing international educational comparisons are the International Association for the Evaluation of Education (IEA) and the Organization for Economic Cooperation and Development (OECD), and their tests TIMSS, PIRLS, and PISA.

Many other global organizations impact American schools, such as intergovernmental organizations like UNESCO and the United Nations' Internet learning program the Cyberschool Bus. UNESCO pursues a number of global educational objectives, including Learning throughout Life, Education for All, Early Childhood, Technical and Vocational Education and Training, Science and Technology, Literacy, Teacher Education, Inclusive Education, Education for Sustainable Development, and Human Rights Education.[55] Cyberschool Bus offers curricula, lesson plans, games, and other activities to promote human rights, environmental protection, and peace. As I discuss later in this book, there are many other global intergovernmental organizations that directly or indirectly influence American education.[56]

Global nongovernmental organizations, as I discuss in Chapter 8, also influence American schools. International publishers and software makers seek global acceptance of their products including in the United States. Education organizations are now international in scope, such as the American Education Research Association. ESL programs are global. Nongovernment special interest groups such as human rights and environmental groups seek global influence. In other words, the U.S. school system is nested in a global set of influences which, as I will explore later, are sometimes in conflict.[57]

Civil Society

As indicated in Figure 3.1, governance at all levels is impacted by America's civil society. As I am using the term, civil society refers to nongovernmental organizations that influence federal, state, and local governments. For instance, special interest groups, such as business, animal rights, religious, environmental, conservative and liberal, gun control, and a host of other organizations, try to influence federal, state, and local education legislation and policies. Private foundations, such as the Heritage and Fordham Foundations, and think tanks, such as the Manhattan Institute, try to influence thinking about educational policies.

There are a variety of professional organizations representing the interests of those concerned with particular education topics ranging from reading to science. These professional organizations sometimes advocate particular curricular and teaching approaches and try to influence federal, state, and local officials. Teachers unions play an important role in supporting and opposing federal and state legislation impacting teachers. And, of course, collective bargaining of unions in local school districts has a major impact on school policies.

Therefore, civil society is an important and complicated part of the governance structure of American schools. Also included in my definition of civil society are the education industries, including publishing and testing corporations, private and for-profit school management groups, including those associated with charter schools, and software producers. These influences will be discussed in Chapter 6.

Conclusion: School Governance and Ideology

The trend in school governance is greater nationalization of school policies and centralization of decision-making about what knowledge is most worth teaching to students and the best conditions and organizational structure for teaching that knowledge. With the call for internationally benchmarked standards and tests based on those standards, the decision over the content of the curriculum has been moved to a global arena. Consequently, state and local school governance is now concerned with carrying out national and global agendas. For states and local school districts governance is primarily a managerial function concerned with allocation of resources and organizational issues. Trustee forms of representation are favored by current trends.

Nationalization and centralization of decision-making about the curriculum, surely the most important part of schooling, has occurred over time. The first stage was decreasing public influence on school boards through nonpartisan and at-large elections scheduled at times different from that of the general election. The next stage was the linking of national policy objectives to school funding through federal categorical aid. These linkages, particularly with No Child Left Behind, strengthened the power of state education authorities over local schools. States became conduits for federal policies. For instance, No Child Left Behind requires states to create academic standards which are in turn imposed on local school systems. President Obama intends to carry this process one step further by requiring a consortium of states to create common national standards.

From the local to the global there is a diversity of educational ideologies. However, the global standards referred to by American politicians are most often those embodied in the international testing activities of the Organization for Economic Cooperation and Development (OECD). In its publications, OECD is firmly wedded to human capital ideology. OECD develops and implements the Programme for International Student Assessment (PISA). In describing the knowledge and skills tested, OECD's *PISA 2003 Assessment Framework* states:

> These are defined not primarily in terms of a common denominator of national school curricula but in terms of what skills are deemed to be *essential for future life* . . . They [national curricula] focus even less on more general competencies, developed across the curriculum, to solve problems and apply ideas and understanding to situations *encountered in life* [author's emphasis].[58]

In other words, PISA is creating global standards for the knowledge required to function in what OECD defines as the everyday life of a global economy.

What is the global influence of international assessment? International assessments like PISA create global standards that are used to compare the achievement of national school systems. A similar international assessment is Trends in International Mathematics and Science Study (TIMSS). Wanting to impress their national leaders, school officials hope their students do well on these tests in comparison to other countries. The consequence is a trend to uniformity of national curricula as school leaders attempt to prepare their students to do well on the test. Writing about the effect of PISA and TIMSS on world education culture, David Baker and Gerald LeTendre assert that,

> After the first set of TIMSS results became public, the United States went into a kind of soul searching . . . The release of the more recent international study on OECD nations called PISA led Germany into a national education crisis. Around the world, countries are using the results of international tests as a kind of Academic Olympiad, serving as a referendum on their school system's performance.[59]

The centralization and globalization of education might favor human capital ideology. As control is removed from those with possible alternative ideologies it is more and more given over to politicians and world leaders. This pattern favors the continuing dominance of human capital thinking as multinational companies pressure nations to supply them with trained workers. Certainly centralization of control does not seem to benefit those who believe that education should prepare the next generation to actively pursue social justice issues or who seek to improve the quality of life.

Within this governance structure, as I discuss in Chapter 5, politicians and political parties struggle to influence American school policies.

Another source of influence is from nongovernment organizations that comprise America's civil society. I will explore the effect of this civil society on education policy in the next chapter.

Notes

1 Alan Richard, "National Governors' Group Raises Education Profile," *Education Week* (October 22, 2003), p. 21.
2 Education Commission of the States, "A Brief History of the Education Commission of the States." Retrieved from http://www.ecs.org/ecsmain. asp?page=/html/aboutECS/mission.asp on January 5, 2010.
3 The Constitution of the State of New York as Revised, with Amendments adopted by the Constitutional Convention of 1938 and Approved by Vote of the People on November 8, 1938 and Amendments subsequently adopted by the Legislature and Approved by Vote of the People as Amended and in Force Since January 1, 2009. Retrieved from http://www.dos.state.ny.us/info/ constitution.htm on December 11, 2009.
4 Ibid.
5 "About the Board of Regents." Retrieved from http://www.regents.nysed.gov/ about/ on December 11, 2009.
6 Constitution of the State of Mississippi. Retrieved from http://www.mscode. com/msconst/ on December 13, 2009.
7 Ibid.
8 Constitution of California. Retrieved from http://www.leginfo.ca.gov/const-toc.html on December 16, 2009.
9 Ibid.
10 "State Board Agenda," *Education Week* (October 22, 2003), p. 21.
11 Constitution of the State of Kansas. Retrieved from http://www.kslib.info/ constitution/index.html on December 13, 2009.
12 Jim Sanders, "Governor's run put aside, California schools chief O'Connell eyes next move," *Sacramento Bee* (October 23, 2009), p. 3A.
13 "Biography Jack O'Connell, State Superintendent of Public Instruction," California Department of Education. Retrieved from http://www.cde.ca. gov/eo/bo/jk/ on November 30, 2009.
14 Joetta L. Sack, "Calif. Vote Brings New Voices To Policy Debates," *Education Week* (March 13, 2002). Retrieved from http://www.edweek.org/ ew/articles/2002/03/13/26calif.h21.html?qs=Jack+O'Connell on December 15, 2009.
15 Julie Blair, "Kansas Primary Seen as Signaling Shift in Evolution Stance" (September 6, 2000). Retrieved from http://www.edweek.org on December 3, 2009. Julie Blair and David Hoff, "Evolution Restored to Kansas Standards, but Called 'Controversial' in Alabama" (February 21, 2001). Retrieved from http://www.edweek.org on December 3, 2009. Jessica Tonn, "Kansas Board Primaries Seen as Win for Moderates" (August 9, 2006). Retrieved from http://www.edweek.org on December 3, 2009. Jessica Tonn, "Kansas's New Schools Chief Sparks Conflict" (December 14, 2009). Retrieved from http://www.edweek.org on December 3, 2009.
16 Sean Cavanagh, "Legislators Debate Bills on the Teaching of Evolution," *Education Week* (April 5, 2006). Retrieved from http://www.edweek.org/ ew/articles/2006/04/05/30evolve.h25.html?tkn=PXQFyAfM79XtvAxMMni SnxFMjDldQ%2F0a04Z4&print=1 on December 15, 2009.

17 Joseph H. McGivney, "State Educational Governance Patterns," *Educational Administration Quarterly*, 20(2) (Spring 1984), pp. 43–63.

18 Lawrence Iannaccone, *Politics in Education* (West Nyack, NY: Center for Applied Research in Education, 1967).

19 McGivney, "State Educational Governance Patterns," p. 54.

20 Frederick Wirt, "School Policy Culture and State Decentralization," in *The Politics of Education*, edited by Jay D. Scribner (Chicago: University of Chicago Press, 1977), pp. 186–187.

21 Ibid.

22 McGivney, "State Educational Governance Patterns," pp. 56–57.

23 Catherine Marshall, Douglas Mitchell, and Frederick Wirt, "The Context of State Level Policy Formation." Paper presented at the annual meeting of the American Educational Research Association, San Francisco (April 16–20, 1986).

24 "The Right Place for Education," *The New York Times* (August 18, 1981). Retrieved from http://www.nytimes.com/ on March 2, 2009.

25 See Joel Spring, *The American School from the Puritans to No Child Left Behind*, 7th edn. (New York: McGraw-Hill, 2008), pp. 339–404.

26 "Elementary and Secondary Education Act of 1965, Public Law 89-10," reprinted in Stephen Bailey and Edith Mosher, *ESEA: The Office of Education Administers a Law* (Syracuse, NY: Syracuse University Press, 1968), pp. 235–266.

27 Public Law 107–110, 107th Congress, "An Act to Close the Achievement Gap with Accountability, Flexibility, and Choice, so that No Child is Left Behind" (Washington, D.C.: U.S. Printing Office, 2002), pp. 15–16.

28 The State Department of Education, "Development of New York's Race to the Top Application," Statement released by the New York Department of Education, Albany, New York, on September 10, 2009.

29 Ibid.

30 Ibid.

31 Erik W. Robelen, "Stimulus is Spurring Legislation: States Position Themselves to Win Competitive Grants," *Education Week* (January 6, 2010), p. 1.

32 Sam Dillon, "Texas Shuts Door on Millions in Education Grants," *The New York Times* (January 14, 2010), p. A22.

33 Ibid.

34 Ibid.

35 Ibid.

36 Sam Dillon, "Education Grant Effort Faces Late Opposition," *New York Times* (January 19, 2010), p. A18.

37 Ibid.

38 David Tyack, *The One Best System: A History of American Urban Education* (Cambridge, MA: Harvard University Press, 1974), pp. 38–39, 61.

39 For a discussion of these political changes, see Joseph Cronin, *The Control of Urban Schools* (New York: Free Press, 1973), pp. 39–123; Joel Spring, *Education and the Rise of the Corporate State* (Boston: Beacon Press, 1972), pp. 85–135; and Tyack, *The One Best System*, pp. 126–167.

40 Willis D. Hawley, *Nonpartisan Elections and the Case for Party Politics* (New York: Wiley, 1973).

41 See Joseph M. Cronin, *The Control of Urban Schools: Perspectives on the Power of Educational Reformers* (New York: Free Press, 1973).

42 Ann Allen and David N. Plank, "School Board Election Structure and Democratic Representation," *Educational Policy* (August, 2005), p. 511.

43 Ibid., p. 512.
44 United States Conference of Mayors, *Mayoral Leadership and Involvement in Education: An Action Guide for Success* (Washington, D.C.: United States Conference of Mayors, 2006), p. 4.
45 Joseph Viteritti, "Why Governance Matters," in *When Mayors Take Charge: School Governance in the City*, edited by Joseph Viteritti (Washington, D.C.: Brookings Institution, 2009), Kindle location 70–72.
46 Ibid., Kindle location 157–159.
47 Prepared for Betsy Gotbaum, Public Advocate for the City of New York, Final Report of the Commission on School Governance, September 2008, pp. i–ii.
48 Ibid., p. i.
49 Donald McCarty and Charles Ramsey, *The School Managers: Power and Conflict in American Public Education* (Westport, CT: Greenwood, 1971).
50 Ibid., pp. 27–79.
51 Ibid., pp. 79–127.
52 Ibid., p. 97.
53 William Boyd, "The Public, the Professionals, and Educational Policy Making: Who Governs?" *Teachers College Record*, 77(4) (May 1976), pp. 547–549.
54 Department of Education, "Race to the Top Fund; State Fiscal Stabilization Fund Program; Institute of Education Sciences; Overview Information; Grant Program for Statewide Longitudinal Data Systems; Notice Inviting Applications for New Awards Under the American Recovery and Reinvestment Act of 2009" (Washington, D.C.: Federal Register, 2009), p. 37808.
55 UNESCO, "Themes." Retrieved from http://www.unesco.org/en/education/themes-ed/ on January 8, 2010.
56 United Nations Cyberschool Bus, "About Us." Retrieved from http://www.un.org/cyberschoolbus/aboutus.html on January 8, 2010.
57 See Joel Spring, *Globalization of Education: An Introduction* (New York: Routledge, 2009).
58 OECD, *The Pisa 2003 Assessment Framework—Mathematics, Reading, Science and Problem Solving, Knowledge and Skills* (Paris: OECD, 2003), p. 14.
59 David Baker and Gerald LeTendre, *National Differences, Global Similarities: World Culture and the Future of Schooling* (Palo Alto, CA: Stanford University Press, 2005), p. 150.

Chapter 4

Civil Society and Schooling

America's civil society is composed of voluntary associations with many trying to influence what knowledge is taught in schools, how it is taught, and the organizational structure of schooling. Commentators on America's political life point to the important role of civil society where legislation often follows the actions of civil organizations. In *The Idea of Civil Society*, Adam Seligman writes, "social movements and not political parties have been the chief form of articulating and furthering demands for social change in the United States—the uniquely American response to social crises."[1] In recent times, the civil rights and anti-Vietnam War protests, popular movements against drunk driving, smoking and drugs, the concerns of religious associations, and the struggles between liberal and conservative groups have influenced or determined educational legislation at all levels of government. For example, the civil rights movement not only resulted in legislation and court rulings supporting school integration but also initiated the 1960s "War on Poverty" legislation which included Head Start and the Elementary and Secondary Education Act. Christian associations concerned about the U.S. Supreme Court's 1960 decisions involving school prayer and Bible reading initiated a movement for school choice and home schooling to protect children from the secular nature of schools, resulting in legislative proposals and in some legal requirements embodied in the 2001 No Child Left Behind legislation. Also, conservative and liberal foundations and think tanks actively seek to influence school legislation.

Civic organizations are indirectly supported by the government through tax exemptions and deductions. In 2006, the Internal Revenue Service certified an estimated 1.85 million formal organizations that were part of the United States' civic society. A 2004 Internal Revenue report put the revenues of civic organizations at over $1.1 trillion. This figure does not include religious organizations such as churches and temples. The Bureau of Labor Statistics estimated that 65.4 million Americans volunteered at least once during recent years. These figures indicate the importance of America's civil society.[2]

There is a moral tone to America's civil society resulting from the strong historical influence of Protestant religious thought. Protestant emphasis on individual salvation and covenant theology linked individual moral actions to the good of the community. In this conceptual framework, a good society results from individual salvation which makes Christian behavior possible. According to nineteenth-century mainstream Protestant thought, once saved, a person was capable of Christian acts and should work for the salvation of others. Associations of the saved were considered the key to social improvement. This approach to civil society can be found in nineteenth-century abolitionist, temperance, and clean government movements. This thinking found expression in No Child Left Behind with its support of voluntary and faith-based organizations in school reform.

Besides resting on a belief in a Christian community of good works, America's civil society is based on a belief in rational resolution of potentially conflicting interests between social organizations. By rational, I mean that individuals make choices in their own best interests that are then actualized in a community of shared interests. For example, if I feel that school prayer is important then I might make a choice to join an association that will work to allow school prayers. The assumption is that there are competing associations of people opposed to school prayer. Again, the assumption is that these oppositional associations will balance each other and result in decisions that will be in the best interest of the whole society. This reflects the economic argument for a free market where rational decisions by participants result in the best exchange of goods.

Therefore, the American concept of civil society rests on morality, individualism, and reason. Rienhart Bendix lists as a key component of America's civil society: "The stress on individual autonomy and agency as the core principles of social solidarity."[3] Bendix stresses that the lack of a feudal tradition in the United States opened the door to broader participation in society, resulting in "The high degree of commitment and participation of these individuals [U.S. citizens] to society and to its social and political orders—that is, in essence, the right of all members of the national community to participate in public life."[4]

Civil society's role in American politics received eloquent support in the now famous words of President George H.W. Bush's 1988 acceptance speech to the Republican National Convention—a speech that was later called the "thousand points of light" speech. The "thousand points of light" referred to voluntary associations that comprise America's civil society:

And there is another tradition. And that's the idea of community—a beautiful word with a big meaning . . . we're a nation of community; of thousands and tens of thousands of ethnic, religious, social, business, labor union, neighborhood, regional and other organizations, all of them varied, voluntary and unique.

This is America: the Knights of Columbus, the Grange, Hadassah, the Disabled American Veterans, the Order of Ahepa, the Business and Professional Women of America, the union hall, the Bible study group, LULAC, "Holy Name"—a brilliant diversity spread like stars, like a thousand points of light in a broad and peaceful sky.

Does government have a place? Yes. Government is part of the nation of communities—not the whole, just a part.[5]

As President George H.W. Bush emphasized, government is only part of the reigning structure of power. The other part is America's civil society or what President Bush eulogized as a "thousand points of light." It is this civil society along with politicians and their political parties that interacts with the political structure of education to generate school policies.

Power, Money, and Civil Society

A problem with President Bush's idealistic portrayal of America's civil society is that some voluntary associations have more money and power than others. Civil society does not simply act as a balance wheel for conflicting interests. The civil rights movement of the 1950s and 1960s owes its success to the large numbers joining the movement and cash contributions which eventually overwhelmed the resistance of racist organizations, such as the Klu Klux Klan, and local and state governments. Also, the civil rights movement hardly involved just rational players making rational decisions in a free market of competition between opposing groups. Emotions ran high, and some might argue that racism itself is driven by emotion and not reason. Using emotional appeal, the civil rights movement was able to gain support from a large percentage of the American population. The emotional appeal of the civil rights movement gained the spotlight of the media and the media ensured the success of the movement. The organization that can shine brighter among the thousand points of light can often claim victory over others.

In recent times the unbalanced power and wealth of some voluntary associations ensures that they will attract the attention of the media and have a larger national voice and influence than others. This is particularly true in the arena of private foundations and think tanks—associations formed to create and influence public policies. As I will discuss, foundations and think tanks are created by private wealth and they serve as a shadow government influencing media and government officials. Those with large amounts of private wealth may share a common ideology which is supportive of the means used to attain and maintain their wealth.

Certainly, human capital ideology as reflected in school policies is supportive of those with wealth by promising to supply educated workers for their companies and avoiding any educational program that promotes social justice and a redistribution of wealth.

Consequently, the majority of foundations and think tanks reflect a variation of human capital ideology that embodies conservative free market economics. There are two possible economic models that can be included in human capital ideology. One model, which is most often associated with the Democratic Party, envisions human capital goals being achieved by regulation of markets and by public schools rather than competition between for-profit and nonprofit schools. The second variation of human capital ideology, and the one reflected by the majority of think tanks and foundations, embodies a free market economic model that favors competition between for-profit and nonprofit schools.

The conservative economic model embodies the very principles used to justify the importance of America's civil society, including a belief in rational choice in a free market and a moral community. With regard to school policies, this conservative ideology has supported, as I explain in this chapter, school choice, home schooling, vouchers, and for-profit educational organizations.

Therefore, America's civil society should be analyzed from both the perspective of promoting the public good and the use of private wealth and power to protect particular interests. In this context, President Bush's image of a "thousand points of light" takes on a slightly different meaning. Not all of the "thousand points of light" shine with equal intensity. Some shine brighter than others resulting in the public focusing on the more brightly illuminated educational ideas and policies.

Types of Associations

Keeping in mind the imbalances in wealth and power between voluntary associations affecting education policies, I am dividing them into four categories:

1. Special interest groups
2. Foundations and think tanks
3. Professional organizations
4. Teachers unions

Special interest groups usually focus on a single issue such as religion in schools, obesity, drug and tobacco use, language, culture, and a host of other issues. For instance in recent years the Christian Coalition has been a major advocate of school prayer, protection of religious rights in schools, and abstinence sex education. Countering the work of the

Christian Coalition is the People For the American Way which remains vigilant in stopping what it considers "right-wing" religious efforts to stop the teaching of evolution and impose religious values in schools. These types of special interest associations have been at the center of America's civil society.

Foundations and think tanks have been relatively recent arrivals to civil society. Beginning in the late nineteenth century, entrepreneurs, such as Andrew Carnegie and John D. Rockefeller, established foundations through which they funneled their wealth to support pet projects including libraries, concert halls, and schools. Think tanks are primarily concerned with funding research and policy reports designed to influence public thinking. They often operate from a "trickle-down" theory of ideas with elite policy-makers influencing the media which in turn pass on their ideas to the public. The end goal of think tanks is to influence the thinking of politicians, administrators, and the voting public.

Professional organizations range from those representing particular school disciplines, such as the National Council of Teachers of Mathematics and National Council of Teachers of English, to research groups like the American Educational Research Association. All of these professional groups have their own political agendas tied to the interests of their professional organization. These professional agendas can include influencing educational legislation that might impinge on a particular discipline, such as laws related to the teaching of history or geography. Or a professional organization might try to influence the content of national tests. For example, a decade ago I went to the Educational Testing Services as a representative of the American Educational Studies Association to lobby for more social foundation questions in the National Teachers Examination. This was an activity that was clearly designed to ensure the continuation of social foundation courses in teacher training and, consequently, was of great interest to members of the organization.

Since the 1970s the two teachers unions, the National Education Association (NEA) and the American Federation of Teachers (AFT), have been extremely active in federal, state, and local education politics. The political power of the NEA, the largest of the two teachers unions, was first felt in national politics during the 1975 campaign of President Jimmy Carter. Since that election both have become active in national politics. In recent years, the two unions have been very active in relation to state and federal policies regarding teacher evaluations. Of particular concern was the Race to the Top advocacy of using student test scores for teacher evaluations.

The four categories of voluntary associations interact with each other and the political structure to influence educational legislation and policies. For instance, Christian evangelical voices have been heard from the Christian Coalition, the Home School Legal Defense Association, and the Heritage Foundation which have provided each other with mutual support regarding school policies. These organizations have also had a common voice in influencing federal and state legislation and policies and local schools. Teachers unions support legislative agendas that reflect their organizational goals. The Obesity Society supports public education and legislation that will aid in reducing America's health problems, with an obvious spinoff to influencing school instruction on diet and food choices in school cafeterias. The list of voluntary associations engaged in attempts to influence the political structure is almost endless. The important point is that any consideration of the politics of education must take into account the influence of civil society on legislation, government regulations, and the actions of politicians.

Special Interest Groups

The vast number of special interest groups precludes me from reviewing all of their activities. Consequently I will focus on the actions of only a few that are influential regarding school policies and legislation. As my examples I am choosing two opposing groups: the Christian Coalition and the People For the American Way. The Christian Coalition plays an important role in winning elections for candidates professing support for prolife, abstinence education, school prayer, choice plans that include religious schools, and opposition to gay/lesbian marriage.

The Christian Coalition was organized in 1989 by televangelist Pat Robertson and Ralph Reed after Pat Robertson's unsuccessful Presidential campaign in 1988. In 2009, the organization described itself as "the largest conservative grassroots political organization in America."[6] The organization, as self-described on its website, "offers people of faith the vehicle to be actively involved in impacting the issues they care about—from the county courthouse to the halls of Congress."[7] The Christian Coalition represents the interests of evangelical Christians. Ralph Reed, first executive director of the Christian Coalition, claims that evangelical Christians became politically active in the late 1970s when the head of the Internal Revenue Service in the Democratic Carter administration required Christian schools to prove that they were not established to preserve segregation. During the early 1970s there were rumblings that many of the Christian academies in the South were created as havens for White students fleeing integration. In Reed's words, "More than any other single episode, the IRS move against Christian schools sparked the explosion of the movement that would become known as the religious right."[8] Claiming to carry on America's traditional relationship between religion and politics, Reed announced, "In this greater moral context faith as a political force is not undemocratic; it is the very essence of democracy."[9]

The Christian Coalition clearly defines itself as a political organization: "The Coalition is a political organization, made up of pro-family Americans . . . we work continuously to identify, educate and mobilize Christians for effective political action."[10] Political action for Christian causes is clearly spelled out in its 2009 mission statement:

- Represent the pro-family point of view before local councils, school boards, state legislatures and Congress
- Speak out in the public arena and in the media
- Train leaders for effective social and political action
- Inform pro-family voters about timely issues and legislation
- Protest anti-Christian bigotry and defend the rights of people of faith[11]

The Christian Coalition, through its headquarters in Washington, DC, maintains close tabs on legislation. It immediately alerts its membership about any bill in Congress that is important to the interests of its members. Members are given the postal and e-mail addresses and the fax and telephone numbers of their Congressional representatives so that they can express their viewpoints on pending legislation. However, the real political activity is in local churches. This raises the issue of religious involvement in politics.

In 2004, the Christian Coalition provided the following justification for blending religion and politics. The organization's 2004 website stated,

We are driven by the belief that people of faith have a right and a responsibility to be involved in the world around them. That involvement includes community, social and political action. Whether on a stump, in print, over the airways the Christian Coalition is dedicated to equipping and educating God's people with the resources and information to battle against anti-family legislation.[12]

In 2009, the Christian Coalition described its political methods including the distribution of voter guides through churches.

Our hallmark work lies in voter education. Each election year, Christian Coalition distributes tens of millions of voter guides throughout all fifty states (up to seventy million in 2000 alone!). These guides help give voters a clear understanding of where candidates stand on important pro-family issues—*before they go to the polls on Election Day* [author's emphasis].[13]

Distributing voter guides through churches threatens their tax-exempt status. Therefore, the Christian Coalition provides a carefully crafted list of do's and don'ts. In the official words of the organization, "And although a church's tax status does limit the amount of political activity it may engage in, it does not prohibit a church from encouraging citizenship."[14] The Christian Coalition informs ministers that the list of

> do's and don'ts will help guide you, without jeopardizing your church's tax-exempt status, as you lead your congregation into the God-given duties of citizenship. Remember, as Edmund Burke warned, "All that is necessary for the triumph of evil is for good men to do nothing".[15]

The Christian Coalition's list of permissible political actions by churches provides an actual guide to the methods ministers can use to influence their congregations. The Christian Coalition provides ministers with the following instructions:

What Churches May Do

Conduct non-partisan voter registration drives

Distribute non-partisan voter education materials, such as Christian Coalition voter guides and scorecards

Host candidate or issue forums where all viable candidates are invited and allowed to speak

Allow candidates and elected officials to speak at church services; if one is allowed to speak, others should not be prohibited from speaking

Educate members about pending legislation

Lobby for legislation and may spend no more than an insubstantial amount of its budget (five percent is safe) on direct lobbying activities

Endorse candidates in their capacity as private citizens—A pastor does not lose his right to free speech because he is an employee of a church

Participate fully in political committees that are independent of the church

The Christian Coalition also provides boundaries for the political action of churches:

What Churches May Not Do

Endorse candidates directly or indirectly from the pulpit on behalf of the church

Contribute funds or services (such as mailing lists or office equipment) directly to candidates or political committees

Distribute materials that clearly favor any one candidate or political party

Pay fees for partisan political events from church funds

Allow candidates to solicit funds while speaking in church

Set up a political committee that would contribute funds to political candidates[16]

Attempting to combat the activities of religious organizations like the Christian Coalition, the People For the American Way was organized in 1981 by Norman Lear, Barbara Jordan, Father Theodore Hesburgh, and Andrew Heiskell. The original mission statement expressed alarm:

> that some of the current voices of stridency and division may replace those of reason and unity . . . People For the American Way was established to address these matters. Our purpose is to meet the challenges of discord and fragmentation with an affirmation of "the American Way." By this, we mean pluralism, individuality, freedom of thought, expression and religion, a sense of community, and tolerance and compassion for others. If these voices continue unchallenged, the results will be predictable: a rise in "demonology."[17]

A major area of disagreement between the People For the American Way and the Christian Coalition is the influence of religion on public schools. People For the American Way criticizes the Christian Coalition for the following:

1. "Strident opposition to educational efforts to prevent AIDS and cut teen pregnancies."
2. Support of "government sponsored organized prayer in the schools."
3. Support of teaching creationism alongside evolution in science classrooms.
4. Support of "government sponsored censorship of public broadcasting and the arts."
5. Support of "new curbs on reproductive freedom."
6. Support of "elimination of Head Start and other preschool programs."
7. "The vilification of gays, lesbians and other minorities."[18]

Evolutionary theory is a major point of contention between the two organizations. For instance, the Christian Coalition posted the following news item lauding a Louisiana Law:

> Governor Bobby Jindal of Louisiana . . . recently signed into law the Louisiana Science Education Act, allowing the state's teachers to freely

teach the scientific evidence both for and against Darwinian evolution
. . . Besides opening the door to critiquing leading theories of evolution, the bill also protects teachers from being harassed, intimidated,
and sometimes fired for offering evidence critical of Darwinian theory.
Several other states are considering similar legislation.[19]

One of the features of 2009 Vice-Presidential Republican candidate Sarah
Palin was her appeal to religious conservatives. Touching on the theme of
evolution, the Christian Coalition posted "Picking Palin Rally Conservative
Base at RNC" which included the welcomed fact that, "Palin opposes
legalized abortion, even in cases of rape and incest; has supported constitutional bans on same-sex marriage and opposed other gay-rights
measures; and *has voiced support for the teaching of religious alternatives
to evolution in public schools* [author's emphasis]."[20]

In contrast, People For the American Way expressed concern about
Governor Jindal in their *Right Wing Watch: The Right Retools as a
"Resistance Movement"*:

> Louisiana Governor Bobby Jindal, a conservative Catholic and close
> political ally of conservative evangelical activists, was touted as a
> potential vice presidential candidate in 2008 . . . was widely seen as
> having bombed while giving the GOP response to President Obama's
> address to the joint session of Congress, but the movement moved
> quickly to circle the wagons and protect Jindal's political future.
> [Rush] Limbaugh, increasingly acting as an ideological enforcer for
> the GOP, threatened conservative leaders that they would, in effect,
> be dead to him if they joined the bipartisan criticism of Jindal's
> remarks.[21]

In their opposition to attempts to introduce religious-based creationist
and intelligent design arguments into public school science, the People For
the American Way issued "Defending Science Education in Your
Community: An Online Toolkit for Students and Parents Whose Public
School Science Curriculum is Under Attack." The kit includes methods
and arguments that parents, students, and community members can use
to resist religious attacks on evolutionary theory. Included in the Toolkit
is the statement:

Creationism Isn't Science
- Science is a way of acquiring knowledge about the natural world
  through rigorous testing and observable data. Other explanations
  for life, like Intelligent Design, are based on super-natural,
  unobservable and unprovable phenomena and are not science.
  Non-scientific theories do not belong in a science classroom.
  Remember: if you can't see it or prove it, it's not science.

- Intelligent Design is not science; it is religion. Everyone's right to religion must be respected, and that means that no particular religion should be given special preference in public school.
- The campaign against evolution is not a scientific movement or an educational movement. It is a political campaign being waged by people who think their religious beliefs should be taught as science in our public school classrooms. It's not good science and it's not good education.[22]

The topics of sex education, abortion rights, and gay marriage create a sharp divide between conservative and liberal religious organizations. The Christian Coalition campaigns for abstinence-only sex education, against abortion, gay marriage, and recognition of lesbian and gay rights in schools.

Planned Parenthood, an organization considered an enemy by the Christian Coalition, rejects abstinence-only sex education courses and advocates instruction in birth control and supports women's right to an abortion. There was an angry reaction from the Christian Coalition when Planned Parenthood began offering sex education courses in the Cleveland Schools, as illustrated by remarks that appeared on the Christian Coalition's associated Cybercast News Service:

It's too late when their eighth grader comes up pregnant. uh? Planned Parenthood's whole goal is to get that 8th grader pregnant. why? unplanned pregnancy = abortion = $$$$$$ for PP. They're in the abortion business. they don't give a cr*p about the health and well-being of our kids . . . PP [Planned Parenthood] is profiting off the backs of our young girls! we've been "Hood" winked by this disguisting [sic] organization!

They've been trying for a long time to get inside the public school systems to teach our children about *** ed. soon, they'll be teaching all the other sexually immoral & filthy things too! When I was in middle school {1984/1985}, our *** ed teacher brought bananas & condems [sic] to class for the girls to practice while the boys watched us. I refused to do it, stating that my parents taught me the importance of "waiting" to have *** until AFTER marriage.

As a Cleveland resident I can tell you something. The school system here is near collapse. When criminal organizations [Planned Parenthood] teach your students, you know the end is not far behind.[23]

An extremely contentious issue is gay marriage. The Christian Coalition expressed concern when President Obama's administration rejected abstinence-only sex education in favor of sex education that included birth control and recognition of other sexual preferences besides heterosexual. The religious right warned: "A coalition of liberal sex education advocates says the Obama administration and the Democrat-controlled Congress will end support for abstinence-only programs that emphasize marriage and heterosexual relationships."[24] Typical of responses to this news were: "The sickies [sic] should stay in the closet and not disgust everyone. Teach by example you intolerant pervert" and "Since most liberals have neither Ethics nor Morals, why should we listen when they preach perversion to us and our children?"[25]

The People For the American Way attacked the religious right for their homophobic attitudes in its report "Back to School with the Religious Right":

> The Religious Right may have become more circumspect in its language when it comes to creationism and textbook censorship, but its anti-gay rhetoric is as strident as ever. Of course, this does not mean that the landscape for gay students remains the same as it was a decade ago. On the contrary, many public schools have made great strides towards becoming safer and more open places for lesbian, gay, bisexual and transgendered youth, largely due to the strength and courage of such students and their friends and supportive family. But along with a stronger gay rights movement come new Religious Right strategies to counter every advance.[26]

The Christian Coalition and the People For the American Way exemplify conflicting voluntary associations pushing their own educational agendas. As illustrated in this example, voluntary associations that comprise America's civil society play a large role in influencing educational policies.

Foundations and Think Tanks: America's Shadow Government

Foundations and think tanks operate outside of the public's immediate purview. They can be thought of as a shadow government influencing politicians, media, and public opinion. Except for tax law requirements that prohibit foundations and think tanks from supporting political candidates and engaging in legislative lobbying, foundations and think tanks are free to use their wealth on any social project or to support any policy statement that does not violate any laws. As I will discuss, foundations and particularly think tanks make no secret of trying to influence the direction of social change and public thinking.

It is sometimes hard to make a clear distinction between a foundation and a think tank. A basic difference is that foundations give financial support to actual working projects designed to bring about social change, while think tanks support experts to do scholarly research and write policy statements designed to influence public thinking and legislative action. However, foundations also support policy reports designed to influence politicians and public opinion regarding school policies. For instance, in the 1960s, the Carnegie Corporation, a foundation, provided funding to the Children's Television Workshop for the development of the very successful educational television program *Sesame Street*.[27] In contrast, the Cato Institute, a think tank, issued a 2009 policy report researched and written by Cato scholar Adam Schaeffer which concluded, "Head Start improved children's language and literacy development during the program year but not later and had only one strongly confirmed impact on math ability in a negative direction."[28] Reflecting the advocacy work of some think tanks, the Cato report asserted, "President Obama should scuttle all plans to expand government childhood programs. It's past time we turn to the education reform that has proven itself through multiple random-assignment studies: school choice."[29]

Foundations as Shadow Educational Policy-Makers

Foundations established in the late nineteenth and early twentieth centuries primarily funded projects to improve social conditions. For instance, the Rockefeller Foundation and Carnegie Corporation sponsored projects to end poverty without giving money directly to the poor. Charity in this context was redefined as eliminating causes of poverty. John D. Rockefeller reflected this attitude about philanthropic work:

> The gift that matters is not to the individual beggar but to the situation represented by the beggar. To attend to the situation rather than the symptom was an idea that permanently and fundamentally altered the relationship between great private wealth and public purpose.[30]

There was concern about the use of immense private wealth to initiate social change, particularly since foundations were not, in most cases, accountable to anyone but their own staffs and donors.[31] This concern was expressed in education circles in 1914 when the Normal Department (responsible for teacher training) of the National Education Association passed a resolution about the growing power of foundations to shape educational policies.

> We view with alarm the activity of Carnegie and Rockefeller foundation [*sic*], agencies not in any way responsible to the people,

in their efforts to control the policies of our state educational institutions; to fashion after own conceptions and to standardize after their own notion our courses of study; and to surround the institutions with conditions which menace true academic freedom and which defeat the primary purpose of democracy as heretofore preserved inviolate in our common schools, Normal schools, and Universities.[32]

Foundations have been particularly interested in education. In *The Foundation: A Great American Secret*, Joel L. Fleishman writes, "Consider, for example, the problems of elementary and secondary education in the United States. For years, foundations have struggled to improve the quality of American schools, and they have made a positive difference in some areas of education."[33] Fleishman gives as an example the Carnegie Corporation's sponsorship and planning of the National Board for Professional Teaching Standards.

Major foundations established in the nineteenth and early twentieth centuries, like Carnegie, Rockefeller, and Ford, are now considered progressive and liberal in their policies regarding social change. However, their work has been criticized for trying to improve social conditions without threatening the wealth and power of the American elite. These foundations have promoted welfare capitalism. The basic tenet of welfare capitalism is to avoid serious social discontent in a capitalist society by giving aid to those in dire economic and social need.[34]

Alan Pifer best expresses the general attitude of these large U.S. foundations. In his last report issued in 1982, after serving eighteen years as president of the Carnegie Corporation, Pifer warns that without welfare capitalism,

> there lies nothing but increasing hardship for ever-growing numbers, a mounting possibility of severe social unrest, and the consequent development among the upper classes and the business community of sufficient fear for the survival of our capitalist economic system to bring about an abrupt change of course. Just as we built the general welfare state in the 1930s and expanded it in the 1960s as a safety valve for the easing of social tension, so will we do it again in the 1980s. Any other path is simply too risky.[35]

A good example of the power of foundations is Carnegie Corporation's sponsorship of the 1986 Task Force on Teaching as a Profession which issued the report *A Nation Prepared: Teachers for the 21st Century*.[36] This report set the terms of the ensuing policy debate on teacher education. The Carnegie Corporation was concerned about the faltering American educational system which, according to the critics, was causing the U.S.

economy to fall behind those of West Germany and Japan. Thus, the primary issue was to shore up a failing capitalist economy by educating a better labor supply for global competition. The Carnegie Corporation's report reflected these concerns.

The opening statement of the Carnegie report on teaching stressed the basic needs of welfare capitalism. First, it recognized that poor and minority groups would continue to have economic problems in a rapidly changing technological world. The report states, "As the world economy changes shape, it would be fatal to assume that America can succeed if only a portion of our school children succeed."[37] The report emphasizes that by the year 2000 one out of every three Americans will be a member of a minority group and that currently one out of every four children is born in a state of poverty. Stressing the consequences of this situation, the report warns, "it is increasingly difficult for the poorly educated to find jobs. A growing number of permanently unemployed people seriously strains our social fabric."[38]

In addition, the report voices concern about the supply of well trained workers: "A heavily technology-based economy will be unable to invest vast sums to maintain people who cannot contribute to the nation's productivity. American business already spends billions of dollars a year retraining people who arrive at the workplace with inadequate education."[39]

Therefore, for welfare capitalism, improving the quality of teachers—which is the intention of the report—will result in better trained workers. Better trained workers, in turn, can find jobs, thus reducing the social tensions caused by unemployment and saving the corporations millions of dollars in training program costs.

In 1987, based on its report *A Nation Prepared: Teachers for the 21st Century*, the Carnegie Corporation developed and funded the National Board for Professional Teaching Standards for improving the status and skills of teachers through a system of national certification. As part of its plan for continued funding of the organization and to gain the support of the federal government, the Carnegie Corporation lobbied for federal financial support. At first the George W.H. Bush administration was reluctant to seek funding for the organization, but in July 1991 Bush's Secretary of Education Lamar Alexander relented and provided funds. Funding would closely link government and foundation policies.[40]

The establishment of the National Board for Professional Teaching Standards exemplifies how foundations can affect educational policies. *A Nation Prepared* was issued with full media coverage. Cooperation and funding were sought and received from the federal government for the support of the National Board for Professional Teaching Standards. Eventually, the report hoped, local school districts would be persuaded to hire teachers certified by the national board. The report recommended that "state authorities should begin drafting plans to offer districts incentives to engage such teachers in appropriate roles and at higher rates of pay than teachers without board certification."[41] In addition, the National Board for Professional Teaching Standards recommended that states take steps to ensure the equitable distribution of board-certified teachers.

The growth of conservative-oriented foundations has countered the work of so-called liberal or centrist foundations. Fleishman contends that, "starting in the 1970s, some foundations began to develop program strategies to foster conservative policies in a wide range of fields from regulatory policy, education, and welfare to immigration and the environment."[42]

In recent years conservative foundations have had a major influence on the Republican Party's educational policies. "Conservative foundations are investing wisely to bring their clearly articulated vision of America into being," claims Carole Shields, president of People For the American Way. She goes on to say, "Their success is troubling . . . because there is no equivalent funding pattern to support a more progressive vision."[43]

One foundation that has a major influence on the Republican Party is the Heritage Foundation. Established in 1973, its expense budget as reported in 2010 was $61 million, with a staff of 244.[44] The Heritage Foundation proclaims its conservative orientation: "Our Mission: To formulate and promote conservative public policies based on the principles of free enterprise, limited government, individual freedom, traditional American values, and a strong national defense."[45] One of the organizers of the Heritage Foundation, Edwin Fuelner, referred to it as a "second-hand dealer in ideas."[46] The Heritage Foundation originated in a plan developed by Pat Buchanan at the request of President Richard Nixon. Shortly after Nixon's 1972 election, Buchanan proposed the creation of an institute that would be a repository of Republican beliefs and would provide a Republican talent bank for conservative thinkers. Buchanan, along with Fuelner and Paul Weyrich, solicited $250,000 in financial support from Joseph Coors, the Colorado brewer and a supporter of conservative causes. Opening its doors in 1973, the Heritage Foundation received further support from the John Olin Foundation and John Scaife, a Mellon heir and another supporter of conservative causes.[47]

The Heritage Foundation's education agenda reflects its concern with school choice and the application of free market principles to create competition between public, private, religious, and for-profit schools. Under educational issues the foundation lists the following:

- Parental Choice: Empower parents with the opportunity to choose a safe and effective school by promoting a competitive market of public, private, charter, and home school opportunities at the state-level.

- K-12: To restore good governance in education, including returning authority to the states and empowering parents with the opportunity to choose a safe and effective school for their child.[48]

In addition, the Heritage Foundation provides a state guide on school choice.

The Heritage Foundation receives support from a large number of other conservative foundations. This creates an entanglement of conservative foundation activities. For example, listed as the major contributors in its 2008 annual report are the Heritage Foundation Founders Chairman's Circle which includes:

> The Richard and Helen DeVos Foundation, Howard Charitable Foundation, Samuel Roberts Noble Foundation, Inc., Jaquelin Hume Foundation, Sarah Scaife Foundation, Lillian S. Wells Foundation, Anschutz Foundation, Armstrong Foundation, Barney Family Foundation, Lynde and Harry Bradley Foundation, Deramus Foundation, Gleason Foundation, Grover Hermann Foundation, Herrick Foundation, Kern Family Foundation, F.M. Kirby Foundation, Claude R. Lambe Charitable Foundation, Frederick and Julia Nonneman Foundation, Roe Foundation, B.K. Simon Family Foundation, Gordon V. and Helen C. Smith Foundation, and John Templeton Foundation.[49]

An investigation of this entangling set of conservative foundations reveals the extent of their work. For instance, one supporter of the Heritage Foundation, the Sarah Scaife Foundation, is described as follows:

> The Scaife Foundations consist of the Sarah Mellon Scaife Foundation, the Carthage Foundation, the Allegheny Foundation and the Scaife Family Foundation. All four have been heavily involved in financing conservative causes under the direction of reclusive billionaire Richard Mellon Scaife, whose wealth was inherited from the Mellon industrial, oil, uranium and banking fortune . . . The Foundation commenced funding conservative "causes" in 1973 when Richard Mellon Scaife became the foundation's chairman. During the 1960s, Richard inherited an estimated $200 million from his mother, Sarah. His net personal worth was estimated at $800 million by *Forbes* magazine, which would make Richard the 38th richest person in the United States. Richard controls the Scaife, Carthage, and Allegheny foundations. In 1993 alone, the Scaife and Carthage foundations donated more than $17.6 million to conservative think tanks.[50]

Another Heritage Foundation supporter is the Templeton Foundation which has in recent years supported research designed to prove the existence of God. Writing in the *Nation*, Barbara Ehrenreich says,

> John Templeton Jr., the president of the foundation, turns out to be one of the funders of Freedom's Watch, the new right-wing group . . . This is not John Templeton Jr.'s first or only venture into right-wing politics. In 2004 he started the group Let Freedom Ring, aimed at getting out the evangelical Christian vote for George Bush. He recently joined the Romney campaign's National Faith and Values Steering Committee, a group that includes an antiabortion activist and a fellow from the Heritage Foundation.[51]

Another Heritage Foundation supporter is the Lynde and Harry Bradley Foundation, which advocates school choice: "And, consistent with its national education program, it identifies and supports specific choice and charter schools and supports organizations that, in Milwaukee's dynamic education marketplace, are beacons of excellence to which others should aspire."[52] The admittedly biased Right Wing Watch reports:

> Lynde and Harry Bradley Foundation
> One of the country's largest and most influential right-wing foundations, the Bradley Foundation is known for its clearly articulated political and ideological vision. In addition to providing funding for a host of right-wing organizations, Bradley contributes to conservative and often highly controversial scholarship, publications and "academic" research aimed at legitimizing far-right policy positions . . . Bradley's philanthropy supports right-wing organizations, privatized educational programs, as well as many non-partisan social programs and civic organizations . . . Bradley supports include: private school vouchers, faith-based social services, and welfare reform.[53]

In general, these so-called conservative foundations are active in funding educational causes involving:

- Choice and voucher plans
- Evolution and creationism
- School prayer
- Abstinence sex education
- Charter schools
- English-only in schools (anti-bilingualism)
- Teaching traditional American history and values

Think Tanks as Shadow Educational Policy-Makers

As I mentioned earlier, there is a thin line between what is called a foundation and what is called a think tank. For instance, the Heritage Foundation, among its many functions, is listed as one of the fifteen largest think tanks by Andrew Rich in his *Think Tanks, Public Policy, and the Politics of Expertise*.[54] As Rich points out, think tanks are engaged in a "war of ideas" by trying to influence public opinion. Regarding the Heritage Foundation, Rich quotes the 1994 Speaker of the House Newt Gingrich: it "is without question the most far-reaching conservative organization in the country in the *war on ideas*, and one which has had a tremendous impact not just in Washington, *but literally across the planet* [author's emphasis]."[55] In 2009, the Heritage Foundation explained its role in marketing ideas: "We believe that ideas have consequences, but that those ideas must be promoted aggressively. So, we constantly try innovative ways *to market our ideas* [author's emphasis]."[56]

Think tanks are designed to bring together experts to study public policy issues. These experts can be either working full-time for a think tank or contracted. Similar to foundations, tax laws prohibit think tanks from directly supporting legislation or political campaigns. However, think tanks can issue policy statements and reports that are ideologically consistent with particular political perspectives. During their early years think tanks were considered politically neutral organizations that applied expertise to the study of public policy. In recent years, think tanks have openly adopted ideological stances such as liberal and conservative.

As a result, Rich is able to classify the fifteen largest think tanks as either "Liberal, Centrist/No Identifiable Ideology" or "Conservative." He classifies the majority of the fifteen largest think tanks as "Liberal, Centrist/No Identifiable Ideology." The largest think tank, and one classified as "Liberal, Centrist/No Identifiable Ideology," is the Rand Corporation which often does contracted work for the federal government. Others in this category include the Population Council, Urban Institute, Aspen Institute, American Institute for Research, Brookings Institution, Council on Foreign Relations, Manpower Demonstration Research Corporation, Center for Strategic and International Studies, Urban Land Institute, Pacific Institute for Research and Evaluation, and Carnegie Endowment for International Peace. The top three "conservative" think tanks are the Heritage Foundation, Hoover Institute, and American Enterprise Institute.[57] There are three important think tanks for educational policy that didn't make Rich's list of the top fifteen. These are the Progressive Policy Institute (liberal), the Manhattan Institute (conservative) and the Thomas B. Fordham Institute (conservative). The Fordham Institute bills itself as "Advancing Educational Excellence."[58]

The majority of think tanks disseminate ideologically-oriented messages. Rich notes the growth of ideological think tanks in the war of ideas:

What is remarkable . . . is that a majority of think tanks in 1996 were avowedly ideological in character, either conservative or liberal. In 1996, 165 of the 306 think tanks—54 percent—were avowedly conservative or liberal, broadly defined. By contrast, only 14 of the 59 think tanks that existed in 1970 and that were still in existence in 1996 were identifiably conservative or liberal . . . Particularly noteworthy . . . [is that] conservative think tanks substantially outnumbered liberal organizations. Of the 165 ideological think tanks, roughly two-thirds (65 percent) were avowedly conservative; only one-third were identifiably liberal.[59]

There are many examples of the involvement of think tanks in education. For instance, the liberal Progressive Policy Institute fed ideas to Democratic Presidential candidate Al Gore during his 2000 campaign. The Progressive Policy Institute was created by the Democratic Leadership Council. The Council formed the Progressive Policy Institute to support scholars formulating a new vision for the Democratic Party. The Institute defined its ideological position as:

PPI's mission arises from the belief that America is ill-served by an obsolete left-right debate that is out of step with the powerful forces re-shaping our society and economy. The Institute advocates a philosophy that adapts the progressive tradition in American politics to the realities of the Information Age and points to a "third way" beyond the liberal impulse to defend the bureaucratic status quo and the conservative bid to simply dismantle government. The Institute envisions government as society's servant, not its master—as a catalyst for a broader civic enterprise controlled by and responsive to the needs of citizens and the communities where they live and work.[60]

The Progressive Policy Institute issued the 21st Century Schools Project report on June 29, 2000. The report, while not explicitly supporting the Democratic Party, reiterated a favorite Democratic educational theme by claiming that it was "foster[ing] innovation to ensure that America's public schools are an engine of equal opportunity in the knowledge economy."[61] The report stated:

American schools are based on an industrial-era model matched to an economy that is disappearing. The information-based economy requires greater skills and knowledge and demands that students reach higher levels of education.[62]

During the 2004 national elections, the Progressive Policy Institute released its report "National Strategy to Expand Early Childhood

Education."[63] The report supported the expansion of childhood education to prepare 4-year-old children to compete in a global work force and contribute to national economic development. According to the plan: "While a national preschool initiative must set clear guidelines, states should set specific curricula and program delivery models."[64] And, as mentioned previously, federal guidelines would require a "science-based" curriculum.

After his election in 2009, President Barack Obama's rhetoric regarding preschool education paralleled that of the Progressive Policy Institute. President Obama linked preschool to the math and science skills needed for the global economy.

> Studies show that children in early childhood education programs are more likely to score higher in reading and math, more likely to graduate from high school and attend college, more likely to hold a job, and more likely to earn more in that job. For every dollar we invest in these programs, we get nearly $10 back in reduced welfare rolls, fewer health care costs, and less crime. That's why the American Recovery and Reinvestment Act that I signed into law invests $5 billion in growing Early Head Start and Head Start, expanding access to quality child care for 150,000 more children from working families, and doing more for children with special needs. And that's why we are going to offer 55,000 first-time parents regular visits from trained nurses to help make sure their children are healthy and prepare them for school and for life.[65]

At the other end of the political spectrum, conservatives have also used think tanks to initiate and support education policies. As Andrew Rich noted, there are more conservative think tanks than liberal. These think tanks play an active role in spreading ideas about education. The two largest conservative think tanks most concerned with education issues are the Heritage Foundation and the American Enterprise Institute. As noted previously, the Heritage Foundation has proclaimed its conservative values. The American Enterprise Institute also states its conservative values "[our] purposes are to defend the principles and improve the institutions of American freedom and democratic capitalism—limited government, private enterprise, individual liberty and responsibility, vigilant and effective defense and foreign policies, political accountability, and open debate."[66]

The interconnection between the goals of special interest groups like the Christian Coalition and conservative think tanks is highlighted by Matthew Spalding's comments at the 25th Annual Resource Bank Meeting of the Heritage Foundation:

Republican government was possible only if the private virtues needed for civil society and self-government remained strong and effective. The civic responsibility and moderation of public passion also requires the moderation of private passion through the encouragement of individual morality. And the best way to encourage morality is through the flourishing of religion and the establishment of traditional moral habits.[67]

This combination of religious groups like the Christian Coalition and think tanks like the Heritage Foundation propagated ideas calling for a closer relationship between government and religion. One consequence was the inclusion in No Child Left Behind of faith-based organizations to provide school services. Praising President George W. Bush's support of faith-based organizations as exemplified by No Child Left Behind, the Heritage Foundation's William E. Simon [Olin Foundation] Fellow in Religion and a Free Society, Joseph Loconte, commented on July 7, 2003 that attacks on Bush's faith-based policies,

> don't trump the freedom of all religious groups to live out their moral vision in a pluralistic society. Indeed, Americans of faith are likely to punish lawmakers who attack their religious institutions. That fact alone might, in the end, inspire a little more charity toward the nation's Good Samaritans.[68]

In contrast to the often religiously-themed messages of the Heritage Foundation, the American Enterprise Institute focuses on free market economics particularly as it is related to school choice and charter schools. Originally organized in 1943 to educate the public about business, the American Enterprise Institute dramatically changed in the 1960s under the leadership of William J. Baroody, who applied the concepts of Austrian economics to the world of ideas. Baroody believed there existed a liberal monopoly of ideas. He argued that "a free society can tolerate some degree of concentration in the manufacture of widgets. But the day it approaches a monopoly in idea formation, that is its death knell."[69]

Baroody wanted to break the supposed liberal monopoly and create a free market of ideas by establishing conservative think tanks. Once competition was created, he believed, the invisible hand of the marketplace would determine the value of particular ideas. During the early 1970s, Melvin Laird, Secretary of Defense in the Republican Nixon administration, kicked off a $25 million fund-raising campaign for the American Enterprise Institute in a Pentagon dining room. By the 1980s, the Institute had a staff of 150 and an annual budget of more than $10 million.

Education is one area of public debate that the American Enterprise Institute is trying to influence. The Institute announced in 2010 that:

AEI [American Enterprise Institute] is devoting significant attention to education policy, examining such topics as school financing, the No Child Left Behind Act, educational accountability and entrepreneurship, education research, student loans, teacher education and certification, higher education, and urban school reform.[70]

In 2010, the American Enterprise Institute was engaged in what they called the "Future of American Education Project." The project's research "encompasses a wide range of important issues including federal education policy (such as No Child Left Behind), school governance, choice-based reform (such as vouchers, charter schools, and tax incentives), school and district leadership, and teacher quality."[71] Influencing public opinion regarding education is the stated goal of the project: "to influence and encourage the national education debate for years to come."

Both the Heritage Foundation and the American Enterprise Institute supported No Child Left Behind. On September 4, 2004 the Heritage Foundation, a traditional supporter of school choice, issued educational guidelines to parents praising No Child Left Behind:

As the summer winds down, children everywhere race to finish their summer reading assignments and parents begin their search for new notebooks, bigger backpacks, and maybe even better schools.

Two years after the enactment of the No Child Left Behind Act parents have access to more information about the quality of public schools than ever before. No Child Left Behind's reporting requirements make schools more accountable to parents. Schools must issue certain specific information about achievement in reading and math, and schools that persistently fail to educate children at grade level must offer new options, such as tutoring and school choice. Armed with information and empowered by this new authority, parents are in a better position than ever before to choose where their children attend school.[72]

Eleven days after the Heritage Foundation issued its 2004 parental guide, the American Enterprise Institute hosted a conference on No Child Left Behind where Chester Finn and Frederick Hess, director of education policy studies at the American Enterprise Institute, offered their analysis of the legislation.[73] At the meeting Finn and Hess primarily complained about the legislation not completely carrying out the conservative education agenda and that the legislation required some internal tinkering. Finn worried that choice options supported by No Child Left Behind were lagging:

The supply of high-achieving schools, alternative options, and support programs do not keep up with the demand for choice provided by NCLB [No Child Left Behind]. More creative options need to be explored, including charter schools, home schools, cyber-schools, private schools, and inter-district transfers.[74]

Hess contended that,

NCLB is today too lenient about the skills and knowledge that students must acquire and too prescriptive about calendars, state improvement targets, and school sanctions. We suggest that there is a reasonable level of nationwide agreement as to what children should learn in reading and mathematics. Federal lawmakers should take advantage of that consensus.[75]

In 2007, as part of NCLB's reauthorization, the Heritage Foundation gave its support to federal legislation titled "Academic Partnerships Lead Us to Success (A-PLUS) Act" sponsored by Republican Senators Jim DeMint of South Carolina and John Cornyn of Texas and Republican Representative Pete Hoekstra of Michigan. While supporting the basic tenets of NCLB, Heritage Foundation officials were concerned about its extension of federal power over local schools. This has been a major dilemma for conservatives who on the one hand call for limiting and reducing federal power and on the other hand have supported one of the greatest invasions of federal power in local education in the form of NCLB. According to the Heritage Foundation both the Senate and House forms of the "A-PLUS Act ... promote greater state and local control in education while maintaining true accountability through state-level testing and information reporting to parents to ensure transparency."[76]

The Heritage Foundation continues to market educational ideas. In 2007, the organization published *A Parent's Guide to Education Reform.*[77] The goal of the guide was increasing parental control of education through school choice, which in this case included choice of public, private sectarian, and religious schools. The guide's major sections were devoted to school choice, including "Why America's Parents Need Greater Choice in Education," "School Choice: A Growing Option in American Education," "Private School Choice," and "Other Forms of School Choice."[78]

The American Enterprise Institute continues its efforts to influence education policies. On April 6, 2009 it sponsored a conference titled "Race to the Top? The Promise—and—Challenges of Charter School Growth."[79] The conference was in response to President Obama's efforts to provide more money for charter schools. As well as receiving Democratic support, charter schools are also favored among conservatives. Headlining the conference was an important American Enterprise Institute scholar, Frederick Hess. Staging a conference to disseminate the ideas of the Institute is a favorite marketing tactic. After asking a string of questions about the future of charter schools, the conference invitation announced, "A new report coauthored by AEI [American Enterprise Institute] director of education policy studies *Frederick M. Hess* . . . considers these and other questions."[80]

In summary, foundations and think tanks attempt to influence politicians, school officials, and the general public through sponsorship of policy research, dissemination of ideas, and actual educational programs. Except for tax laws, these centers of influence operate without any direct public control. Most importantly, these foundations and think tanks attempt to influence the media, which has become an important element in a democracy because of its ability to shape public opinion. It could be argued that most of the public are not aware of debates about education policy. The media, as I have noted in Chapter 2, provide only superficial coverage of education issues. Despite this superficiality, the media can affect public opinion by giving a positive or negative spin on education issues. In the war of ideas, foundations and think tanks can influence how the media spin these issues. In other words, the media may shape public opinion according to the influences of policy-making foundations and think tanks.

Professional Organizations

By their very nature professional organizations are openly self-serving. This statement is not meant to give them a negative tinge. It is just a statement of the obvious. Professional education organizations advance agendas that are in the interests of their memberships. These agendas are supposed to influence public opinion and legislative actions. In Chapter 2, I discussed the policy positions of the American Association of School Administrators, the National Alliance of Black School Educators, and the Association of Latino Administrators and Superintendents. While the policies of these organizations are designed to advance their membership, such as helping black and Latino educators become school administrators, they also advance sincere concerns about student learning.

As an example of the combination of self-serving and altruistic policies consider the umbrella educational research organization the American Educational Research Association (AERA). AERA claims to represent the interest of researchers in all fields of education. The organization is not shy about admitting that it is self-serving: "As a research association, AERA has a primary responsibility to its members to support and promote policies and programs that advance education research and its tools, resources, and infrastructures."[81] The reference to advancing "education research and its tools, resources, and infrastructures" includes lobbying federal and state governments for more research money or, as stated in its policies, "advocacy on behalf of education research and education researchers."[82] As a result, the Association states that it "needs to be well positioned and highly credible to give voice and visibility to the field and to policy issues essential to its continued advancement."[83]

Similar to other parts of civil society, professional organizations like AERA are concerned with influencing educational policies through the dissemination of ideas. In its guidelines for policy-making, AERA asserts:

> It is certainly the case that associations like AERA have educative responsibilities to *disseminate knowledge*—to make research known, useful, and useable to its *primary consumers (practitioners and policy makers involved in education) and to other external communities (e.g., the media, policy makers with a broader portfolio)* [author's emphasis].[84]

It is impossible in this limited space to review the missions and policy objectives of all professional education organizations. Below is a list of a few that the reader might want to explore regarding how they serve their memberships and how they try to influence legislative agendas and public opinion.

American Association for the Mentally Retarded (AAMR) [www.aamr.org]

American Alliance for Health, Physical Education, Recreation and Dance (AAHPERD) [www.aahperd.org]

Association for Experiential Education (AEE) [www.princeton.edu/~rcurtis/aee. html]

Association for Retarded Citizens (ARC) [www.thearc.org/welcome.html]

ENC Online Resources for Math and Science Education [www.enc.org/stan.htm]

National Association for Bilingual Education (NABE)

National Association for the Education of Young Children (NAEYC) [naeyc.org/naeyc]

National Council of Teachers of Mathematics (NCTM) [www.nctm.org/]

National Council for the Social Studies (NCSS) [www.socialstudies.org/]

National Council of Teachers of English (NCTE) [www.ncte.org]

National Science Teachers Association [www.nsta.org/]

Organization of American Historians (OAH) [www.oah.org]

Teachers Unions

Since the 1970s, the two teachers unions, the National Education Association (NEA) and the American Federation of Teachers (AFT), have been actively involved in politics. As noted in Wayne Urban's excellent history of teachers unions, *Why Teachers Organized*, teachers organized for two major reasons: to improve wages and working conditions and to secure seniority. Urban notes, "Through the pursuit of salary scales and other policies, teachers sought to institutionalize experience, or seniority, as the criterion of success in teaching."[85]

In 1976, Democratic Presidential candidate Jimmy Carter promised the NEA, in exchange for its support, to establish a Department of Education with a Secretary of Education to represent educational interests at presidential cabinet meetings. It was the first time the NEA endorsed a presidential candidate. This opened a new era of teacher union involvement in politics. After his election, Carter fulfilled his promise to the NEA. During the 1980 Democratic primary campaigns the NEA backed Jimmy Carter while the AFT supported Democratic Senator Edward Kennedy. The AFT ended up backing Carter after Kennedy lost in the primary elections.[86]

During the 1980s, Republican President Ronald Reagan's administration was an outspoken critic of the two unions. As a result, the two unions began pouring money into the coffers of the Democratic Party. One concern of President Reagan was the continuing expansion of federal involvement in local schools as symbolized by the creation of the U.S. Department of Education. By 1989 the two unions were spending $5.2 million on political action including $3.23 million in contributions to U.S. Congressional and Senate campaigns, mostly for Democrats.[87]

In 2000, Larry J. Sabato, director of the Center for Governmental Studies at the University of Virginia, concluded,

> It's fair to say that the Democrats would be nowhere without them [the two teachers unions]. And in my view, the NEA and AFT are the most effective union players out there, because they not only have the money and the muscle, they also have a positive public image from representing teachers that much of labor lacks.[88]

Professor Sabato was still stressing the political power of the two teachers unions in 2006:

> The NEA and the AFT are very influential in party politics. The most important element is actually manpower and womanpower. Volunteers in the campaigns and people getting out the vote—that counts far more than money, although money is also important.[89]

There has been a heated political debate about teacher evaluations using student test scores. Both unions have been leery about going down this road. This debate has put a crimp on union support of the Democratic Party. President Barack Obama gave support to using student test scores for teacher evaluation shortly after entering office. It should be noted that he did not push this position on teacher evaluations until after the election, possibly out of fear of losing the support of the two teacher unions. In a speech to the Hispanic Chamber of Commerce on March 10, 2009, on a "Complete and Competitive American Education," he asserted: "*Good teachers will be rewarded with more money for improved student achievement*, and asked to accept more responsibilities for lifting up their schools [author's emphasis]."[90]

What was the reaction of the teachers unions? Immediately after the speech, Randi Weingarten, president of the AFT, issued a press release praising President Obama's speech. The short news release referred to rewards for teaching excellence: "The president's vision of education—and the AFT's—includes world-class standards for all students, new and better tools for teachers, greater effort to recruit and retain good teachers and competitive teacher salaries with innovative ways to reward teaching excellence."[91] However, Weingarten did emphasize the importance of teachers' involvement in developing any new pay plans: "As with any public policy, the devil is in the details, and it is important that teachers' voices are heard as we implement the president's vision."[92]

In his press release, NEA president Dennis Van Roekel praised the speech but avoided any reference to Obama's call for extra pay based on student achievement and simply referred to raising pay for teacher knowledge and skills:

> We, like President Obama, advocate for improving professional development and mentoring for new and less effective teachers; a national investment in recruiting some of the most talented individuals into the field of teaching, as well as investing in scaling up innovative teacher preparation and induction models; and *raising teachers' compensation based on their knowledge and skills* [author's emphasis].[93]

In his short press release, Roekel did make reference to the National Board: "NEA is working to improve teacher quality through promotion of National Board for Professional Teaching Standards and support of Teacher Working Condition Surveys."[94]

The two unions were shocked when the Obama administration announced that one of the criteria for states gaining federal monies under the Race to the Top plan was: "that to be eligible under this program, a State must *not have any* legal, statutory, or regulatory barriers to linking student achievement or student growth data to teachers for the purpose of teacher and principal evaluation."[95]

The Obama administration's break with the teachers unions over teacher evaluations may have marked the end of their honeymoon with the Democratic Party but it did not end their role in trying to influence political decisions. For instance, the NEA issued the following 2010 guide to its membership:

NEA'S FEDERAL POLICY GUIDE: ISSUES
1. Expand and Improve Early Childhood Education and Children's Program
2. Overhaul the Elementary and Secondary Education Act (ESEA)
3. Help More Students Graduate
4. Meet the Needs of English Language Learner Students
5. Ensure Teacher Quality
6. Strengthen and Fully Fund the Individuals with Disabilities Education Act (IDEA)
7. Support All School Staff, Vital Members of the Team
8. Create Effective Learning Environments
9. Expand Learning Opportunities for All Students
10. Strengthen Family Involvement and Community Engagement
11. Invest in America's Future
12. Improve College Affordability and Support Excellence in Higher Education
13. Use Education Research to Identify and Support Promising Practices.[96]

The AFT continued to urge members to apply pressure on Congress and state legislatures to achieve its policy goals. Typical of the union's approach was that it gave members form letters to be sent to politicians. For example, the form letter below reflects the type of political pressure the AFT is trying to exert over changes in No Child Left Behind.

Tell Congress To Overhaul NCLB

The No Child Left Behind Act is due to be reauthorized by Congress. Now is the time to send a letter to your representative and senators outlining the problems with NCLB and offering constructive ideas for changing the law.

Dear [Decision Maker],

I care about and support public education, and I believe that the No Child Left Behind Act (NCLB) is hurting, not helping, our nation's schoolchildren . . .

Congress, with real input from educators working on the frontlines, should design a law that first and foremost provides a framework for providing students a high-quality, well-rounded education. That framework should include high standards, real accountability that gives credit for progress, a commitment to focusing on interventions that work rather than on sanctions that don't, and to providing the resources needed to meet the law's requirements.

The fact is, NCLB is not about teaching and learning, it is primarily about testing and punishment. Today, our schools are more focused on test preparation than on actual teaching and learning. The result is that our children are not being exposed to the well-rounded curriculum that will prepare them for the challenges and opportunities of the 21st century.

We have an opportunity and a responsibility to do more and to do better for our children. I urge you to keep these thoughts in mind as you consider changes to NCLB.[97]

In summary, teachers unions like other parts of civil society are trying to shape educational policy to meet their needs, particularly regarding working conditions and salaries. The two unions also have an altruistic dimension, namely creating teaching and learning conditions that their membership think are best for students. Like other parts of civil society, the two unions' policies combine self-interest with a moral vision; a moral vision of working to improve education.

Conclusion: A Thousand Points of Light

As I discuss at the beginning of the chapter, American civil society was traditionally organized around the religious principles of community service and a competitive marketplace of self-interested groups. This was captured in President George H.W. Bush's reference to a "thousand points of light." Special interest groups, foundations and think tanks, professional associations, and teachers unions claim to be lighting the sky with their visions of the knowledge that is most worth teaching and the best conditions for teaching that knowledge. Of course, these lights are tinged with self-service, including promotion of religious and political ideologies and economic and political interests. Not all lights shine with the same brightness. Some are powered by more money and connections than others. However all of them want their moral and self-serving visions of education to influence the media and the public and light the path for politicians.

Notes

1   Adam B. Seligman, *The Idea of Civil Society* (New York: Free Press, 1992), Kindle location 2010.
2   Joel L. Fleishman, *The Foundation: A Great American Secret: How Private Wealth is Changing the World* (New York: Public Affairs, 2007), Kindle location 393–400.
3   Seligman, *The Idea of Civil Society*, Kindle location 1990–1994.
4   Ibid.
5   George H.W. Bush, *1988 Republican National Convention Acceptance Address*. Retrieved from http://www.americanrhetoric.com/speeches/george hbush1988rnc.htm on January 13, 2009.
6   Christian Coalition, "About Us." Retrieved from http://www.cc.org/about_us on April 10, 2009.
7   Ibid.
8   Ralph Reed, *Active Faith: How Christians Are Changing the Soul of American Politics* (New York: Free Press, 1996), p. 105.
9   Ibid., p. 9.
10 Ibid.
11 Ibid.
12 Christian Coalition, "About Us."
13 Ibid.
14 Christian Coalition, "Dos and Don'ts." Retrieved from http://www.cc.org on March 2, 2005.
15 Ibid.
16 Ibid.
17 People For the American Way, "Mission of People For the American Way." Retrieved from http://site.pfaw.org/site/PageServer?pagename=about_mission_statement on November 14, 2009.
18 I received these objections in a letter dated June 20, 1996 from the People For the American Way, 2000 M Street Suite 400, Washington, DC 10036. The letter was signed by the organization's president, Carole Shields.
19 Christian Coalition, "Governor Bobby Jindal of Louisiana is being praised for signing what is being hailed as a historic education act." Retrieved from http://www.cc.org/userlink/039historic039_education_bill_louisiana on November 14, 2009.
20 Christian Coalition, "Picking Palin Rally Conservative Base at RNC." Retrieved from http://www.cc.org/news/picking_palin_rally_conservative_base_rnc on November 15, 2009.
21 People For the American Way, *Right Wing Watch: The Right Retools as a "Resistance Movement."* Retrieved from http://site.pfaw.org/pdf/rww-in-focus-resistance-movement.pdf on November 18, 2009.
22 People For the American Way, "Defending Science Education in Your Community: An Online Toolkit for Students and Parents Whose Public School Science Curriculum is Under Attack." Retrieved from http://site. pfaw.org/site/PageServer?pagename=issues_religious_defending_science_education on November 19, 2009.
23 Penny Starr, "Planned Parenthood Teaches Sex Ed Classes in Cleveland Public Schools" (October 19, 2009). Retrieved from http://www.cnsnews.com/news/article/55660 on November 20, 2009.
24 Penny Starr, "Sex Ed Should Not Promote Only Marriage or Heterosexual Relationships, Advocates Say" (October 16, 2009). Retrieved from http://www.cc.org/user_submitted_news/education on November 10, 2009.

25 Ibid.
26 People For the American Way, "Back to School with the Religious Right." Retrieved from http://www.pfaw.org/media-center/publications/back-to-school-with-the-religious-right on January 17, 2010.
27 See Gerald S. Lesser, *Children and Television: Lessons from Sesame Street* (New York: Vintage, 1975).
28 "Failing Grade for Head Start." Retrieved from http://www.cato.org/ on January 18, 2010.
29 Ibid.
30 Fleishman, *The Foundation*, Kindle location 773–775.
31 Ibid., Kindle location 805–806.
32 Ibid., Kindle location 744–747.
33 Ibid., Kindle location 338–340.
34 See Waldemar Nielsen, *The Big Foundations* (New York: Columbia University Press, 1972).
35 Alan Pifer, "When Fashionable Rhetoric Fails," *Education Week* (February 23, 1983), p. 24.
36 Task Force on Teaching as a Profession, *A Nation Prepared: Teachers for the 21st Century* (New York: Carnegie Corporation of New York, 1986).
37 Ibid., p. 14.
38 Ibid.
39 Ibid., p. 20.
40 Julie Miller and Karen Diegmuller, "Bush Shift Seen on Federal Aid to Teacher Board," *Education Week* (July 31, 1991), pp. 1, 22.
41 Ibid., p. 13.
42 Ibid., Kindle location 752–756.
43 People For the American Way, "Buying a Movement: A Report by the People For the American Way Foundation, 1996." Retrieved from http://site.pfaw.org/site/PageServer?pagename=report_buying_a_movement on January 20, 2010.
44 Heritage Foundation, "About Heritage." Retrieved from http://www.heritage.org/about/ on January 20, 2010.
45 Ibid.
46 James Smith, *The Idea Brokers and the Rise of the New Policy Elite* (New York: Free Press, 1991), p. 197.
47 Ibid., pp. 197–202.
48 Heritage Foundation, "Issues: Education." Retrieved from http://www.heritage.org/research/ on January 20, 2010.
49 Heritage Foundation Reports, "2008 Annual Report." Retrieved from http://www.heritage.org/about/reports.cfm on January 20, 2010.
50 Source Watch, "Scaife Foundations." Retrieved from http://www.sourcewatch.org/index.php/Scaife_Foundations on January 20, 2010.
51 Barbara Ehrenreich, "John Templeton's Universe," *The Nation* (October 15, 2007). Retrieved from http://www.thenation.com/doc/20071022/ehrenreich on January 20, 2010.
52 The Lynde and Harry Bradley Foundation, "Current Program Interests." Retrieved from http://www.bradleyfdn.org/program_interests.asp on January 21, 2010.
53 Right Wing Watch, "The Lynde and Harry Bradley Foundation." Retrieved from http://www.rightwingwatch.org/content/lynde-and-harry-bradleyfoundation on January 21, 2010.
54 Andrew Rich, *Think Tanks, Public Policy, and the Politics of Expertise* (Cambridge: Cambridge University Press, 2004), Kindle location 2572–2575.

55 Ibid., Kindle location 64–67.
56 Heritage Foundation, "About Us."
57 Rich, *Think Tanks*, Kindle location 2572–2575.
58 See Thomas B. Fordham Institute website http://www.edexcellence.net/template/index.cfm.
59 Rich, *Think Tanks*, Kindle location 231–236.
60 Progressive Policy Institutes, "About The Progressive Policy Institute," Retrieved from http://www.ppionline.org/ppi_ci.cfm?knlgAreaID=87&subsecID=205&contentID=896 on August 14, 2004.
61 PPI Project Description, "About PPI's 21st Century Schools Project." Retrieved from http://www.ppionline.org/ppi_ci.cfm?contentid=1125&knlgAreaID=110&subsecid=204 on June 29, 2000.
62 Ibid.
63 Progressive Policy Institute Press Release (September 8, 2004), "PPI Unveils National Strategy to Expand Early Childhood Education, Report Outlines Federal–State Partnership to Close Preparation Gap and Foster Accountability." Retrieved from http://www.ppionline.org/ppi_ci.cfm?contentid=252868&knlgAreaID=85&subsecid=108 on September 24, 2004.
64 Ibid., p. 3.
65 "Remarks by the President to the Hispanic Chamber of Commerce on a Complete and Competitive American Education" (March 10, 2009). Retrieved from http://www.whitehouse.gov/the_press_office/Remarks-of-the-President-to-the-Hispanic-Chamber-of-Commerce/ on March 10, 2009.
66 "American Enterprise Institute: About Us." Retrieved from http://www.aei.org/about/filter.all/default.asp on April 8, 2009.
67 Matthew Spalding, "Character and the Destiny of Free Government," *Building a Culture of Character, Heritage Lectures* (Washington, DC: The Heritage Foundation, 2002).
68 Joseph Loconte, "The Importance of Believing in Charity" (July 7, 2003). Retrieved from http://www.heritage.org/Press/Commentary/ed070703a.cfm?RenderforPrint=1 on September 2, 2003.
69 Quoted in Smith, *The Idea Brokers*, p. 178.
70 American Enterprise Institute, "Education." Retrieved from http://www.aei.org/ra/29 on January 18, 2010.
71 American Enterprise Institute, "Future of American Education Project." Retrieved from http://www.aei.org/yra/100001?parent=3 on January 18, 2010.
72 Grace Smith, "What Parents Should Know for Back to School," WebMemo #561 (September 3, 2004), p. 1. Retrieved from www.heritage.org on July 24, 2005.
73 "No Child Left Behind: Mend It, End It, or Let It Work?" Retrieved from http://www.aei.org/events/eventID.878,filter./event_detail.asp. on July 24, 2005.
74 "Summary: No Child Left Behind: Mend It, End It, or Let It Work?" Retrieved from http://www.aei.org/events/eventID.878,filter./event_detail.asp on July 24, 2005.
75 Ibid.
76 Dan Lips, "Reforming No Child Left Behind by Allowing States to Opt Out: An A-Plus for Federalism," *Backgrounder* (Washington, DC: Heritage Foundation, June 19, 2007), p. 1.
77 Dan Lips, Jennifer Marshall, and Lindsey Burke, *A Parent's Guide to Education Reform* (Washington, DC: Heritage Foundation, 2007).
78 Ibid., pp. 13–29.

79 "Race to the Top? The Promise—and—Challenges of Charter School Growth." Retrieved from http://www.aei.org/events/eventID.1904,filter.all, type.past/event_detail.asp on April 8, 2009.

80 Ibid.

81 American Educational Research Association, "AERA Position Taking and Policymaking Processes Guidelines Joint Report of the Government Relations Committee and the Social Justice Action Committee to the AERA Council" (January 2005). Retrieved from http://www.aera.net/AboutAERA/Default. aspx?menu_id=90&id=1914 on January 21, 2010.

82 Ibid.

83 Ibid.

84 Ibid.

85 Wayne Urban, *Why Teachers Organized* (Detroit: Wayne State University Press, 1982), p. 22.

86 See Fredrick Wirt and Michael Kirst, *The Political Dynamics of American Education*, 3rd edn. (Riverside, CA: McCutchan Publishing Corporation, 2005), pp. 43–44; and Eileen White, "N.E.A. Steps Up Anti-Reagan Lobbying Effort" (January 12, 1982). Retrieved from *Education Week* http://www.edweek.org on February 26, 2009.

87 Mark Pitsch, "Teachers' Unions' PAC's Gave $5.2 Million in '89–'90 Elections" (November 28, 1990). Retrieved from *Education Week* http://www.edweek.org on February 26, 2009.

88 Quoted in ibid.

89 Vaishali Honawar and Bess Keller, "Unions Provide Money and Personnel for Key Races with Control of Congress at Stake" (November 1, 2006). Retrieved from *Education Week* http://www.edweek.org on March 3, 2009.

90 "Remarks by the President to the Hispanic Chamber of Commerce."

91 "Statement by Randi Weingarten, President, American Federation of Teachers,on President Obama's Remarks Today to the U.S. Hispanic Chamber of Commerce" (March 10, 2009). Retrieved from http://www.aft. org/presscenter/releases/2009/031009.htm on March 11, 2009.

92 Ibid.

93 "NEA President Welcomes 'Cradle to Career' Plan Outlined by President Obama" (March 10, 2009). Retrieved from http://www.nea.org/home/ 30945.htm on March 11, 2009.

94 Ibid.

95 U.S. Department of Education, "Education Race to the Top Fund; State Fiscal Stabilization Fund Program; Institute of Education Sciences; Overview Information; Grant Program for Statewide Longitudinal Data Systems; Notice Inviting Applications for New Awards Under the American Recovery and Reinvestment Act of 2009," *Federal Register*, 74(144) (July 29, 2009), p. 37806.

96 National Education Association, "NEA's Federal Policy Guide." Retrieved from http://www.nea.org/home/NEAs%20Federal%20Policy%20Guide.htm on January 10, 2010.

97 American Federation of Teachers, "Tell Congress to Overhaul NCLB." Retrieved from http://www.unionvoice.org/campaign/NCLB070708 on January 17, 2010.

Chapter 5

Politicians and Educational Ideologies

The educational ideologies of conservative Republicans and liberal Democrats influence the educational policies emerging from the governance structure discussed in Chapter 3. The educational ideas of conservatives and liberals are in turn influenced by the public and civil society as discussed in Chapters 2 and 4. Many of civil society's organizations espouse different variations on human capital ideology including those that embody a conservative religious agenda, socially liberal values, and free market and government regulated economic models. There exist alternative educational ideologies that reject human capitalism and focus on education for social justice and environmentalism and the arts. These educational ideologies have found their place nationally in the third party campaigns of Ralph Nader and the Green Party. However, human capital ideology with its different variations remains dominant.

Since the 1960s the Republican and Democratic parties have espoused different variations on human capital ideology. The major divide between the two political parties has been over cultural values. What is now called the "culture wars" between conservative social values and liberal social values can be traced back to events of the 1960s, such as the civil rights movement, pro- and anti-Vietnam War demonstrations, rebellion in high schools, increased illegal drug usage, sexual freedom, and the U.S. Supreme Court's school prayer and Bible decisions. While some burned flags others proclaimed America was destined to lead the world to peace and democracy.

Just as the 1960s kindled angry and opposing emotions between Americans, both major political parties developed ideologies designed to appeal to voters' emotions. In *The Political Brain: The Role of Emotion in Deciding the Fate of the Nation*, Drew Westen argues that the Republican Party since the 1960s has developed what he calls a master narrative designed to appeal to the emotions of voters. From his perspective, emotional appeals play a more important role than reasoned appeals in persuading voters to support a particular candidate or political party.

Westen identifies these components of the Republican or the conservative master narrative which I consider to represent differences in cultural values within the framework of human capital ideology:

- Republicans protect traditional American values
- Republicans protect traditional religious faith and values
- Republicans consider poverty to be the result of poor character and every American has the chance to be financially successful through hard work
- Republicans protect the free market and rely on the "invisible hand" of the market[1]

In contrast, I have concluded that the Democratic or liberal cultural values that have evolved since the turbulent 1960s are:

- Democrats protect pluralism and multicultural values
- Democrats protect the secular nature of American government
- Democrats believe poverty is the result of social conditions that impede equality of opportunity and that government programs can help to eliminate poverty
- Democrats believe that government has a positive role to play in ensuring equality of opportunity

These cultural differences exist within an accepted framework that the primary purpose of schooling is to grow the economy and ensure America's place in global economic competition. For instance, consider the similar statements in both parties' 2008 national platforms. The Republican 2008 Party Platform under the section titled "Education Means a More Competitive America" proclaims:

> Maintaining America's preeminence requires a world-class system of education, with high standards, in which all students can reach their potential. That requires considerable improvement over our current 70 percent high school graduation rate and six-year graduation rate of only 57 percent for colleges.[2]

Using similar language even in reference to the high school dropout rates, the 2008 Democratic platform under its section titled "A World Class Education for Every Child" claims:

> In the 21st century, where the most valuable skill is knowledge, countries that out-educate us today will out-compete us tomorrow. In the platform hearings, Americans made it clear that it is morally and economically unacceptable that our high-schoolers continue to

score lower on math and science tests than most other students in the world and continue to drop-out at higher rates than their peers in other industrialized nations.[3]

In addition, both those professing conservative and those professing liberal economic and cultural values support creation of state curriculum standards and use of test scores to evaluate schools and teachers.

Similarities in educational ideas quickly disappear when discussion turns to culture, values, religion, and the role of the free market in education. It is important to note that differences in culture, values, and religion directly affect the answer to the question: What knowledge is most worth teaching?

Cultural Conservatism and American Exceptionalism

Central to conservative cultural values is a belief in what is called American "exceptionalism" which means that the history of the United States has been guided by the hand of a Christian God and that the country's unique and superior set of republican values should be spread around the world. A belief in American exceptionalism is usually accompanied by a heightened sense of patriotism and a belief that America was founded on Christian values. For example, 2008 Republican candidate John McCain expressed in his autobiography a belief in American exceptionalism in regard to the cultural rift caused by the Vietnam War:

> Disagreements about the purpose and conduct of the war as well as its distinction of being the first lost war in American history left some Americans bereft in confidence in *American exceptionalism—the belief that our history is unique and exalted and a blessing to all humanity. Not all Americans lost this faith* [author's emphasis].[4]

The belief in American exceptionalism is expressed in the following educational goal appearing in the 2008 Republican national platform (it is important to note that a similar statement did not appear in the 2008 Democratic platform).

> Education is essential to competitiveness, but it is more than just training for the work force of the future. It is through education that we ensure the transmission of a culture, a set of values we hold in common. It has prepared generations for responsible citizenship in a free society, and it must continue to do so. Our party is committed to restoring the civic mission of schools envisioned by the founders of the American public school system. Civic education, both in the

classroom and through service learning, should be a cornerstone of American public education and should be central to future school reform efforts.[5]

In the framework of American exceptionalism, conservative Republicans are particularly concerned with the values imparted by history instruction. Conservatives want schools to promote patriotism, a positive view of American history, a traditional religious-based morality, and a unified American culture. Of particular concern for conservatives is multiculturalism with its emphasis on teaching history from a variety of cultural perspectives. In addition, multiculturalism suggests that the school curriculum should give an equal space to the literature and history of other cultures alongside that of Western culture.

The reaction to the multicultural challenge to American exceptionalism occurred during the Republican administration of President Ronald Reagan (1980–1988). President Reagan's Secretary of Education William Bennett, who besides serving under Reagan spent nine years in public office as head of the National Endowment for the Humanities and was the first drug czar under George H.W. Bush, expressed the conservative sentiment that multiculturalism was undermining American values. In 1986, Secretary Bennett publicly criticized the Stanford University faculty for replacing a freshman undergraduate course entitled "Western Culture," in which students read fifteen works on Western philosophy and literature, with a course entitled "Cultures, Ideas, and Values," with readings by "women, minorities, and persons of color."[6] Bennett argued that students should be required to study Western culture because it provided the framework for American government and culture. And adding Western exceptionalism to American exceptionalism, Bennett asserted, "Probably most difficult for the critics of Western culture to acknowledge is that 'the West is good'." Western culture, according to Bennett, "set the moral, political, economic, and social standards for the rest of the world."[7]

Secretary Bennett criticized liberals for undermining a belief in the superiority of American and Western values. Liberals, Bennett contended, rejected many traditional Christian values and looked with scorn on Americans who believe in the value of hard work and economic individualism.

Another protector of American exceptionalism during the Reagan years was Lynne Cheney, the wife of the future Republican Vice-President Dick Cheney. President Reagan appointed her head of the National Endowment for the Humanities where she served from 1986 through the administration of George H.W. Bush. Reflecting her commitment to protecting the teaching of American exceptionalism in schools, she distributed a report in 1987 titled "American Memory: A Report on the Humanities in the Nation's Public Schools."[8] In the report, she criticized the general neglect of history in the public schools in favor of the generalized field of social studies. "The culprit is 'process'," Cheney wrote, "the belief that we can teach them how to understand the world in which they live without conveying to them the events and ideas that have brought it into existence." In her conclusion, she warned, "we run the danger of unwittingly proscribing our own heritage."[9]

In the same year as Lynne Cheney's report a dispute over history standards broke out in California. California Superintendent of Public Instruction Bill Honig appointed a panel to rewrite California's social studies curriculum which included Diane Ravitch, who at the time was a noted educational conservative and adjunct professor at Teachers College, Columbia University, and Charlotte Crabtree, a professor of education at UCLA. Ravitch would later be appointed in 1991 by Republican President George H.W. Bush to the post of Assistant Secretary of Education in charge of the Office of Educational Research and Improvement. After her appointment to the U.S. Department of Education, Ravitch promoted "the creation of academic standards."[10]

Ravitch's office and the National Endowment for the Humanities headed by Lynne Cheney provided a combined $1.6 million to the National Center for History in Schools to develop national history standards. To the surprise of Ravitch and Cheney, the first set of national standards in history did not support the notion of American exceptionalism and its role as a moral model for other nations. The standards contained teaching examples, which in the words of Cheney, "make it sound as if everything in America is wrong and grim." She complained that the teaching examples contained seventeen references to the Ku Klux Klan and nineteen references to McCarthyism, whereas there was no mention of Paul Revere, Thomas Edison, and other "politically incorrect White males."[11] Outraged, Lynne Cheney founded a Washington-based Committee to Review National Standards to apply political pressure for a revision of the history standards.

In 1995, the National Center for History in Schools announced that it was revising the history standards and teaching examples. Claiming a victory, Diane Ravitch hoped that "we can declare this particular battle-front in the culture wars to be ended."[12] In reporting Ravitch's statement, *Education Week*'s reporter Karen Diegmueller explained that Ravitch was "a panelist who not only had criticized the documents but had commissioned their creation when she served as an assistant secretary in the U.S. Department of Education."[13] Diegmueller reported that the criticisms of the history standards were primarily from conservative Republicans who contended, in Diegmueller's words, that "the standards undercut the great figures that traditionally have dominated the landscape of history and portray the United States and the West as oppressive regimes that have victimized women, minorities, and third world countries."[14]

What the critics wanted, Diegmueller wrote, was a history that emphasized U.S. accomplishments and provided students with uplifting ideals or, as I have been referring to it, a history that promoted American exceptionalism. With a cynical tone, Diegmueller opened a later *Education Week* article with these words: "Timbuktu has disappeared. Pearl Harbor has ascended. George Washington is in; Eleanor Roosevelt is out. And names and places like Joseph McCarthy and Seneca Falls, N.Y., whose prominence irked critics . . . have been allotted one mention apiece."[15] Also, she reported an attempt to give a more upbeat tone to the introductions to the ten eras of U.S. history delimited by the standards.

In their 1996 campaign book, Republican Presidential candidate Bob Dole and his running mate Jack Kemp joined the chorus demanding a more upbeat history instruction. Among three failures of public schools, Dole and Kemp identified this one: "Where schools should instill an appreciation of our country and its history, often they seem to reflect a blindness toward America and its finer moments."[16] The conservative Heritage Foundation, discussed in Chapter 4, joined the chorus demanding that schools teach from the perspective of American exceptionalism. The Foundation even published an article giving an upbeat spin to the enslavement of Africans. Dinesh D'Souza, who at the time was the John Olin scholar at the conservative American Enterprise Institute, wrote in a 1995 article in the Heritage Foundation's monthly *Policy Review*, "Slavery was an institution that was terrible to endure for slaves, but it left the descendants of slaves better off in America. For this, the American Founders are owed a measure of respect and gratitude."[17] In a previous book sponsored by the American Enterprise Institute, D'Souza argued that multiculturalism and feminism were destroying liberal education through the replacement in college courses of significant books written by White males with inferior books written by minorities and women.[18]

The struggle over traditional American values continued into the twenty-first century. In 2004 the conservative Thomas B. Fordham Institute published Diane Ravitch's *A Consumer's Guide to High School History Textbooks*.[19] The book reviewed thirteen American and World History textbooks for senior high schools. The reviews were written by scholars who were asked if the textbooks were biased. None of the reviewers found a *conservative* bias to the books. However, some books were charged with being "left-liberal" and "leftist." For instance, Morton Keller, Spector Professor of History at Brandeis University, asserted that Gary B. Nash's *American Odyssey: The United States in the Twentieth Century* is "the most biased and partisan of the texts reviewed here: unabashed in its politically (if not historically) correct definition of diversity, and in its adherence to a left-liberal view of modern America."[20] Another reviewer, Edward J. Renehan, Jr., author of the *Kennedys at War*, charged that there was "a leftist political bias" to *The Americans* by

Gerald Danzer et al. Renehan claimed, "The book's section on HUAC (House Un-American Activities Committee), Joseph McCarthy, etc. could easily have been written by Paul Robeson [noted Communist of the period]."[21] Ravitch reported that Jeffery Mirel, Associate Dean for Academic Affairs at the University of Michigan, found the *American Odyssey* to have

> a "deeply pessimistic" view, in which the nation's failures consistently out weight its commitment to its ideals . . . Mirel concludes that "it is difficult to judge a book as even-handed and fair that devotes so much time to violations of people's civil liberties [in the U.S.] . . . but does not even mention the millions of deaths under Soviet Communism".[22]

In summary, conservative support for teaching American exceptionalism continued into the unsuccessful 2008 campaign of Republican Presidential candidate John McCain. The "culture wars" over U.S. history highlight a negative aspect of the drive to create state and national curriculum standards. Should a particular interpretation of U.S. history be embodied in curriculum standards? While cultural conservatives call for a celebratory and patriotic history, cultural liberals want one that exposes flaws in American development and provides a rich tapestry of American diversity. The important point for this book is the fact that politics will determine which interpretation of history is taught in schools and not which interpretation is correct. Either historical interpretation can create a particular image of American life in students' minds.

Liberal Cultural Values and Multiculturalism

While culturally conservative Republicans are clear in their support for teaching American exceptionalism, culturally liberal Democrats have sent out a confused message about what should be taught in American schools. As I will be using the term in this section, liberal refers to support for particular cultural values and an economic vision that includes government regulation of the economy. As stated previously, liberals accept the human capital paradigm for education.

A significant problem for Democratic efforts to win voter support from cultural minorities is the risk of offending traditional White supporters. Democrats have been successful in recruiting votes from cultural minorities. According to the Pew Hispanic Center, in 2008 67 percent of the Hispanic community voted for Democratic President Barack Obama while Republican candidate John McCain received only 31 percent of the Hispanic vote. In the election 55 percent of Whites voted Republican and only 4 percent of Blacks voted Republican.[23]

When the "culture wars" began in the 1960s cultural liberals were associated with protection of minorities as cultural conservatives marched to the drumbeat of American exceptionalism. In addition, liberals supported women's rights, abortion, sexual freedom, internationalism (in contrast to patriotism), a secular government and schools, government programs to aid the poor, and multiculturalism (in contrast to the U.S. being a single culture society).

The branding of liberal Democrats as multiculturalists resulted from their support of civil rights legislation and bilingual education. In the 1960s, liberal Democrats supported protection of minority languages and cultures for Native Americans, Mexican Americans, and Puerto Ricans. Liberal Democratic Senator Ralph Yarborough of Texas, believing that he would lose the 1970 election to a wealthy and conservative Democrat, decided that Hispanic support was crucial to his coalition of African Americans, Mexican Americans, and poor Whites. In an effort to win Hispanic support, Yarborough, after being appointed to a special subcommittee on bilingual education of the Senate Committee on Labor and Public Welfare, launched a series of hearings in major Hispanic communities.[24] The testimony at these hearings came primarily from representatives of the Mexican American and Puerto Rican communities, not educational experts or linguistic theorists. Yarborough supported bilingual legislation that focused on students whose "mother tongue is Spanish." The legislation included programs to impart knowledge and pride about Hispanic culture and language and to bring descendants of Mexicans and Puerto Ricans into the teaching profession. Yarborough's efforts resulted in the passage of the Bilingual Education Act of 1968. Native Americans, along with Mexican Americans and Puerto Ricans, reacted favorably to the bilingual legislation which promised that their cultures and languages would be preserved by the public schools. Bilingual education, as it was conceived of in Hispanic and Native American communities, involved teaching both English and Spanish or Native American languages.[25]

The 1968 legislation left open the question of whether bilingual education was simply to help students with limited English proficiency, or whether it was also to maintain native languages and cultures. Later in the 1980s this distinction became important as some conservative Republicans agitated for English-only in schools. The language of the legislation suggested that the goal was compensatory because it targeted children who were both poor and "educationally disadvantaged because of their inability to speak English." A statement by Senator Yarborough to other members of Congress suggested that the legislation's goal was primarily compensatory, "It is not the purpose of the bill to create pockets of different languages throughout the country . . . not to stamp out the mother tongue, and not to make their mother tongue the dominant language, but just to try to make those children fully literate in English."[26]

Liberals seemed to be on the road to supporting multiculturalism in schools when during the 1974 reauthorization of the Bilingual Education Act liberal Democratic Senators Edward Kennedy and Walter Mondale tried to expand bilingual education programs by requiring them to include instruction in students' native languages and cultures. This turned the program into bilingual–bicultural education.[27]

The ambivalence of liberals about multiculturalism appeared in the 1976–1980 administration of President Jimmy Carter. When Carter ran for office in 1976 the Democratic platform asserted, "We recognize the right of all citizens to education, pursuant to Title VI of the Civil Rights Act of 1968, and the need in affected communities for *bilingual and bicultural educational programs* [author's emphasis]."[28] However, President Carter backed away from support of bicultural programs when he declared to his Cabinet, "I want English taught, not ethnic culture."[29]

Liberals backtracked on their original support of bilingual and bicultural education when conservative Republicans argued that bilingual education might somehow be against American traditions. As quoted by Garcia and Baker, Republican President Reagan commented that while supporting aid to non-English-speaking students to learn English, "it is absolutely wrong and against American concepts to have a bilingual education program that is now openly, admittedly dedicated to preserving their native language. . . ."[30]

In their 1980 national platform, Democrats gave terse support to bilingual instruction without any reference to biculturalism or multi-culturalism. The Democratic platform simply stated: "We support an effective bilingual program to reach all limited-English-proficiency people who need such assistance. The Democratic Party supports efforts to broaden students' knowledge and appreciation of other cultures, languages and countries."[31]

During the 1980s, the special interest group, the National Association for Bilingual Education, increased its political activities and intensified its public relations efforts. Like any special interest group, as discussed in Chapter 4, this organization adopted self-serving responses to criticism of multiculturalism and bilingualism. Gene T. Chavez, the president of the Association, warned that "those who think this country can only tolerate one language" were motivated by political rather than educational concerns. The incoming president of the organization, Chicago school administrator Jose Gonzalez, accused the conservative Reagan admin-istration of entering an "unholy alliance" with right-wing groups opposing bilingual education, groups such as U.S. English, Save Our Schools, and the Heritage Foundation.[32]

By the 1990s, liberals continued to withdraw support for maintaining minority cultures in schools. For instance, when, in 1995, Democratic President Bill Clinton pledged support for bilingual education at a fundraiser for the Hispanic Caucus Institute, he argued for bilingualism as a method for teaching English and providing non-English speakers access to the curriculum while in transition to learning English:

> The issue is whether children who come here, while they are learning English, should also be able to learn other things. The issue is whether American citizens who work hard and pay taxes and are older and haven't mastered English yet should be able to vote like other citizens.[33]

Liberal Democrats further retreated from their original support of bilingual education and multiculturalism when they supported the 2001 No Child Left Behind legislation. Symbolically, the legislation's section titled "English Language Acquisition, Language Enhancement, and Academic Act" changed the name of the federal government's Office of Bilingual Education to Office of English Language Acquisition, Language Enhancement, and Academic Achievement for Limited English Proficient Students; its shortened name became Office of English Language Acquisition. The director of bilingual education and minority languages affairs became the director of English language acquisition. While recognizing programs designed to maintain Native American languages and Spanish, the law mandated that the major thrust of these programs has to be English proficiency. The legislation declared that programs serving

> Native American (including Native American Pacific Islander) children and children in the Commonwealth of Puerto Rico may include programs . . . designed for Native American children learning and studying Native American languages and children of limited Spanish proficiency, except that an outcome of programs serving such children *shall be increased English proficiency among such children* [my emphasis].[34]

Also, in 2004, Democratic Presidential candidate John Kerry did not make bilingual education a priority issue. In an online chat, Robert Gordon, who was an advisor to the Kerry campaign and had been policy director for Democrat John Edwards' campaign and an aide in the Clinton White House, explained John Kerry's views regarding Native American education and bilingual education: "He has offered detailed initiatives to improve the quality of teaching and afterschool programs in American Indian schools. And he is committed to strongly supporting bilingual education programs based on the methods that have proven most successful in the community."[35]

In the 2008 election President Barack Obama criticized the media's portrayal of the culture wars. President Obama described a nation where identities and cultural values are constantly changing. In *The Audacity of*

Hope, Obama argued that America's cultural values are more centrist than portrayed by the media. For instance, in contrast to the media, Obama argued, many evangelicals are more tolerant, many secularists are more spiritual, some rich want the poor to succeed, and many poor want to succeed. Obama claimed that many political commentators point to "moral" issues such as gay marriage and abortion as being crucial to some elections. But, he stated, the number one election issue is often national security with moral values taking second place.[36]

In 2008, Democrats, influenced by the previously mentioned book by Drew Westen, created a centrist master narrative. I am using the term "centrist" for their master narrative because it was an attempt to bridge the gap between the perceived values of conservative Republicans and so-called counter-cultural values of liberal Democrats.

"I think Democrats," Obama wrote, "are wrong to run away from a debate about values, as wrong as those conservatives who see values only as a wedge to pry loose working-class voters from the Democratic base."[37] Obama stated his belief that most issues can be negotiated from the perspective of American values. These American values, to be included in the Democratic centrist master narrative, Obama asserted, are beliefs:

- in equality of opportunity and the possibility of upward social mobility;
- that society will prosper through individual pursuit of self-interest;
- that individualism should be bounded by communitarian values embodied in the family, neighborhood and community;
- in patriotism and the obligations of citizenship;
- in a faith bigger than ourselves that are embodied in religion or secular ethical principles;
- in humanitarian values including honesty, fairness, humility, kindness, courtesy, and compassion.[38]

The culture wars continued despite Obama's professed efforts to create a centrist position. Rejecting the original liberal support for schools to maintain minority languages and cultures, the 2008 Democratic platform simply stated,

> We also support transitional bilingual education and will help Limited English Proficient students get ahead by supporting and funding English Language Learner classes. We support teaching students second languages, as well as contributing through education to the revitalization of American Indian languages.[39]

In summary, liberals might have a public image of supporting multi-culturalism, but there is nothing in their recent political record to support that image. While cultural conservatives consistently support the idea of American exceptionalism, liberals project an image of patriotism that is bounded by communitarianism and mutual responsibility. Also, liberals link patriotism to both religious and secular values. Cultural conservatives and liberals mutually agree that equality of opportunity and social mobility are part of traditional American culture.

Cultural Conservatives, Moral Instruction, and Evolution

Many culturally conservative supporters of teaching American exceptionalism also consider the country's foundations to be Christian and resent any attempts to portray the United States as a secular nation. In this section, I will be using conservative to refer to those holding conservative cultural values and a belief that the free market is the best economic system. Reflecting a conservative view of American history, noted historian Arthur Schlesinger commented,

> For better or worse, the White Anglo-Saxon Protestant tradition was for two centuries and in crucial respects still is the dominant influence on American culture and society . . . The language of the new nation, its laws, its institutions, its political ideas, its literature, its customs, its precepts, its prayers, primarily derived from Britain.[40]

By linking American exceptionalism to Christianity, religious-oriented conservatives believe that any attack on the role of religion in government is an attack on the very foundations of American life. Consequently, allowing school prayer and teaching abstinence sex education are high on the agenda of many conservatives; it should be noted that not all conservatives are religious or Christian.

In the 1960s and 1970s the Republican leadership recruited voters who were upset by U.S. Supreme Court rulings. Three important U.S. Supreme Court decisions galvanized some religious groups into political action. The first was the 1962 U.S. Supreme Court case *Engel* v. *Vitale*, which denied the official use of prayer in public schools. Since the founding of common schools in the early nineteenth century, many public school days opened with a prayer and reading from the Protestant Bible. The 1962 decision denied the right of a public school system to conduct official prayer services within school buildings during regular school hours.

The second decision was *Abington School District* v. *Schempp* involving a Pennsylvania law permitting the reading of ten verses from the Bible at the opening of each public school day. Again, the U.S. Supreme Court ruled that this violated the establishment clause of the First Amendment. Religious texts could be read, the Court argued, as part of an academic course, such as literature or history.[41] As anger swelled over the school prayer and Bible reading decisions, the U.S. Supreme Court added more fuel to the fire with the 1973 decision *Roe v. Wade*, legalizing abortion. As a result of these decisions many evangelical Christians declared the public school system an enemy of Christianity and began sending their children to newly created private Christian academies.

Up to the 1980s, there was no specific political movement by organized Christians to influence federal and state policies. It was during Republican President Ronald Reagan's administration in the 1980s that the Moral Majority was organized through Jerry Falwell's "electronic church" which broadcast through his television program the "Old-Time Gospel Hour."[42]

The marriage between Ronald Reagan and the Moral Majority occurred shortly after the 1980 Republican convention when Reagan was asked to address 20,000 evangelicals at a rally in Dallas. Reagan told the group, "I know that you cannot endorse me [because of the tax-exempt status of the Moral Majority], but I endorse you and everything you do."[43] Giving hope to evangelicals opposed to evolutionary theory, Reagan expressed doubts about the plausibility of Darwinian ideas. After the 1980 election, Reagan supported the religious right's agenda by endorsing legislation for a tuition tax credit to allow parents to choose between public and private schools and by promising to support a school prayer amendment. After 1980, school choice and school prayer became a standard fixture in Republican platforms.

After 1980, conservative Republicans were committed to protecting the values of evangelical Christians. As I discussed in Chapter 4, the Moral Majority was eventually replaced by the Christian Coalition as the major political organization representing evangelical Christians. Conservative Republicans became aligned with the values of evangelical Christians. For instance, in the 2008 national elections, Republican candidate John McCain, who was not known for being religious, found it necessary to select a running mate who would appeal to the evangelical base of the Republican Party. Consequently, he chose Alaskan Governor Sarah Palin, an evangelical Christian, to share the ticket with him.

Governor Palin was a good representative of evangelical values. She favored teaching creationism in schools alongside evolutionary theory, supported abstinence-only sex education, and denied that global warming was caused by humans. The *Education Week*'s Michele McNeil and Sean Cavanaugh reported that during a televised debate in Alaska's 2006 gubernatorial campaign, "Ms. Palin said she thought creationism, the biblically based view that God created humans in their current form, should be taught alongside evolution in public school classrooms."[44] In an online interview in 2008, Palin claimed that climate change was not a result of human activities. Governor Palin also drew attention to her position on abstinence-only sex education when it was announced during the 2008 campaign that her unmarried 17-year-old daughter was pregnant.[45] McNeil and Cavanaugh quoted Jerry Bowen, a Republican delegate from Tennessee attending the 2008 national convention, about why he thought Governor Palin was an excellent person to defend abstinence-only sex education. "I think Governor Palin is the poster child for that message," Bowen asserted. "We cannot condemn her daughter for being human and making a mistake."[46]

In summary, the ideology of many conservative Republicans includes a belief that American exceptionalism is based on Protestant Christian values and that the future of the Republic is dependent on those values. Regarding the question of what knowledge is most worth teaching, these conservative Republicans defend religion and prayers in schools, advocate the teaching of the importance of Christianity in the development of America, oppose the teaching of birth control in favor of abstinence-only sex education, oppose instruction that supports abortion, oppose the recognition of lesbians and gays in the curriculum and in student clubs, and advocate that creationism be taught alongside evolutionary theory. It is important to emphasize that not all conservative Republicans adhere to these religious values.

Cultural Liberals and Moral Values

The culture wars emerging from the 1960s pitted secular-leaning cultural liberals against religious-oriented cultural conservatives in struggles over sex education and abortion. Liberals support teaching about birth control and women's right to an abortion. Gay marriage added another element to already existing ideological divisions. The 2004 Democratic platform declared, "We support full inclusion of gay and lesbian families in the life of our nation and seek equal responsibilities, benefits, and protections for these families." It also stated, "Because we believe in the privacy and equality of women, we stand proudly for a woman's right to choose, consistent with Roe v. Wade . . . We stand firmly against Republican efforts to undermine that right."[47] While Democrats avoided the issue of abstinence-only sex education in their 2004 platform they did make reference to family planning and, in the context of abortion and adoption: "we strongly support family planning and adoption incentives."[48]

In the 2008 elections, President Obama provided a liberal response to the "hot" cultural issues of abstinence education, abortion, and gay marriage. While President Obama stated that there could be no compromise over the right to an abortion, he argued that both sides could work together to reduce unwanted pregnancies through "education (including about abstinence), contraception, adoption, or any other strategies that have broad support and have been proven to work."[49] In keeping with liberal values, Obama evaluated gay marriage in the framework of fairness and compassion. Gay marriage would allow loving same-sex couples mutual access to hospital insurance and visitation rights.[50]

Addressing the concern about religion in public schools, President Obama stated that he was never bothered by the "under God" phrase in the Pledge of Allegiance or faith-based organizations working in public schools. Several sentences capture Obama's position on the religious use of public schools:

> Allowing the use of school property for meetings by voluntary student prayer groups should not be a threat, any more than its use by the high school Republican Club should threaten Democrats. And one can envision faith-based programs—targeting ex-offenders or substance abusers—that offer a uniquely powerful way of solving problems.[51]

In summary, there are major ideological differences between liberals and conservatives regarding explosive cultural issues like gay marriage, abortion, and birth control, which can affect public school instruction regarding these issues. In addition, liberals adopt a more secular view of the role of the school in society. Despite Obama expressing a lack of concern about "under God" in the Pledge of Allegiance, some liberals might prefer a more secular version.

Free Markets and School Choice

In answer to the question "What is the best organization for teaching?" many conservatives, who envision the best economic system as being the free market, answer that the best is one based on parental choice and competition between schools, including private, religious, public, charter, and for-profit schools. Competition, it is argued, will improve schools and teaching by causing failing schools to close and the best schools to survive and influence other schools. In the words of free market economists, "the invisible hand of the marketplace" will ensure quality schools. In addition, religious complaints about the secular nature of public schools following the school prayer and Bible decisions of the 1960s caused some parents to seek public financing for their choice of private religious schools. This combination of economic arguments and religious motives justified plans for school vouchers, a parent's right to choose a public or private school at public expense, and for-profit education.

Contemporary ideas on school choice can be traced to the work of Friedrich Hayek, an Austrian economist and Nobel Prize winner, who moved to the United States to teach at the University of Chicago from 1950 to 1962. Hayek influenced a number of American economists, including Milton Friedman who first proposed school vouchers. In the 1930s, Hayek debated with English economist John Maynard Keynes over the role of government in a capitalist system. Keynes argued that for capitalism to survive governments needed to intervene in the economy. Classical liberals, such as John Stuart Mill, opposed government intervention, but the progressive liberals of the 1930s justified government intervention to ensure equality of opportunity and provide a social safety net to ensure the survival of capitalism.[52]

In *The Road to Serfdom*, Hayek set the stage for later conservative criticisms of government bureaucracies, including educational bureaucracies. He argued that the difficulty of determining prices or the value of goods would inevitably cause the failure of centrally planned economies. According to Hayek, pricing determines the social value of goods: What should a car cost in relation to food? What should the price of health care be in relation to education? In a free market, Hayek asserted, prices or social values are determined by individual choice. In a planned economy, pricing or social value is determined by a government bureaucracy. What criterion is used by a government bureaucracy? Hayek's answer was that the inevitable criterion is one that promotes the personal advantage of bureaucracy members. In addition, bureaucrats and intellectuals supported by a bureaucracy will advance social theories that vindicate the continued existence and expansion of the bureaucracy.[53] In this context, the problem with public schools was their control by a self-serving bureaucracy.

Milton Friedman, a colleague of Hayek's at the University of Chicago and a 1976 Nobel Prize winner, became the first American, at least to my knowledge, to advocate the use of vouchers as a means of providing school choice. Friedman argued that the benefits of maintaining a stable and democratic society justified government support of education, but not government-operated schools. Friedman proposed a government-financed voucher that parents could redeem "for a specified maximum sum per child per year if spent on 'approved' educational services."[54] Friedman believed the resulting competition between private schools for government vouchers would improve the quality of education. Also, he believed that vouchers would overcome the class stratification in education caused by the existence of rich and poor school districts. As Friedman suggested, "Under present arrangements, stratification of residential areas effectively restricts the intermingling of children from decidedly different backgrounds."[55] Except for a few parochial schools, Friedman argued, private schools were too expensive for most families, which resulted in further social class divisions in education.

Conservatives embrace Hayek's concept of the free market and Friedman's idea of a voucher system to support school choice. Free market ideologists contend that competition in the education market will result in improving the quality of education available to the American public. An unusual aspect of this argument is the support given to for-profit education. It is argued that a school operating for a profit will be more attuned to balancing costs with quality school instruction and appeal to parents. A for-profit education institution will want to market a good product to attract customers and control costs to ensure a profit.

Conservative Republicans were unsuccessful in achieving a free and competitive school market with parental choice being financed by vouchers or some form of tuition tax credit. However, some of these ideas did find their way into the 2001 legislation No Child Left Behind. Under the legislation, parents with children in failing schools are allowed to choose other schools in the district. And scattered throughout No Child Left Behind are provisions to support for-profit companies. For instance, the legislation states that assistance to schools requiring improvement because of low test scores can be provided by a "for–profit agency."[56]

Under the Reading First section, reading and literacy partnerships can be established between school districts and for-profit companies.[57] Also, state and local school districts are provided funds to contract with for-profit companies to provide advanced placement courses and services; to reform teacher and principal certification; to recruit "highly qualified teachers, including specialists in core academic subjects, principals, and pupil services personnel"; "to improve science and mathematics curriculum and instruction"; "to develop State and local teacher corps or other programs to establish, expand, and enhance teacher recruitment and retention efforts"; to integrate "proven teaching practices into instruction"; for professional development programs; to provide services to teachers of limited English proficient students and for developing and implementing programs for limited English proficient students; to create and expand community technology centers; to accredit basic education of Indian children in Bureau of Indian Affairs Schools; and to train prospective teachers in advanced technology.[58] In other words, No Child Left Behind opens the door to the education business to profit from schooling.

So in answer to the question about the best school organization, the answer of free market conservatives is competition between charter, public, private, religious, and for-profit schools financed through either a voucher or tax-credit system. Conservatives believe the "invisible hand of the marketplace" will ensure that the "best" schools will win the competition. Religious-oriented parents hope that choice will allow them to choose a religious education for their children.

Liberals and Regulated Markets

Liberals support public education and resist efforts to publicly fund private and religious schools. Any support liberals have expressed for choice has been limited to choice between public schools rather than between public, private, and religious schools. Unlike conservatives, liberals do not support the free market ideology of economist Friedrich Hayek and his followers. Liberals feel that economic conservatives live in a dreamland for believing that the free market works fairly and for the best interests of all citizens. American liberals do not reject the importance of a free market but argue that it cannot exist without government intervention.

In *The Audacity of Hope*, President Obama stated the liberal position on free markets:

> our free market system is the result neither of natural law nor of divine providence . . . although the benefits of our free-market system have mostly derived from individual efforts . . . in each and every period of great economic upheaval and transition we've depended on government action to open up opportunity, encourage competition, and make the market work better.[59]

Referring to liberal Democratic Franklin D. Roosevelt's administration, Obama referred to "FDR saving capitalism from itself through an activist federal government that invests in its people and infrastructure, regulates the marketplace, and protects labor from chronic deprivation."[60] For liberal Democrats, the public school is one of the government institutions designed to "open up opportunity" and "make the market work better."

In the 1990s liberals accepted competition in government services as part of "reinventing government." In this context, government services could be improved if competition were introduced, such as competition between government-funded schools and public charter schools. The idea of reinventing government and schools was put forth by David Osborne and Ted Gaebler in their book *Reinventing Government: How the Entrepreneurial Spirit Is Transforming the Public Sector*.[61] Political writer Jacob Weisberg commented in the 1990s, "The most influential New Democratic idea—and perhaps the only widely read New Democratic book—is Reinventing Government."[62] The lead author of *Reinventing Government*, David Osborne, was a senior fellow at the liberal Democratic think tank, the Progressive Policy Institute, discussed in Chapter 4, and he served as senior advisor to Al Gore's National Performance Review, which attempted to reform the federal government. Osborne's coauthor, Ted Gaebler, was a former city manager.

The basic thesis of *Reinventing Government* is that "the kind of government that developed during the industrial era, with their sluggish, centralized bureaucracies, their preoccupations with rules and regulations, and their hierarchical chains of command, no longer works very well."[63] Osborne and Gaebler offered suggestions for reinventing government and public schools. One of their most influential ideas was that competition between government service providers meant creating competition between public schools. Anticipating the strong liberal push for public charter schools, Osborne and Gaebler asserted that, "the school districts would not operate public schools. Public schools would be run—on something like a contract or voucher basis—by many different organizations: teachers, colleges, even community organizations."[64]

In the twenty-first century, liberal Democrats continue to campaign for public school choice and public charter schools while condemning the idea of giving public money to private and religious schools. The 2000 Democratic Party Platform declares,

> The Democratic Party supports expansion of charter schools, magnet schools, site-based schools, year-round schools, and other non-traditional public school options. Charter schools and other nontraditional public school options can free school leaders, teachers, parents, and community leaders to use their creativity and innovation to help all students meet the highest academic standards.[65]

The 2004 Democratic Party Platform states: "Instead of pushing private school vouchers that funnel scarce dollars away from the public schools, we will support public school choice, including charter schools and magnet schools that meet the same high standards as other schools."[66] In a speech on March 10, 2009, to the Hispanic Chamber of Commerce, President Obama called charter schools the fourth part of his education strategy. He told the gathering,

> One of the places where much of that innovation [reinventing the school] occurs is in our most effective charter schools. And these are public schools founded by parents, teachers, and civic or community organizations with broad leeway to innovate—schools I supported as a state legislator and a United States senator.[67]

In order to pursue this reinvention of schooling President Obama urged states to remove caps on the number of charters because, in his words, the caps weren't "good for our children, our economy, or our country."[68]

In conclusion, unlike conservative economists who put unquestioned faith in the "invisible hand of the marketplace" and, consequently, support a free market for education with competition between public, private, and religious schools, liberals question the fairness of the "invisible hand of the marketplace" and argue that government intervention is necessary to ensure that the marketplace works fairly. However, in accepting the idea of "the reinvention of government," Democrats support competition between public schools using choice plans and place a great deal of hope in improving public education by expanding the role of public charter schools.

Cultural Conservatives: Poverty is a Matter of Character in a Free Market

Both Democrats and Republicans link poverty to schooling and economic opportunity. Both support equality of opportunity to compete for jobs and wealth. However, there are sharp differences between cultural liberals and conservatives about the causes of poverty and how schooling contributes to equality of opportunity. In this section, I will discuss culturally conservative views of poverty, equality of opportunity, and schooling. Liberal cultural responses to these issues will be discussed later in the chapter.

Many conservatives believe that the free market in the United States gives everyone who is willing an equal opportunity to escape from poverty. For religious conservatives good character is needed to utilize the opportunities of a free market to improve one's economic condition. In this framework, poverty is not a result of growing up in poor economic and social conditions, but it is the result of individual failure to exploit the benefits of the American economic system. Schools can help students escape poverty by giving them the tools and character traits needed to advance in the free market system.

In the early twenty-first century this conservative view of poverty was embodied in what Republican President George W. Bush called compassionate conservatism. "Compassionate conservatism," President Bush asserted, "places great hope and confidence in public education. Our economy depends on higher and higher skills, requiring every American to have the basic tools of learning. Every public school should be the path of upward mobility."[69]

Compassionate conservatism rejects direct charity or government welfare because it might reinforce negative character traits. Ending poverty, according to conservatives, involves providing the conditions by which people can help themselves. In the context of this argument, self-help will result in a transformation of character and the acquisition of positive values. This character transformation is aided by exposure to religious values. Consequently, according to compassionate conservatives, the imposed discipline of educational standards and testing is to help students to develop the character traits of self-discipline and hard work. Aiding in this process are character education, student-initiated school prayer, and exposure to religious values.

The importance of values was emphasized by George W. Bush when, as Governor of Texas, he wrote that,

> *Dream and the Nightmare* by Myron Magnet crystallized for me the impact the failed culture of the sixties had on our values and society. It helped create dependency on government, undermine family and

eroded values which had stood the test of time and which are critical if we want a decent and hopeful tomorrow for every single American.[70]

Myron Magnet was editor of the conservative Manhattan Institute's *City Journal* and a former member of the editorial board of *Fortune* magazine. Similar to other conservatives, he considers the 1960s and early 1970s the cultural watershed of American history. During this period American values, he argues, deteriorated as a result of a cultural revolution led "by an elite of opinion makers, policymakers, and mythmakers—lawyers, judges, professors, political staffers, journalists, writers, TV and movie honchos, clergymen—and it was overwhelmingly a liberal, left-of-center elite."[71] Out of this cultural revolution, according to Magnet, emerged a whole host of liberal programs, including the War on Poverty, court-ordered busing, affirmative action, drug treatment programs, and the political correctness movement at colleges.

Magnet argues that the 1960s cultural revolution overturned traditional American values that supported hard work and family life as the basis for economic success and good living. The new values were represented by two "epochal" expressions. The first was the sexual revolution, which Magnet claims caused increased divorce, illegitimacy, and female-headed families. The second was the 1960s counterculture that rejected the idea of equality of opportunity being based on hard work.

These conservative arguments stress that the liberal failure to end poverty is because of a reliance on changing the economic system rather than changing the values of the poor. Magnet presented the following argument:

> On the grandest level, if you believe that human choices and actions, rather than blind, impersonal forces, determine the shape of history, then the ideas and visions impelling the human actors become crucial causes of the reality that unfolds. Men don't simply have their environment handed to them from on high; they collectively make and remake it from the cultural and material resources that lie ready at hand. And great men augment those resources by inventing new techniques and new ideas.[72]

Magnet argued that American society advanced because of the Protestant values that promoted a free economy. Citing Max Weber, Magnet identified these values as individualism, hard work, and a belief that success is a sign of God's blessing.

Other conservatives echoed Magnet's sentiments. Pat Buchanan, the conservative political commentator and 2000 Presidential candidate for the Reform Party, provided the following description of these beliefs: "Among the social conservatives [of the Republican Party] resides the

Religious Right to whom the expulsion of God from the classroom, the rise of the drug culture, and the 'sexual revolution' are unmistakable symptoms of cultural decadence and national decline."[73]

Also, Bush and other religious-oriented Republicans were influenced by the work of University of Texas journalism professor Marvin Olasky who is editor of the weekly news magazine *Christian* and author of two important books, *The Tragedy of American Compassion* and *Renewing American Compassion: How Compassion for the Needy Can Turn Ordinary Citizens into Heroes*. Olasky blames government welfare programs for worsening the moral conditions of the poor and, as a result, perpetuating poverty in the United States.[74] Olasky's answer to helping the poor was returning welfare programs to faith-based organizations. Federal programs operated by faith-based groups, according to Olasky and other religious-oriented conservatives, ensure the teaching of traditional moral values to America's poor. To Olasky, humans are basically sinful, and their inherent sinfulness must be curbed by moral instruction. The danger of providing welfare funds without demanding work in return, he argues, is that humans could easily slip into a depraved condition. Olasky maintains that in "orthodox Christian anthropology . . . man's sinful nature leads toward indolence, and that an impoverished person given a dole without obligation is likely to descend into pauperism."[75] Olasky emphasizes the traditional American nature of his argument by quoting seventeenth-century Puritan divine Cotton Mather: "Don't nourish [the idle] and harden'em in that, but find employment for them. Find'em work; set'em to work; keep'em to work."[76]

Conservatives stress the importance of ideas in affecting values and character and not social conditions. Consequently, control of schools and media is important. Conservative Pat Buchanan quotes Mazzini: "Ideas rule the world and its events. A revolution is a passage of an idea from theory to practice. Whatever men say material interests never caused and never will cause a revolution."[77] Agreeing with Buchanan, former Secretary of Education William Bennett states,

> I have come to the conclusion that the issues surrounding the culture and our values are the most important ones . . . They are at the heart of our resolution of the knottiest problems of public policy, whether the subject be education, art, race relations, drugs, crime, or raising children.[78]

For Bennett, the solution to public problems was teaching morality and Western cultural values.

Conservative values can justify an educational system regulated by standards and tests that forces students to work hard and, consequently, instills behaviors and values associated with success. In addition, the use of faith-based organizations is considered necessary to instilling a morality needed for economic success. Consequently, No Child Left Behind supports public funding of faith-based organizations. In July, 2004, the U.S. Department of Education issued a pamphlet describing the relationship between No Child Left Behind and faith-based organizations. The pamphlet asserted, "With No Child Left Behind, schools and religious organizations can become even more powerful allies in the effort to ensure that all children—regardless of their race, family income or the language spoken in their homes—receive a high-quality education."[79]

For conservatives character education is important at school for preparing students for success. "Character education," according to a press release from the U.S. Department of Education, "is a key feature of No Child Left Behind, the landmark education reform law designed to change the culture of American schools."[80]

No Child Left Behind links character education to democracy and a free market economy. The legislation's "Section 2345: Cooperative Civic Education and Economic Education" supports research to determine the "effects of educational programs on students' development of the knowledge, skills, and *traits of character essential* for the preservation and *improvement of constitutional democracy*; and . . . effective participation in, and the preservation and improvement of, *an efficient market economy* [author's emphasis]."[81]

No Child Left Behind's "Section 5431: Partnerships in Character Education Program" supports "the design and implementation of character education programs that . . . are able to be integrated into class-room instruction and to be consistent with State academic content standards."[82] This section of the legislation even listed possible elements of character education instruction; this may be the first time in history where federal legislation actually identified elements of character considered important for the functioning of American society. The legislation provides the following examples:

(A) Caring.
(B) Civic virtue and citizenship.
(C) Justice and fairness.
(D) Respect.
(E) Responsibility.
(F) Trustworthiness.
(G) Giving.[83]

In summary, conservative attitudes about poverty center on the failure of individual character to take advantage of the rewards of equality of opportunity in the United States. Standards, testing, character education, and the work of faith-based organizations are the means by which schooling can instill values that will help people escape poverty. Conservatives do not question the economic organization of society. They argue that the rich are rich because they work hard and the poor are poor because their ethical failures keep them from taking advantage of the equality of opportunity offered by the American economic system. For conservatives, schools can help people escape poverty by teaching the knowledge and skills needed for employment and instilling values of hard work and discipline.

Cultural Liberals: Poverty and Equal Educational Opportunity

Cultural liberals do not reject conservative concerns with shaping individual character for success in the labor market, but liberals do put more emphasis on providing equality of educational opportunity through government-financed programs. Liberals believe that public education is necessary to ensure equal opportunity to compete in the economic system. Liberals also believe that if public education is to be successful in providing equality of opportunity it must ensure that all students receive an equal education.

The 2008 Democrat platform identified historic liberal concern with poverty and belief in education as a remedy.

> When Bobby Kennedy [brother of President John F. Kennedy assassinated in 1968] saw the shacks and poverty along the Mississippi Delta, he asked, "How can a country like this allow it?" Forty years later, we're still asking that question. The most American answer we can give is: "We won't allow it." One in eight Americans lives in poverty today all across our country, in our cities, in our suburbs, and in our rural communities.
>
> Most of these people work but still can't pay the bills. Nearly thirteen million of the poor are children. We can't allow this kind of suffering and hopelessness to exist in our country. It's not who we are.
>
> Working together, we can cut poverty in half within ten years. *We will provide all our children a world-class education, from early childhood through college* [author's emphasis].[84]

Since Bobby Kennedy's 1960s remarks about poverty, liberals have pushed an agenda of preschool and compensatory education as the remedy for the social and economic conditions of poverty that left children poorly prepared to do school work. The liberal 1960s War on Poverty included the 1965 Elementary and Secondary Education Act which contained funding for compensatory education programs designed to help students who at the time were labeled "culturally disadvantaged." The emphasis on compensatory education was dropped when Title I of the 1965 Elementary and Secondary Education Act was reauthorized in 2001 as No Child Left Behind. With this legislation, liberal rhetoric about equality of educational opportunity shifted from compensatory education to equality of exposure to a state-mandated curriculum and standards and tests, with failing schools being closed or restructured.

In the twenty-first century liberals define equality of educational opportunity as all students, including rich and poor, being taught the same curriculum and being assessed by the same tests. According to liberals, the goal of equality of educational opportunity would be achieved by reducing the achievement gap between the dominant and minority cultures and the rich and poor. The 2008 Democratic platform declares, "We cannot accept the persistent achievement gap between minority and white students or the harmful disparities that exist between different schools within a state or even a district."[85]

Preschool is another liberal remedy for poverty. Accepting the conservative argument that character traits are important for success, liberals argue that preschool can instill character traits for success in school which would lead to equality of opportunity in the pursuit of wealth. As part of the War on Poverty, President Lyndon Johnson announced in 1965 the funding of the preschool program Head Start designed for children from low-income families. After the 1960s, liberal Democrats continued to push for preschool education to end poverty. The 1968 Democratic national platform—the Democrats lost the Presidency to Richard Nixon in the election—promised: "We will marshal our national resources to help develop and finance new and effective methods of dealing with the educationally disadvantaged—including expanded pre-school programs to prepare all young children for full participation in formal education."[86]

Reflecting the continued liberal push for preschool education, the Democratic Party's 2008 platform declares,

> Early Childhood
> We will make quality, affordable early childhood care and education available to every American child from the day he or she is born. Our Children's First Agenda, including increases in Head Start and Early Head Start, and investments in high-quality Pre-K, will improve quality and provide learning and support to families with children ages zero to five. Our Presidential Early Learning Council will coordinate these efforts.[87]

In *Audacity of Hope*, President Obama supported universal preschool education because it would have the highest impact on reducing the so-called achievement gap. He claimed that, "we already have hard evidence of reforms that work . . . early childhood education."[88] *New York Times* reporter Sam Dillon commented about President Obama's support of preschool education:

> Driving the movement [for increased spending on preschool education] is research by a Nobel Prize-winning economist, James J. Heckman, and others showing that each dollar devoted to the nurturing of young children can eliminate the need for far greater government spending on remedial education, teenage pregnancy and prisons.[89]

Using a human capital model, Heckman, after carrying out a cost-benefit analysis of many proposed school reforms, concluded that preschool education yielded the highest financial returns for invested dollars.[90]

After being elected, President Obama made these remarks, reflecting Heckman's influence:

> Studies show that children in early childhood education programs are more likely to score higher in reading and math, more likely to graduate from high school and attend college, more likely to hold a job, and more likely to earn more in that job. For every dollar we invest in these programs, we get nearly $10 back in reduced welfare rolls, fewer health care costs, and less crime. That's why the American Recovery and Reinvestment Act that I signed into law invests $5 billion in growing Early Head Start and Head Start, expanding access to quality child care for 150,000 more children from working families, and doing more for children with special needs. And that's why we are going to offer 55,000 first-time parents regular visits from trained nurses to help make sure their children are healthy and prepare them for school and for life.[91]

In summary, the liberal educational antidote for poverty is equality of exposure of all students to the same curriculum standards and assessments and preschool education. For liberals, the free market cannot be fair if children are given unequal educations.

Conclusion: Human Capital and Alternative Ideologies

In conclusion, both culturally liberal and conservative Democrats and Republicans espouse the goals of human capital, with variations in their educational platforms reflecting their differing cultural values. Is there any alternative to the set of ideas that see the value of education in its contribution to economic growth and preparation for work in a global economy? One lonely alternative voice in the political landscape is that of Ralph Nader who ran for President in 1996 and 2000 on the Green Party ticket and as an independent in the 2004 and 2008 elections.

The ideology of the Green Party with its emphasis on protecting the environment challenges the very idea that economic growth and global competition are good for everyone. Human capital education is primarily directed at helping people and nations acquire more material goods. The Green Party argues that there are other values that are just as important. The 2004 Green Party Platform asserts,

> The Green Party strongly believes that the quality of life is determined not only by material aspects that can be measured and counted but also by elements that cannot be quantified . . . We believe that artistic expression and a thriving structure of art institutions are key to community well-being.[92]

Within this framework, the platform asserts,

> We advocate a diverse system of education that would introduce children early to the wonders of the Great School (Nature), and would cultivate the wisdom of eco-education, eco-economics, eco-politics, and eco-culture. We seek to protect our children from the corrosive effects of mass culture that trains them to regard themselves first and foremost as consumers.[93]

The Green Party's reference to children being trained as consumers is an indirect attack on the human capital model. Among other things, the human capital model values a mass consumption society where economic growth is spurred on by the desire of citizens to purchase more and more products. Success in a mass consumption society is measured by the material goods that can be purchased from earned income. The better the pay, the more goods a person can consume. Education for jobs in the global economy, the mantra of human capital, places the value of education on personal income and consumption.

On the surface, education for economic growth neglects the effect of that growth on the environment. It is striking that neither the Democratic nor the Republican Party called for environmental education as part of its school reform platform in the 2008 election. In the midst of concerns about environmental destruction and climate change one would think that environmental education would be highlighted in the platforms of the two major parties.

The anti-materialist and environmental ideology of the Green Party offers a vision of education that does not focus on a standardized curriculum and tests, and on measuring the worth of teachers, principals, and students according to test results. The Obama administration's push for a single national standardized curriculum is rejected by the Green Party. The Green Party platform rejects standardization of education and proclaims: "Greens support educational diversity. We hold no dogma absolute, continually striving for truth in the realm of ideas. We open ourselves, consciously and intuitively, to truth and beauty in the world of nature."[94] Unlike human capital ideology, the Green Party ideology embraces art education and their platform calls for:

> Funding and staffing to incorporate arts education into every school curriculum. We encourage local artists and the community to contribute time, experience, and resources to these efforts.

> Diversity in arts education in the schools including age-specific hands-on activities and appreciative theoretical approaches, exposure to the arts of various cultures and stylistic traditions, and experiences with a variety of media, techniques and contents.

> The integration of the arts and artistic teaching methods into other areas of the curriculum to promote a holistic perspective.[95]

The stark contrast between human capital and Green ideology is highlighted by the following from the 2004 Green platform: "We advocate creative and noncompetitive education at every age level, and the inclusion of cultural diversity in all curricula. We encourage hands-on approaches that promote a multitude of individual learning styles."[96] Rather than embracing the work of the global economy, the Green platform proclaims: "We are deeply concerned about the intervention in our schools of corporations that promote a culture of consumption and waste."[97]

Rather than applying a business model of accountability that measures the worth of school teachers and principals according to standardized test scores of students, the Green Party Platform declares:

> Classroom teachers at the elementary and high school levels should be given professional status and salaries comparable to related professions requiring advanced education, training and responsibility.

> Principals are also essential components in effective educational institutions. We encourage State Departments of Education and school boards to deliver more programmatic support and decision-making to the *true grassroots level—the classroom teacher and school principal* [author's emphasis].[98]

There are a number of educational ideologies that find their place in alternative private schools and in the thinking of many academics.

Foremost among these alternatives are varying forms of progressive education that eschew a system dominated by standardization and testing for one based on learning by doing and individual interest. There are also human rights and environmental curricula which usually incorporate progressive methods derived from the work of John Dewey. There are also truly radical educational ideologies that are designed to teach students how to apply knowledge to reconstruct society. Currently, these radical educators derive their inspiration from the works of Paulo Freire and envision an education that results in greater social justice. These alternative educational ideologies reject the call for a public school system organized to educate workers who will improve America's ability to compete in global markets.[99] I will discuss these other educational ideologies when I consider American education in a global context.

Notes

1 Drew Westen, *The Political Brain: The Role of Emotion in Deciding the Fate of the Nation* (New York: Public Affairs, 2007), pp. 145–169.
2 Republican Party Platform of 2008, p. 43. Retrieved from the American Presidency Project Document Archive http://www.presidency.ucsb.edu/papers_pdf/78545.pdf on February 10, 2009.
3 Democratic National Convention Committee, "Report of the Platform Committee: Renewing America's Promise." Presented to the 2008 Democratic National Convention, August 13, 2008, p. 18. Retrieved from the American Presidency Project Document Archive http://www.presidency.ucsb.edu/papers_pdf/78283.pdf on November 13, 2008.
4 John McCain with Mark Salter, *Faith of My Fathers: A Family Memoir* (New York: Harper, 1999), pp. 345–346.
5 Republican Party Platform of 2008, p. 43.
6 William J. Bennett, *The De-Valuing of America: The Fight for Our Culture and Our Children* (New York: Simon & Schuster, 1992), p. 170.
7 Ibid.
8 Lynne Cheney, "American Memory" (Washington, DC: National Endowment for the Humanities, 1987).
9 Ibid.
10 Diane Ravitch Curriculum Vitae. Retrieved from http://www.dianeravitch.com/vita.html on March 28, 2009.
11 "Plan to Teach U.S. History Is Said to Slight White Males," *The New York Times* (October 26, 1994), p. B12.
12 Karen Diegmueller, "Revise History Standards, Two Panels Advise," *Education Week* (October 18, 1995), p. 11.
13 Ibid.
14 Ibid.
15 Karen Diegmueller, "History Center Shares New Set of Standards," *Education Week* (April 10, 1996), p. 1.
16 Bob Dole and Jack Kemp, *Trusting the People: The Dole-Kemp Plan to Free the Economy and Create a Better America* (New York: HarperCollins, 1996), p. 92.
17 Dinesh D'Souza, "We the Slaveowners: In Jefferson's America, Were Some Men Not Created Equal?" *Policy Review* (Fall 1995), p. 74.

18 Dinesh D'Souza, *Illiberal Education: The Politics of Race and Sex on Campus* (New York: Vintage Books, 1992), and *The End of Racism* (New York: Free Press, 1995).
19 Diane Ravitch, *A Consumer's Guide to High School History Textbooks* (Washington, DC: Fordham Institute, 2004).
20 Ibid., p. 33.
21 Ibid., p. 42.
22 Ibid., p. 35.
23 Mark Hugo Lopez, "How Hispanics Voted in the 2008 Election." Retrieved from the Pew Hispanic Center http://pewresearch.org/pubs/1024/exit-poll-analysis-hispanics on February 12, 2009.
24 Hugh Davis Graham, *Uncertain Triumph: Federal Educational Policy in the Kennedy and Johnson Years* (Chapel Hill: University of North Carolina Press, 1984), pp. 155–156.
25 See ibid.
26 James Crawford, "Bilingual Policy Has Taken Shape Along Two Federal Tracks" (April 1, 1987). Retrieved from *Education Week* http://www.edweek.org/ew/index.html on February 20, 2009.
27 Ibid.
28 Democratic Party Platforms: Democratic Party Platform of 1976 (July 12, 1976), p. 25. Retrieved from the American Presidency Project Document Archive http://www.presidency.ucsb.edu/ws/?pid=29606 on February 8, 2009.
29 Quoted by Crawford, "Bilingual Policy."
30 Quoted in Ofelia Garcia and Colin Baker, *Policy and Practice in Bilingual Education: Extending the Foundations* (Bristol: Multilingual Matters, 1995), p. 6.
31 Democratic Party Platform of 1980, p. 40.
32 James Crawford, "Bilingual Educators Seeking Strategies to Counter Attacks," *Education Week*, 5(28) (April 9, 1986), pp. 1, 9.
33 "Federal File: Supporting Language" (October 18, 1995). Retrieved from *Education Week* http://www.edweek.org/ew/articles/1995/10/18/07fedfil.h15.html?qs=Federal+File on December 18, 2009.
34 Public Law 107–110, 107th Congress, January 8, 2002 [H.R. 1], *No Child Left Behind Act of 2001* (Washington, DC: U.S. Government Printing Office, 2002). For a political history of No Child Left Behind see Patrick J. McGuin, *No Child Left Behind and the Transformation of Federal Education Policy, 1965–2005* (Lawrence: University of Kansas Press, 2006).
35 "Transcript: The Kerry Education Agenda" (October 15, 2004). Retrieved from *Education Week* http://www.edweek.org on February 21, 2009.
36 Barack Obama, *The Audacity of Hope: Thoughts on Reclaiming the American Dream* (New York: Vintage Books, 2006), p. 63.
37 Ibid., p. 64.
38 Ibid., pp. 66–68.
39 Ibid., p. 20.
40 Arthur M. Schlesinger, Jr., *The Disuniting of America* (Knoxville, TN: Whittle Direct Books, 1991), p. 8.
41 See Joel Spring, *The American School from the Puritans to No Child Left Behind*, 7th edn. (New York: McGraw-Hill, 2008), pp. 459–460.
42 Ralph Reed, *Active Faith: How Christians Are Changing the Soul of American Politics* (New York: Free Press, 1996), pp. 109–111.
43 Ibid., p. 111.
44 Michele McNeil and Sean Cavanaugh, "Palin Takes Measured Tack on

Alaska's School Issues" (September 10, 2008). Retrieved from *Education Week* http://www.edweek.org on April 4, 2009.

45 Ibid.
46 Ibid.
47 Democratic Party Platform of 2004, p. 38.
48 Ibid.
49 Ibid., p. 263.
50 Ibid., pp. 263–264.
51 Ibid., p. 262.
52 See Peter Boettke, "Friedrich A. Hayek (1899–1992)." Retrieved from the Department of Economics, New York University, http//www.econ.nyu.edu/user/boettke/hayek.htm on August 2, 2000.
53 Friedrich Hayek, *The Road to Serfdom* (Chicago: University of Chicago Press, 1994).
54 Milton Friedman, *Capital and Freedom* (Chicago: University of Chicago Press, 1962), p. 89.
55 Ibid., p. 92.
56 No Child Left Behind Act of 2001, p. 58.
57 Ibid., p. 122.
58 Ibid., pp. 58, 70, 122, 185, 201, 206, 219, 232, 248, 297, 382, 419, 584, 657.
59 Obama, *The Audacity of Hope*, p. 178.
60 Ibid., p. 183.
61 David Osborne and Ted Gaebler, *Reinventing Government: How the Entrepreneurial Spirit Is Transforming the Public Sector* (New York: Penguin, 1993).
62 Jacob Weisberg, *In Defense of Government: The Fall and Rise of Public Trust* (New York: Scribner's, 1996), p. 132.
63 Osborne and Gaebler, *Reinventing Government*, pp. 11–12.
64 Ibid., p. 316.
65 Democratic Party Platform of 2000, p. 17.
66 Democratic Party Platform of 2004, p. 34.
67 "Remarks by the President to the Hispanic Chamber of Commerce on a Complete and Competitive American Education" (March 10, 2009). Retrieved from http://www.whitehouse.gov/the_press_office/Remarks-of-the-President-to-the-Hispanic-Chamber-of-Commerce/ on March 10, 2009.
68 Ibid.
69 George W. Bush, *On God and Country*, edited by Thomas Freiling (Washington, DC: Allegiance Press, Inc., 2004), p. 122.
70 George W. Bush, Comment on the front cover of Myron Magnet, *The Dream and the Nightmare: The Sixties' Legacy to the Underclass* (San Francisco: Encounter Books, 2000).
71 Magnet, *The Dream*, p. 20.
72 Ibid., p. 24.
73 Patrick J. Buchanan, *Right From the Beginning* (Washington, DC: Regnery Gateway, 1990), p. 14.
74 Marvin Olasky, *The Tragedy of American Compassion* (Wheaton, IL: Crossway Books, 1995), and *Renewing American Compassion: How Compassion for the Needy Can Turn Ordinary Citizens into Heroes* (Washington, DC: Regnery, 1997).
75 Olasky, *Renewing American Compassion*, pp. 41–42.
76 Ibid., p. 36

77 Buchanan, *Right From the Beginning*, p. 14.
78 William J. Bennett, *The De-Valuing of America: The Fight for Our Culture and Our Children* (New York: Simon & Schuster, 1992), p. 36.
79 U.S. Department of Education, "No Child Left Behind and Faith–Based Leaders: Working Together So All Children Succeed" (Washington, DC: U.S. Government Printing Office, 2004). Retrieved from the U.S. Department of Education http://www.ed.gov/nclb/freedom/faith/leaders.pdf. on January 7, 2005.
80 Press Release, "Character Education Grants Awarded" (September 29, 2003). Retrieved from the U.S. Department of Education http://www.ed.gov/news/pressreleases/2003/09/09292003.html on December 10, 2003.
81 *No Child Left Behind Act of 2001*, pp 240–241. Retrieved from the U.S. Department of Education http://www.ed.gov/policy/elsec/leg/esea02/107-110.pdf on April 2, 2009.
82 Ibid., p. 393.
83 Ibid., pp. 394–395.
84 Democratic Party Platform of 2008, p. 15.
85 Democratic Party Platform of 2008: Renewing America's Promise. Presented to the 2008 Democratic National Convention, August 13, 2008, p. 18. Retrieved from the American Presidency Project Document Archive http://www.presidency.ucsb.edu/papers_pdf/78283.pdf on November 13, 2008.
86 Democratic Party Platform of 1968: The Terms of Our Duty, p. 42. Retrieved from the American Presidency Project Document Archive http://www.presidency.ucsb.edu/ws/index.php?pid=29604 on January 14, 2009.
87 Ibid., p. 19.
88 Obama, *The Audacity of Hope*, p. 191.
89 Ibid.
90 See Pedro Carneiro and James J. Heckman, "Human Capital Policy," in *Inequality in America: What Role for Human Capital Policies?* edited by James J. Heckman and Alan Krueger (Cambridge, MA: MIT Press, 2005), pp. 77–241.
91 "Remarks by the President to the Hispanic Chamber of Commerce."
92 Green Party of the United States, "2004 Platform" (Washington, DC: Green Party, 2004), p. 17.
93 Ibid.
94 Ibid., p. 27.
95 Ibid., p. 29.
96 Ibid., p. 28.
97 Ibid.
98 Ibid.
99 For a general review of alternative educational ideologies see Joel Spring, *Wheels in the Head: Educational Philosophies of Authority, Freedom, and Culture from Confucianism to Human Rights*, 3rd edn. (New York: Routledge, 2008); *Pedagogies of Globalization: The Rise of the Educational Security State* (Mahwah, NJ: Lawrence Erlbaum, 2006); and *How Educational Ideologies are Shaping Global Society* (Mahwah, NJ: Lawrence Erlbaum, 2004).

Chapter 6

The Education Business

Making Money and
Influencing Schools

The education business has moved from the days of simply selling books, maps, and other classroom apparatus to being a business with a multiplicity of vendors, including textbook publishers, software, open-source, and information companies, for-profit school management businesses, for-profit tutoring and test preparation centers, for-profit preschools, and for-profit testing corporations. Even nonprofit organizations are driven by a desire to make money which results in high salaries for their managers. Examples of nonprofit organizations that act like profit-making companies range from the testing giant Educational Testing Services to charter school franchises like the Knowledge is Power Program (KIPP). One estimate of the total revenue of the for-profit education business was $68.5 billion in 2010, up by 5 to 6 percent from 2005. The education business is a growth industry and it is the second largest U.S. economic sector after health care.[1]

In 2009, Seeking Alpha, the online stock advisor with ties to Charles Schwab stockbrokers, declared: "For-Profit Education Sector: Recession Proof."[2] Seeking Alpha urged investors to consider the education business because: "As the recession becomes more severe and unemployment increases, there is greater motivation for the broader workforce to join institutions and universities to augment their skills. This benefits educational companies."[3] The online service also noted the close connection between government policies and the for-profit education business: "These companies will also gain from the impetus provided by significant federal spending on pro-education initiatives and preservation of federal grants as part of the new Obama administration's economic stimulus package."[4]

The education business industry wants to influence educational policies that will ensure the purchase of their products. For instance, the 2001 No Child Left Behind federal legislation allows for the use of for-profit tutoring services such as Sylvan Learning Centers and Kaplan. For-profit tutoring companies want to ensure continued funding of their companies in any reauthorizations of No Child Left Behind. Even the most traditional sectors of the education business such as textbook publishers are concerned with state curriculum standards and any government funding of open-source textbooks. Also, providers of open-source materials are interested in promoting their cause in the halls of the federal government and state legislatures.

Consequently, the pursuit of profit creates another shadow government influencing school policies along with foundations and think tanks. Political pressure to sponsor profit-earning legislation is exerted by trade organizations such as the Education Industry Association, the Schools Division of the Association of American Publishers, the Education Industry Forum, and industrial conglomerates such as the Apollo Group. As an example of the operation of a trade organization, the Education Industry Forum posted this announcement for their March 2010 meeting. Note that the meeting is designed to bring together representatives of the education business and government officials:

> Welcome back to the Education Industry Investment Forum, a continually morphing real-time incitement to investment in the U.S. and International for-profit education industry. We have gathered together leading *private equity investors, operational strategists in education, as well as entrepreneurs and experts from foundations and the United States government* to make your experience at our leading industry forum the most exacting and satisfying one to date [author's emphasis].[5]

The Education Industry Association is a lobbying group representing 450 for-profit education management companies, online providers, tutoring services, and other education companies. As a lobbying organization it has focused on those aspects of the No Child Left Behind legislation that allow schools to hire for-profit companies. The Education Industry Association describes its representation as follows:

> The Education Industry Association (EIA) represents the rapidly growing group of education entrepreneurs who are providing products, services, and strategies that both complement and supplement education services. Our 450 members include online education providers, school improvement and management services, charter school operators, alternative education and special education services, professional development providers, after-school tutoring providers, and educational content providers.[6]

The Education Industry Association is very involved in representing for-profit companies in the 2010 reauthorization of No Child Left Behind. In a document titled "Education Industry Association & ESEA [No Child Left Behind] Organizing Principles," the organization notified its membership:

"Expanding access to high quality learning experiences which requires cultivating a policy and regulatory environment that supports innovation with new learning tools, school models, and services provided both by non-profits and *the private sector* [author's emphasis] . . ."[7] Regarding No Child Left Behind, the document called for

> Funding education research and innovation . . . [which] requires focused investment that must include an equal role for the *private sector* . . . The ability of our nation to educate over 55 million students and achieve the President's ambitious education goals is not possible without the active participation and support of the *private sector* [author's emphasis].[8]

Also important to many members of the Education Industry Association is the provision for supplementary education services under No Child Left Behind. As explained by the U.S. Department of Education:

> Supplemental educational services (SES) are additional academic instruction designed to increase the academic achievement of students in schools in the second year of improvement, corrective action, or restructuring. These services, which are in addition to instruction provided during the school day, may include academic assistance such as tutoring, remediation and other supplemental academic enrichment services for failing schools.[9]

The Education Industry Association considers federal monies for supplementary education services so important to its membership that it has created a special subgroup called the SES Coalition. The purpose of the SES Coalition is to unite for-profit providers to lobby for more state and federal funds to spend on supplementary education services. The SES Coalition asks potential members:

> Feeling isolated as a provider?
> Not sure of emerging markets?
> Not getting timely answers from your State or school district?
> Worried about unethical practices?
> Concerned about the future of SES?[10]

The lobbying goals of the SES Coalition of the Education Industry Association are clearly stated by the organization:

> The Coalition represents the interests of providers when it engages local school officials, States, the US Department of Education and the Congress. By working together, organizations can and do amplify their voices with these stakeholder groups so that the special interests of SES providers will be better understood.[11]

The education business is also represented by investment bankers and law firms who lobby members of Congress and state legislatures to protect the industry's economic interests. For example, BerkeryNoyes Investment Bankers defines the education market as "companies that provide instructional materials, education and administrative software, information & services to public and private schools and institutions, and to for-profit, career training and other businesses."[12] BerkeryNoyes Investment Bankers list the following areas for investment:

- Infrastructure / School Management Software
- Schools
- Publishing and Publishing Services
- E-Learning
- Testing & Assessment
- Supplemental Manipulatives
- Tutoring & Afterschool Markets[13]

The law firm Ritzert & Leyton works primarily with the post-secondary and higher education market. The firm advertises as follows:

Ritzert & Leyton's higher/postsecondary education group offers a unique combination of experience and expertise in the highly specialized and regulated areas of federal student financial assistance, accreditation, licensure, corporate and tax related matters, *and mergers and acquisitions of postsecondary institutions from both a corporate and regulated industry perspective*. The firm works with applicable laws, regulations and procedures *and the people who regulate institutions of higher education on a daily basis* [author's emphasis].[14]

The education business does not speak with a unified voice. There are conflicts. For instance, textbook publishers might not support legislation encouraging the use of open-source textbooks, while new companies creating open-source texts might try to influence legislation favorable to their work. For-profit school companies work vigorously to ensure legislation that allows for-profit charter schools, while the teachers unions fight against this legislation because of the threat to recruiting union membership and achieving collective bargaining agreements. In other words, the pursuit of profit in education creates another complex web of interest groups influencing educational policy. In this chapter, I will focus on different sectors of the education business, beginning with textbook publishing.

The Publishing Industry, Texas, and Open-Source Texts

The elementary and secondary education (El-Hi) publishing industry is big business! The Association of American Publishers reported on January 18, 2010 that "the net El-Hi (elementary/high school) basal and supplemental K-12 category posted an increase of 18.4 percent in November with sales of $136.9 million, but sales declined by 15.7 percent for the year."[15] The decline in reported sales can be attributed to the effect on school budgets of the then current economic recession. As a result of the recession and new entrepreneurs entering the field, the textbook industry suddenly found itself confronted with an alternative, namely "open-source" textbooks. In the middle of a 2009 budget crisis, the California state legislature cut funding for textbook purchases, resulting in a call for the use of open-source digitalized texts. *Education Week*'s Kathleen Kennedy Manzo reported, "the changes have also left publishers reeling as they brace for the potential of huge losses of sales in what is their biggest and most influential market."[16]

Before turning to the issue of open-source texts, I would like to consider the politics of traditional textbook publishing. The major political player is the Texas Board of Education because Texas has statewide adoption of textbooks. The Texas Board of Education must approve the content of any texts before adoption. Consequently, publishers eagerly adapt their textbooks to the requirements of the Texas Board. The result is that the Texas Board of Education has a major influence over the contents of textbooks for the entire nation. Mariah Blake, a reporter for the *Washington Monthly*, in reporting an interview with the chair of the Texas Board of Education, described Texas' influence:

> And when it comes to textbooks, what happens in Texas rarely stays in Texas. The reasons for this are economic: Texas is the nation's second-largest textbook market and one of the few biggies where the state picks what books schools can buy rather than leaving it up to the whims of local districts, which means publishers that get their books approved can count on millions of dollars in sales. As a result, the Lone Star State has outsized influence over the reading material used in classrooms nationwide, since publishers craft their standard textbooks based on the specs of the biggest buyers. As one senior industry executive told me, "Publishers will do whatever it takes to get on the Texas list."[17]

Texas' Politics and Textbook Publishing

It is important to note that Texas gained increased influence over textbook content as a result of California's adoption of open-source books and its budget cuts affecting the purchase of traditional textbooks. For instance, in 2002, Carol Jones, the field director of the Texas chapter of Citizens for a Sound Economy, could make this statement about the influence of Texas and California, "The bottom line is that Texas and California are the biggest buyers of textbooks in the country, and what we adopt in Texas is what the rest of the country gets."[18] By 2010, Mariah Blake noted the effect of California turning to open-source textbooks: "Until recently, Texas's influence was balanced to some degree by the more-liberal pull of California, the nation's largest textbook market."[19]

The Texas Constitution, Article VII, Section 3, requires that the State Board of Education set aside sufficient money to provide free textbooks for children attending the public schools in the state. The following are some of the requirements for determining which textbooks will be purchased with state money. These requirements give influential power to state textbook review panels and all Texas residents who submit comments to the State Board of Education.

- Publishers who plan to offer instructional materials for adoption in the state provide finished-format review samples to the Texas Education Agency, each of the 20 regional education service centers, and members of the appropriate state textbook review panels appointed by the Commissioner of Education.
- Members of the state textbook review panels are charged with evaluating instructional materials to determine coverage of essential knowledge and skills and with identifying factual errors. At the close of the review period, panel members submit evaluations to the Commissioner of Education.
- Based on these evaluations, the Commissioner prepares a preliminary report recommending that instructional materials be placed on the conforming list, be placed on the nonconforming list, or be rejected.
- Texas residents are allowed to file written comments regarding instructional materials submitted for adoption. In addition, a public hearing is held before the State Board of Education approximately two months before scheduled adoption.
- After consideration of evaluations submitted by state review panel members, information provided by publishers, and staff recommendations, the Commissioner of Education submits a final report to the State Board of Education recommending that instructional materials submitted be placed on the conforming list, be placed on the nonconforming list, or be rejected. A report detailing any factual

errors to be corrected in instructional materials prior to delivery to school districts is also presented.[20]

In recent years, major concerns of some Texans have included the content of American history, environmentalism, evolution, and birth control and abstinence education. National attention was directed to Texas' adoption policies as far back as the 1980s when Mel and Norma Gabler complained that textbooks were incorrectly calling the American War of Independence a revolution rather than colonial obedience to British laws. Essentially, they wanted to change the image of the United States as a country born from revolution. They told the Texas State Textbook Committee, "In other words, the colonists were obeying the laws. Actually, it was parliament that was breaking the law. Parliament was passing laws contrary to the British rights, the British Constitution."[21] Also, the Gablers believed that one text was undermining a belief in the free enterprise system by discussing government farm subsidies: "[the text] treats agricultural problems, on a number of pages, as something to be solved by government, rather than as problems that government helped to create by interfering with the free market."[22]

Mel Gabler died in 2005 and Norma Gabler in 2007 but their work was continued by Mel Gabler's Educational Research Analysts: Public School Textbook Reform through Textbook Reviews.[23] Currently, the organization provides this description of its activities and priorities. Important in the organization's statement is the recognition of the impact of Texas' textbook decisions.

We are a conservative Christian organization that reviews public school textbooks submitted for adoption in Texas. *Our reviews have national relevance because Texas state-adopts textbooks and buys so many that publishers write them to Texas standards and sell them across the country* [author's emphasis].

Our unique 48 years' experience gives us expertise equal to or beyond that of the education establishment itself in all phases of the public school textbook adoption process, and in that our standard review criteria spell out what public school textbooks often censor on certain topics.

Publishers market textbooks—and many teachers select them—based on convenience of their teaching aids. Unlike them, we review textbooks for academic content only. Parents, teachers, and school board members can all profitably use our materials.

Subject areas of concern include:
• Scientific weaknesses in evolutionary theories
• Phonics-based reading instruction

- Principles and benefits of free enterprise
- Original intent of the U.S. Constitution
- Respect for Judeo-Christian morals
- Emphasis on abstinence in sex education
- Politically-correct degradation of academics[24]

In 2002, groups supporting the Gabler principles added environmentalism and AIDS education to their list of concerns. During the summer of 2002, the Texas state school board began public hearings to select textbooks in history and social studies for its 4 million students. One issue that constantly cropped up was the content of history books. At the opening of the hearings, there already seemed to be agreement among board members not to select for advanced placement classes the Pearson Prentice Hall history text *Out of Many: A History of the American People*, despite it being among the best sellers. The problem was two paragraphs dealing with prostitution in late nineteenth-century cattle towns. "It makes it sound that every woman west of the Mississippi was a prostitute," said Grace Shore, the Republican chairwoman of the Texas State Board of Education. "The book says that there were 50,000 prostitutes west of the Mississippi. I doubt it, but even if there were, is that something that should be emphasized? Is that an important historical fact?"[25]

Out of Many: A History of the American People was criticized not only for its section "Cowgirls and Prostitutes" but also for its mention of Margaret Sanger and the development of contraception, and the gay rights movement. Complaining about the book's content, Peggy Venable, director of the Texas chapter of Citizens for a Sound Economy, said, "I don't mean that we should sweep things under the rug. But the children should see the hope and the good things about America."[26]

The issue of environmentalism gained attention during the 2002 approval of science textbooks. Contrary to expectations that science texts would not be as controversial as history books, the issue of global warming caused a major uproar. Science textbooks were condemned for saying that there was a scientific consensus that the earth's climate was changing because of global warming. This claim was labeled as "anti-technology," "anti-Christian," and "anti-American." The Board rejected Jane L. Person's *Environmental Science: How the World Works and Your Place in It* because of statements such as "Destruction of the tropical rain forest could affect weather over the entire planet" and "Most experts on global warming feel that immediate action should be taken to curb global warming." To gain acceptance by the Texas Board, the statements were changed to: "Tropical rain forest ecosystems impact weather over the entire planet" and "In the past, the earth has been much warmer than it is now, and fossils of sea creatures show us that the sea level was much higher than it is today. So does it really matter if the world gets warmer?"[27]

The concern with environmentalism had been expressed the previous year when the Texas Board singled out for censorship Daniel Chiras' *Environmental Science: Creating a Sustainable Future*. The book opened with phrases such as "Things can't go on as they have been," "We must change our ways," "throwaway mentality," and "obsession with growth." The Board attacked the text for using the "oft-used falsehood that over 100 million Americans are breathing unhealthy air."[28]

One text that did win approval was financed by a consortium of mining companies. Titled *Global Science: Energy, Resources, Environment*, the book was praised before the Texas Board by Duggan Flanakin, formerly of the U.S. Bureau of Mines and a member of the Texas Policy Foundation. The book was also commended by Ms. Shore, chair of the Texas Board and co-owner of TEC Well Service. TEC is a producer of gas and oil and repairs and deepens oil wells. From Ms. Shore's perspective, the oil and gas industries "always get a raw deal" in environmental science textbooks.[29]

Issues were raised regarding health books. A high school health text published by Holt, Rinehart and Winston, Inc. was condemned by Monte Hasie, a member of the Texas Board of Education, who claimed, "They were promoting homosexuality as an acceptable alternative lifestyle and promoting sex as being O.K. if you use a condom. We were going to put *Playboy* and *Penthouse* out of business."[30] In an unusual decision, in March 1994, the publisher decided not to sell its book in Texas rather than make changes demanded by the Texas Board of Education. After months of hearing testimony from family planning, anti-abortion, gay advocacy, fundamentalist Christian, and other groups, the Board mandated that the health book and four others under consideration delete toll free numbers for gay, lesbian, and teenage suicide prevention groups, illustrations for examinations for testicular cancer, and sections on homosexuality. They also asked for inclusion of descriptions of Texas laws against sodomy. It was very unusual for a publishing company to remove a book from the Texas market rather than make suggested changes.[31]

In 2010, conservative Christians were represented on the Texas Board of Education by Don McLeroy. He was first elected to the Board in 1998 and appointed Chair of the Texas Board of Education in 2007 by the then Governor Rick Perry. In 2010, Democrats in the Texas legislature objected to McLeroy's chairmanship. Democratic state Senator Eliot Shapleigh said,

[McLeroy] has demonstrated he is not fit to lead the board of education. He has used his position to impose his extreme views on the 4.7 million schoolchildren in Texas. He has tried to revise the curriculum in a way that is inconsistent with scientific standards, and he has obstructed reading standards on a regular basis.[32]

When interviewed by reporter Mariah Blake, McLeroy asserted, "Evolution is hooey" and "we are a Christian nation founded on Christian principles."[33]

What does it mean to emphasize in a text that the United States is a Christian nation? A project of Peter Marshall and David Barton is to ensure that textbooks reflect this point of view. Peter Marshall gained some notoriety by claiming that "California wildfires and Hurricane Katrina were God's punishment for tolerating gays."[34] Peter Marshall's website, "Peter Marshall Ministries," declares, "there is the urgent necessity of recovering the original American vision, and the truth about our Christian heritage. How can we restore America if we don't know who we are?"[35] In 1977, Marshall began publishing a series of history books emphasizing America's Christian heritage and distributing DVDs with teacher and student guides.

David Barton is former Vice-Chair of the Texas Republican Party. In 2009, the reelection campaign for Governor Rick Perry proudly announced David Barton's support. Barton declared, "Gov. Perry has been a leading voice across Texas and our nation in the effort to strengthen families, protect life, and stand up for the values that have made our nation prosperous."[36] Barton is the founder and president of an organization called WallBuilders which is described on its website as

an organization dedicated to presenting America's forgotten history and heroes, with an emphasis on the moral, religious, and constitutional foundation on which America was built . . . which was so accurately stated by George Washington, we believe that "the propitious [favorable] smiles of heaven can never be expected on a nation which disregards the eternal rules of order and right which heaven itself has ordained".[37]

Both Barton and Peter Marshall represent those who believe in an "American exceptionalism" that envisions a Christian God as not only guiding the founding of the nation but also using it to spread Christianity around the globe. Peter Marshall's website describes his book series as: "Reading like novels, these books tell the stories of God's providential hand in our history."[38]

The WallBuilders website offers this goal for changing textbooks and disseminating American history guides: "we develop materials to educate the public concerning the periods in our country's history when its laws and policies were firmly rooted in Biblical principles." The organization believes that its principles are exemplified in the nineteenth-century textbook, Charles Coffin's *The Story of Liberty*, which refers to God's guidance of the nation or, as the book refers to it, "a divine hand." The WallBuilders website quotes Coffin's text:

You will notice that while the oppressors have carried out their plans and had things their own way, there were other forces silently at work which in time undermined their plans—as if a Divine hand were directing the counter-plan. Whoever peruses the story of liberty without recognizing this feature will fail of fully comprehending the meaning of history. There must be a meaning to history or else existence is an incomprehensible enigma.[39]

David Barton has also suggested that textbooks should emphasize America's early nineteenth-century war against the Barbary Coast pirates as the "original war against Islamic Terrorism."[40]

In March 2010, Don McLeroy was not reelected to the Texas Board, reducing the number of conservatives voting on curriculum and textbook matters. However, he did have ten more months of service after his failed reelection attempt. Working with other religious conservatives on the Board, he vowed to impact the writing of social studies texts by issuing publication guidelines. These guidelines included requiring publishers:

- To include in texts a section on "the conservative resurgence of the 1980s and 1990s, including Phyllis Schlafly, the Contract with America, the Heritage Foundation, the Moral Majority and the National Rifle Association."
- To include material on "the effects of increasing government regulation and taxation on economic development and business planning."
- To not refer to American "imperialism," but to call it "expansionism."
- To add "country and western music" to the list of cultural movements to be studied.
- To remove references to Ralph Nader and Ross Perot.
- To list Stonewall Jackson, the Confederate general, as a role model for effective leadership.
- To highlight the Christian roots of the U.S. Constitution.[41]

While Texas, and particularly Texas' religious conservatives, are influencing the content of nationally distributed textbooks, there is a growing national trend to require science courses to link the questioning of climate change to evolution. In 2009, the Texas Board of Education required that teachers present all sides of the evidence on evolution and global warming. In 2010, a bill was introduced in Kentucky to have teachers discuss "the advantages and disadvantages of scientific theories," including "evolution, the origins of life, global warming and human cloning." Louisiana passed a similar law in 2008 and Oklahoma in 2009. The South Dakota legislature passed a resolution in 2010 calling for the "balanced teaching of global warming in public schools." The resolution declared, "Carbon dioxide is not a pollutant but rather a highly beneficial ingredient for all plant life."[42]

New York Times reporter Leslie Kaufman argues that,

> The linkage of evolution and global warming is partly a legal strategy: courts have found that singling out evolution for criticism in public schools is a violation of the separation of church and state. By insisting that global warming also be debated, deniers of evolution can argue that they are simply championing academic freedom in general.[43]

How fares the politics of knowledge regarding textbooks? On March 12, 2010, *New York Times* writer James McKinley reported, "After three days of turbulent meetings, the Texas Board of Education on Friday voted to approve a social studies curriculum that will put a conservative stamp on history and economics textbooks, stressing the role of Christianity in American history."[44] The vote was eleven to four in favor of the conservative agenda. Conservatives were not the only ones interested in the content of textbooks. Many Mexican Americans wanted to increase their representation in texts. Their efforts were defeated, causing one member of the Texas Board, Mary Helen Berlanga, "to storm out of a meeting late Thursday night, saying, 'They can just pretend this is a white America and Hispanics don't exist.'"

The Politics of Open-Source Textbooks

While Texas' political groups try to influence traditional textbooks, national attention is being focused on open-source textbooks. As mentioned previously, the 2009 budget crisis resulted in California reducing spending for traditional textbooks in favor of open-source texts. Groups concerned about the content of texts worry about open-source books containing material they might find objectionable.

In 2009, the California legislators granted $300 million to be spent on classroom materials with an encouragement to use free digital textbooks. California legislators suspended the textbook adoption process. Also, the state curriculum commission was eliminated in a line-item veto by California's Governor Arnold Schwarzenegger. The commission reviews and advises on the adoption of textbooks.[45] In May 2009, Governor Schwarzenegger announced that the state would be offering free, open-source texts for high school math and science courses. He argued that these digital texts would help relieve the growing school budget crisis. The content of these digital books was to be aligned with California state curriculum standards.[46]

Immediately jumping at the chance of managing and producing open-source textbooks, the California Open Source Textbook Project was created as "a collaborative, public/private undertaking . . . to address the high cost, content range, and consistent shortages of K-12 textbooks in California." The project claims that it will:

- Eliminate $400M+ line item for California's K-12 textbooks
- Increase the range of content afforded to California's K-12 textbooks
- Provide a permanent end to California's textbook shortages
- Create a fully portable content holdings database.[47]

The California Open Source Textbook Project plans to work through an organization called the Creative Commons to deal with copyright issues. The Creative Commons advertises itself:

> Creative Commons is a nonprofit corporation dedicated to making it easier for people to share and build upon the work of others, consistent with the rules of copyright. We provide free licenses and other legal tools to mark creative work with the freedom the creator wants it to carry, so others can share, remix, use commercially, or any combination thereof.[48]

Using creative copyright laws, the California Open Source Textbook Project plans to use already existing K-12 educational content that is in the public domain and the free input of California teachers. Also, and this is where copyright laws become important, the California Open Source Textbook Project will use "innovative copyright tools to secure new and dormant K-12 textbook content that would not otherwise be made available."[49]

Open-source publishing introduces another for-profit education business tied to government funding. This new industry has a political stake in lobbying for laws supporting open-source publishing and government funding. Current entrepreneurs in the field have politicians in their hands. What politician can resist claims that open-source textbooks will save money? Certainly those earning salaries and profits from the California Open Source Textbook Project will wave a cost-saving flag before state politicians.

The founders and leaders of the California Open Source Textbook Project are longtime entrepreneurs in the software industry. The founder of the California Open Source Textbook Project is Sanford Forte who at the time was also "Principal of Interactive Development Systems."[50] Interactive Development Systems is described as a "strategic and business development consultancy that has served many technology, academic publishing, music industry, and new media (including Internet) enterprise groups." In addition, Sanford was listed as "a principal and consulting partner with three Silicon Valley startups: PixCube (consumer imaging);

Snagg, Inc. (RFID-based supply chain and verification systems); and, TeloPhase (a not-for-profit community wireless networking project)." Sanford also has many connections in the publishing industry, having worked with Addison-Wesley, Benjamin-Cummings, Prentice-Hall, Holt-Rinehart-Winston (now part of the Thompson Publishing Group), Millimeter Magazine, Akai, Roland, Gibson/Oberheim, New Media Magazine, On Command Video, Radius, SuperMac, Springer-Verlag (GDR), Samsung, LG (Korea), Apple Computer, Clayton-Dubilier-Ross (Kinko's Corporate Document Solutions Group), Stanford University (Office of Technology and Licensing), San Francisco Museum of Modern Art, and Starr Labs.[51]

The first textbook to be developed by the California Open Source Project is a World History book for 9th grade World History–Social Studies based on California state curriculum standards. This textbook is being developed in cooperation with Wikibooks.[52] At the time, Wikibooks was also hosting a group to create a textbook for advanced placement standards for World History. Wikibooks claims that the California Open Source Project will save California $200 million a year. Wikibooks' website states:

> In order for open-source books to pass peer review (and thus approval for public school adoption) at the California State Board level (this is also true in most other states), textbook content must conform to the written state K-12 education framework standard—this is a sine qua non for adoption, no exceptions are made.[53]

While the world history textbook will conform to California standards there is still the question of what teachers can add to the book. After all, the goal of an open-source text is to allow users to add and subtract material. One of the benefits listed by the California Open Source Textbook Project is that it will draw on the knowledge of California teachers. But how do you keep a teacher from adding material that is blatantly racist or terrorist? For instance, when the open-source digital for-profit company Flat World Knowledge was started in 2008 by two former textbook industry executives, one of them, Eric Frank, explained, "The nice thing about open content is it gives faculty full control, creative control over the content of the book, full control over timing, and it give students a lot more control over how they want to consume it and how much they want to pay."[54]

The possibility of instructors adding objectionable material is discussed but not adequately addressed by open-source publishers. Currently, Macmillan's DynamicBooks is the largest enterprise to sell open-source digital textbooks. While praising open-source books, Neil Comins, one of the authors of DynamicBooks' college text "Discovering the Universe," asserts that if an instructor decides to rewrite paragraphs about the origins of the universe from a religious rather than an evolutionary perspective, "I would absolutely, positively be livid."[55] In response, a Macmillan spokesperson stated, in the words of a *New York Times* reporter, "the publisher reserves the right to 'remove anything that is considered offensive or plagiarism,' and would rely on students, parents and other instructors to help monitor changes."[56] However it is hard to imagine publishers checking every instructor's additions to an open-source book.

Objections quickly followed passage of the law. The League of United Latin American Citizens (LULAC) and the American G.I. Forum complained that open-source threatened or prevented public participation in the textbook review process. LULAC was concerned that without public review of textbooks there would be a decline in representation of Mexican Americans. The organization wanted the ability to ensure greater representation of Mexican Americans. LULAC national president Rosa Rosales worried that, "Texas schoolchildren could end up being taught with material that no one has seen or critically reviewed."[57] From this perspective it meant less representation of Mexican Americans in textbooks. "Latinos make up 40 percent of Texas and many historical Latino figures have made invaluable contributions to the state of Texas. Unfortunately, many of these historical Latino figures will not be included in the new social studies curriculum," President Rosales said. "Let's make our social studies curriculum relevant for all Texas schoolchildren."[58]

Posted comments on the above article about LULAC's concern about open-source texts illustrate the importance of and controversy surrounding textbook content. These comments included the following:

> I believe that all school books should be reviewed by the school board and the parents of the students. We cannot rewrite history or teach history that is false. If you want Mexican History go to Mexico and learn it there.

> If it is relevant to being an American then fine but if it has to do with the teaching of Hispanic history, they can go to Mexico and be indoctrinated on the hate that is being taught over there. This is America and we don't need to change our history for anyone!!

> Yes, LULAC National President Rosa Rosales. If a Spanish person contributed to what has made Texas what she is today, I can agree to that fact of that person being put in a text book.
> But . . . and that is a big BUT . . . do not force and make the Spanish language or something falsely historical to make the Spanish nationality be the BIG part of Texas history! We, our Texas . . . a Republic State in America . . . is an English speaking country, and made up of many nationalities, right here in TEXAS!

I want our children to know the truth about Texas and the rest of America. Not some made up story that makes the Mexicans look better than Davey Crockett! I hope you can help get the facts out to the people.[59]

Geraldine Miller of the Texas State Board of Education was reported to be aghast at the passage of the open-source legislation. The report claimed,

SBOE [State Board of Education] has developed a textbook adoption process that is a model for other states . . . House Bill 2488 ignores a process that has been in place for years and has resulted in great success. It offers no chance for review or public participation . . . The effects of this bill run deep. It will eliminate materials that are aligned with state standards and will allow questionable resources into the system that will be there for years to come.[60]

In summary, open-source books are attractive because they promise to reduce school expenditures. Those making a profit from open-source books will lobby state legislatures to replace traditional texts with these new digitalized versions. The political struggles do not end when a legislature succumbs to budget problems and lobbying by open-source groups. There is still the political struggle over what can be added to open-source texts.

For-Profit and Franchised Educational Services

Basically, any for-profit organization receiving government money has a political stake in ensuring continued funding. Therefore, for-profit educational organizations have an interest in supporting political candidates and lobbying for legislation that will increase or continue the flow of their existing government funding. As mentioned previously, No Child Left Behind opens the door to federal funding of for-profit educational services. Throughout the 670-page legislation there appear statements such as "the term 'provider' means a non-profit entity, a *for profit* entity, or a local educational agency [author's emphasis]."[61]

Charter schools, both for-profit and nonprofit, have created a powerful political force interested in federal and state regulatory laws and funding. The very existence of charter schools is dependent on their continued support by federal and state politicians and their voters. By 2009 there were 95 for-profit educational management organizations operating 689 charter schools, and 103 nonprofit educational management organizations operating 592 charter schools. A major interest group for charter schools is U.S. Charter Schools which has provided its membership with the following history of charter school funding and regulation:

- Minnesota passed the first charter school law in 1991 that allowed for the development and operation of publicly funded charter schools.
- U.S. Congress authorizes the Charter School Expansion Act of 1998 which creates the federally managed and funded Charter Schools Program.
- The purpose of the Charter School Program is to expand the number of high-quality charter schools available to students across the nation by providing financial assistance for planning, program design, and initial implementation of public charter schools; evaluation of the effects of charter schools; and the dissemination of information about charter schools and successful practices in charter schools.
- Charter School Program begins a competitive grant program for alleviating the financial constraints in planning and starting a charter school.
- Since 1995, when CSP started administering start-up grants, the number of states that have passed charter laws has risen to 40, not including the District of Columbia and Puerto Rico. Accordingly, federal policy makers have allocated more funds to the grant program. In fiscal year (FY) 1995, the CSP administered $6 million in grants; in fiscal year (FY) 2005, the CSP administered almost $217 million in grants.[62]

The 2002 No Child Left Behind legislation contained "Part B—Public Charter Schools" with the following stated goals:

SEC. 5201. PURPOSE.

It is the purpose of this subpart to increase national understanding of the charter schools model by—

(1) providing financial assistance for the planning, program design, and initial implementation of charter schools;

(2) evaluating the effects of such schools, including the effects on students, student academic achievement, staff, and parents;

(3) expanding the number of high-quality charter schools available to students across the Nation; and

(4) encouraging the States to provide support to charter schools for facilities financing in an amount more nearly commensurate to the amount the States have typically provided for traditional public schools.[63]

In 2008, the U.S. Department of Education reported the existence of:

over 4,300 schools in 40 states and the District of Columbia, serving more than 1.2 million students—about 3 percent of all public school children. In some cities, charter schools' "market share" is even higher, exceeding 50 percent in New Orleans and 25 percent in Washington, D.C. And charter schools have not yet filled the demand for quality school choice options; tens of thousands of families are on waiting lists.[64]

Major interest groups serving the charter school community are U.S. Charter Schools along with the previously mentioned Education Industry Forum. The U.S. Charter Schools organization monitors state laws and funding, planning and starting a charter school, and links to charter school resources. It publishes a monthly newsletter to inform its membership about laws and policies affecting public schools. For instance, the February 2010 newsletter contained the item:

A Cost Estimation Tool for Charter Schools
This guide helps public charter school developers identify and estimate the range of costs and timing of expenditures they will be obligated to cover during start-up and the early years of operation. The tool provides several worksheets to help public charter school operators identify basic cost assumptions (e.g., student enrollment and facilities needs) and use those assumptions to estimate their operating costs.[65]

During his election campaign and after assuming office, President Barack Obama, as discussed in Chapter 5, announced that charter schools were a major pillar of his school reform plan.

In summary, the Charter School Expansion Act of 1998 and No Child Left Behind set the stage for government funding of for-profit education services and charter school management organizations. This creates a dependent relationship between for-profit education services and charter schools and federal and state governments. The very existence of these services and schools is dependent on federal and state funding and laws. To survive, for-profit education services, charter school management companies, and individual charter schools must be involved in trying to influence politicians and government agencies. In the next section I will explore the economic and political world of charter schools before turning to for-profit education services.

Educational Management Organizations: Charter Schools

A watchdog group overseeing for-profit education exists at Arizona State University and the University of Colorado, involving the Education Policy Research Unit, the Commercialism in Education Research Unit, and the Education and the Public Interest Center. In 2009, these combined groups issued a report through the Commercialism in Education Research Unit titled, "Profiles of For-Profit Educational Management Organizations."[66] This report stated that the number of for-profit educational management organizations had increased from fourteen in the 1997–1998 school year to ninety-five during the 2008–2009 school year, with the number of states having educational management organizations increasing from sixteen to thirty-one during the same period. The report provides the following definition of an educational management organization:

> We define an education management organization, or EMO, as an organization or firm that manages schools receiving public funds, including district and charter public schools. For-profit EMOs are businesses that seek to return a profit to the investors who own them. A contract details the terms under which executive authority to run one or more schools is given to an EMO in return for a commitment to produce measurable outcomes within a given time frame.[67]

Imagine Schools, Inc. is identified as the largest for-profit educational management organization, operating seventy-six schools in the 2008–2009 school year. EdisonLearning, another large for-profit educational management organization, experienced a decrease in the public schools it managed, from sixty-eight in 2007–2008 to sixty-two in 2008–2009, but even with this decline it still had the largest number of students (37,574) managed by a for-profit organization. Another company, K12 Inc., had 37,543 students in its virtual schools. There were a total of fifty-six virtual schools operated by for-profit management organizations.[68]

Charter schools, as opposed to public district schools, represent the overwhelming number of schools managed by for-profit companies. Consequently, one might assume that these companies are interested in supporting politicians advocating for more charter schools and charter school legislation. According to the previously cited report, 94 percent of the for-profit managed schools are charter and 6 percent are district schools.[69] In all, the report identifies 537 schools managed by sixteen large companies, which are defined as those managing ten or more schools. In total, these large companies manage 496 charter schools. Twenty medium-size companies that manage between four and nine schools operate a total of 113 schools, all of which are charter schools. Fifty-nine small companies operate eighty charter schools and three district schools. This means that there are a total of ninety-five for-profit companies managing 689 charter schools and forty-four district schools.[70]

One wonders how many for-profit charter school management companies applaud President Obama's support for charter schools. There is also a stake in online learning. For example, K12 Inc. is listed as a large company operating twenty-two charter and two district schools along with providing other online instruction. The company's founder and chief executive officer, Ron Packard, has direct ties to Wall Street and lacks any background in teaching. His biography posted on the company website indicates that "Mr. Packard worked for McKinsey & Company as well as for Goldman Sachs in mergers and acquisitions . . . and he is a chartered financial analyst." He has direct ties to government, "serving on the Department of Defense Educational Advisory committee." This work is complemented by college degrees in Economics, Mechanical Engineering, and Business. There is no mention in his company biography of having taught or served as an educational administrator. In other words, Mr. Packard would appear from his biography to be motivated by financial gain rather than acting as an educational reformer.[71]

The business emphasis at K12 is highlighted by its partners:

> K12 teams up with a variety of companies and organizations that offer services or products that we believe could be of interest to our families. Below is a current list of our partners. We encourage you to visit their websites to learn more about them, including any current promotions or contests that you and your family can participate in.
>
> Hersheypark
>
> By Kids, For Kids (BKFK)
>
> Education.com
>
> American Junior Golf Association (AJGA)
>
> SkyWay USA[72]

Imagine Schools Inc., founded in 2004 by Dennis and Eileen Bakke, was also developed by individuals with a business rather than an education background. Dennis Bakke was a CEO of the AES Corporation, a global power company.[73] Managing seventy-six charter schools, Imagine Schools Inc. advocates for a free market of choice as the method of regulating school quality in contrast to government regulations and testing. The company's 2009 report states,

PARENT CHOICE
If I had to choose only one criterion for judging the quality of a charter school, it would be Parent Choice. It is a more reliable measure than academic performance because parents are looking for much more in a school than academics alone. Typically, students are assigned to government-operated public schools based on where they live. The uniqueness of a public charter school is that parents must choose to enroll their children. In many cases, the students we recruit for our campuses have never been recruited for anything in their young lives. It is powerful and moving when we state, "We want you to attend our Imagine campus."[74]

The connection between politics and business is revealed in the operation of Altair Learning Management and IQ Innovations Inc. which provide for-profit online learning. The founder of both companies is William Lager who was an assistant to the Ohio Attorney General and worked for Motorola and Xerox.[75] Over the years, William Lager has kept his fingers in politics through campaign donations. One might assume that he does not back candidates opposed to charter schools or who are not interested in advancing the e-learning business.[76] The following sales pitch is given in the company's brochure:

The IQity e-learning platform is high-tech and low-hassle with top-notch hosting services of high-reliability, security and availability. You can tailor the entire IQity system to accommodate your school's needs right down to your mascot. Our extremely *competitive pricing* will accommodate your school's budget [author's emphasis].[77]

Another example of the business orientation of for-profit charter school management companies is White Hat Management which boasts that it "is the largest for-profit charter school operator in Ohio and third largest nationwide. The company contracts and assists non-profit corporations that hold charters or see a need for a charter school in their community." The company operates fifty schools in six states utilizing three separate educational organizations: DELA (Distance & Electronic Learning Academies), HOPE Academies, and Life Skills Centers. The founder and owner is David Brennan who as CEO of a manufacturing company started providing education to his employees.[78] The CEO of White Hat Management, Ed Harrison, is described on White Hat's website:

Mr. Harrison has . . . worked in fields as diverse as automotive parts and fasteners to elevator manufacturing and sheet metal fabricating. Most recently, Ed has served as president of LXD, a liquid crystal display manufacturing company in the Cleveland area and as president of SMT, a sheet metal fabricating company in Raleigh, NC.[79]

The company's Chief Operating Officer, Mark Rice, is described on the same website as a graduate of West Point whose

Army career of more than 20 years included tactical, combat, joint and recruiting assignments throughout the Continental United States, Germany and Southwest Asia. His final assignment was at the Pentagon, where he served as the special assistant for recruiting projects to the Assistant Secretary of the Army for Manpower and Reserve Affairs at the Pentagon. He retired as a Lieutenant Colonel in April of 2008.[80]

In addition to the for-profit educational management companies, there are also 103 nonprofit educational management companies operating 592 charter schools and 17 district schools.[81] The largest of these nonprofit educational management companies is the Knowledge Is Power Program (KIPP), discussed in Chapter 2, which manages sixty-four charter schools. The next largest nonprofit company is Summit Academy Management which oversees twenty-six charter schools in Ohio. These charter schools educate special needs students, particularly those with Asperger's syndrome, attention deficit hyperactivity disorder, high-functioning autism, and related disorders. The company is fully funded by the Ohio Department of Education.[82]

Similar to for-profit companies, nonprofit companies have a stake in what happens to charter school laws and funding. The leadership and staff of nonprofit charter school management companies are interested in laws that increase their funding, regulate their activities, or increase their numbers. Consequently, they represent a political group interested in federal and state legislation and in lobbying for their cause.

In conclusion, since the 1990s an important education sector has developed which consists of over 4,000 charter schools with administrators and staff interested in the education politics related to funding and regulation. This is a new and large political interest group. However, they do not speak with a unified voice. The ninety-five for-profit educational management organizations have a primary interest in ensuring legislation that favors for-profit charter schools. In contrast, the 103 nonprofit educational management organizations may in some cases oppose federal or state legislation favoring for-profit charter schools. Despite this difference, the charter school industry is now an important element in the political landscape of education.

Supplementary Education Services: The Shadow Education System

As I discussed at the beginning of this chapter, No Child Left Behind provides funds to hire for-profit companies to provide supplementary education services to schools identified as needing improvement or restructuring. Supplementary education services provide tutoring and classes for remediation and for test preparation or, in the polite language of industry, achievement enhancement. Across the globe from Japan to India to Cape Town to Buenos Aires to the United States, parents worry about their children's grades and test scores because they are tied to their children's future economic success. Consequently, they seek out private learning services to help their children during the after-school hours.

World culture theorists David Baker and Gerald LeTendre label supplementary education providers as the "shadow education system."[83] From the perspective of the twenty-first century, Baker and LeTendre see a global growth of the shadow education system as pressures mount for students to pass high-stakes tests and the world's governments attempt to closely link student achievement to future jobs. In their words, "Mass schooling sets the stage for the increasing importance of education as an institution, and to the degree that this process creates greater demand for quality schooling than is supplied, augmentation through shadow education is likely."[84]

Baker and LeTendre predict that shadow education systems will continue to grow as nations embrace human capital forms of schooling. Simply put, as schooling is made more important for a child's future, families will invest more money in tutoring services for remedial education and for providing for enhanced school achievement. In 1995, the Organization for Economic Cooperation and Development gathered figures on the size of the shadow education system. These figures are dated and they do not include the effect in the United States of the funding of the shadow education system by No Child Left Behind legislation. In 1995, about 30 percent of U.S. 8th graders participated in the shadow education system while in Japan it was about 60 percent.

The U.S.'s shadow education system is tied to government support and this therefore leads to lobbying efforts by the Education Industry Association. This organization has adopted a self-protective code of ethics. I call this code of ethics self-protective because it provides an internal policing function designed to protect the industry from criticism by politicians and the media. The SES Coalition states: "In its role of providing critical leadership to the education industry, both public and private, EIA [Education Industry Association] has adopted this voluntary code to describe key organizational behaviors and policies that will guide its member companies and others."[85] The actual code focuses on standards involving possible kickbacks to politicians, government officials, and local community leaders along with hiring practices that might create a conflict of interests. The Education Industry Association adopted these compliance procedures:

1. EIA [Education Industry Association] will develop educational materials on these standards for use by providers, States and school district personnel. These materials will be distributed to members and non-members alike for their incorporation into their internal staff development procedures.
2. All EIA members will sign a statement acknowledging their acceptance of these standards. EIA will maintain a list of signers on its website for the public to review.
3. When a State or School District completes an investigation and has a finding that a breach of these guidelines has occurred, EIA may issue its own censure, suspend or terminate the membership status of the Member. Before EIA acts, it will discuss the matter with the party and offer the party the opportunity to present its information to an ad hoc committee of the Board of Directors.

Therefore, the Education Industry Association's SES Coalition not only provides lobbying to maintain a steady flow of government money to these for-profit organizations but it also attempts to provide a blanket of protection from any possible government or media criticism through its self-policing activities. Signatories to the code of ethics include the major for-profit providers of supplementary services and might be considered the major players in the shadow education system.* In addition, the Education Industry Association advertises career opportunities in the education business. The career page of the Education Industry Association website promises:

---

* 100 Scholars, A+ Tutoring Services, A to Z Educational Ctr., Academic Tutoring Centers, Achieve Success, Tutoring-University Instructors, Alternatives Unlimited, American Center for Learning, Anne Martin Educational Services, Applied Scholastics International, ATS Project Success, Basic Skills Learning, Brain Hurricane, Brienza Academic Advantage, Bright Futures, Cambridge Educational Services, Club Z Tutoring, Home Tutoring Plus, Huntington Learning Centers, IEP, Knowledge College, Knowledge Headquarters, Kumon, Learn-It Systems, Learning Disabilities Clinic, Learning Styles, MasterMind Prep Learning Solutions, McCully's Educational Resource Center, Moving Forward Education, Mrs Dowd's Teaching Services, Mytutor24, NESI, New Jersey Student Success, Newton Learning (Edison Schools), Orions Mind, Pinnacle Learning Center, Porter Educational Service, Progressive Learning, Read and Succeed, Renaissance Enrichment Services, Rocket Learning, Rockhaven Learning Center, Si2, Inc., Sunrise East Tutoring Service, Sylvan Learning Center—Peoria, IL, TestQuest, Total Education Solutions, TutorFind, Tutor Train, Tutors-To-You, TutorVista, Village Sensei.

Employment opportunities in the education industry abound. Whether you are just starting out or have substantial executive level professional experience, EIA members may have the position to fit your interests. To help you discover the range of great entry-level or senior level positions for you, the Education Industry Foundation has supported the development and production of the first-ever *Career Opportunities in the Education Industry*.[86]

One economic opportunity that drives the shadow education system is the purchase of a franchise from a major company. Franchising supplementary education services, as I discuss in the next section, increases the base political support for government funding. As the number of franchises increases, so does the number of people interested in ensuring political and government financial support of the for-profit education industry. Therefore, the shadow education system becomes a shadow political system with its own educational interests, which, at times, might be in competition with the public school system for government funding.

Franchising the Shadow Education System

Interested in joining the for-profit shadow education system? One signatory of the Education Industry Association's code of ethics, Sylvan Learning, offers franchises requiring an initial investment of $179,000–$305,000 to people who have a minimum net worth of $250,000. By offering K through 12 tutoring services it is able to take advantage of government funds provided for for-profit educational services. Depending on the location the franchise fee is from $42,000 to $48,000. Why might you choose Sylvan? The company advertises its sale of franchises by pointing out that it has served two million students since 1979, has been ranked twenty-four times in *Entrepreneur* magazine's "Franchise 500 Ranking," and was number 61 overall in its 2009 "Franchise 500 Ranking" and number 52 in the publication's "Top Global Franchises" ranking. It was ranked in Bond's Top 100 Franchises and was number 57 in the *2008 Franchise Times*' "Top 200 Systems." In addition, the Sylvan Learning franchise brand was selected as the best educational provider in Nickelodeon's ParentsConnect's First Annual Parents' Picks Award and as "Favorite Kids Learning Center" by SheKnows.com. If you happen to be Hispanic, you might be tempted to invest in a franchise because Sylvan Learning was identified by "PODER Enterprise magazine as one of the 'Top 25 Franchises for Hispanics' in April 2009."[87]

Sylvan Learning's promotion of its franchises highlights the political stake it has in the continued government funding of for-profit supplementary education services. It functions like any corporation trying to expand its reach and profits. Like any corporation it relies on having a global brand name which is impressed on the public through its $40 million advertising and marketing program. In the midst of the 2010 recession the company claimed, "Despite the economy, now is the right time to enter the supplemental education industry. According to Eduventures, Inc., the current demand is strong and the market is projected to continue with double-digit growth."[88] The company claimed that when in 2008 it decided to focus on "franchising to local entrepreneurs and business operators who can respond to the particular needs of each community while utilizing the tools, resources and brand equity of the Sylvan name," it grew by 150 percent.[89]

It is understandable why Sylvan Learning would want to join the Education Industry Association with its strong lobbying efforts to increase funding for supplementary services and its efforts to protect for-profit education from government investigations. Sylvan Learning is also a global company with tutoring services located in the Cayman Islands, the Bahamas, Hong Kong, Bahrain, Kuwait, Qatar, and the United Arab Emirates.[90] While this global reach is relatively small it does indicate a potential future for Sylvan Learning as a major global education company. As I will explain later in this book, this involves Sylvan Learning in global politics related to the regulation of trade under the auspices of the World Trade Organization.

Kumon Learning Centers is another signatory of the Education Industry Association's code of ethics and a major global company concerned about both American and global political support of supplementary education services. While not having as strong a brand recognition as Sylvan Learning in the United States, Kumon Learning Centers supports a vast number of global franchises. In the United States, where it is partly dependent on government support and therefore joins the Education Industry Association in its lobbying efforts, the company had 1,204 franchises in 2009. In addition, it had over 25,000 franchises in other countries.[91]

The Kumon Learning Centers were founded in Japan in 1958 by Toru Kumon. In 2010 the company was ranked #12 in a list of franchises which included Subway at #1 followed by McDonald's, 7-Eleven Inc., Hampton Inn, Supercuts, H&R Block, Dunkin' Donuts, Jani-King, Servpro, ampm Mini Market, and Jan-Pro Franchising Int'l Inc.[92] This is a pretty impressive list and indicates the growing global importance of the shadow education industry. In 2009, Kumon Learning Centers enrolled 4.2 million students in forty-six countries.[93]

Kumon represents the globalization of the shadow education system with interests in the education policies of countries it serves. This globalized shadow education system has a political interest in national school policies that rely on test scores for entry into the job market or schools and, at least in the United States, on some form of government funding.

This global shadow education system is being transformed into a system of for-profit schools in addition to providing just supplementary education services. One example of this is Kaplan which started as a test preparation company and is now a global company operating for-profit schools along with test preparation and language instruction. Kaplan's operations in Singapore, Hong Kong, Shanghai, and Beijing are advertised as meeting "students' demand for Western-style education." In ten European countries it offers test preparation and English language instruction. "In the UK," Kaplan states, "we are one of the largest providers of accountancy training and private higher education. We also operate the Dublin Business School, Ireland's largest private undergraduate college."[94] Kaplan operates Tel Aviv-based Kidum, the largest provider of test preparation in Israel. In Brazil, Colombia, Panama, and Venezuela, Kaplan operates English language and test preparation programs designed to prepare students for admission to schools in the United States.[95]

In summary, the shadow education system is now an important player in national and global politics. The agenda of these supplementary education services focuses on increasing revenues by lobbying for government financial support and school policies supporting assessment systems that drive students into buying their services. These companies are also seeking to expand revenues through globalization of their products and by expanding into new areas such as for-profit schools and English language instruction.

Multinational Testing Corporations

There is money to be made in the production of tests along with test preparation. Multinational groups involved in test construction and production are also dependent on political support for assessment-driven school systems. These companies share common interests with the shadow education system. As I will discuss in Chapter 8, Educational Testing Services, Pearson, and McGraw-Hill, the three biggest test producers in the United States, are global enterprises that feed parental fears about their child's need for supplementary education services. And, as the English language comes to dominate the commercial world, these companies market English language achievement tests and services.

In summary, global testing enterprises share the same interests as the shadow education industry. Can you imagine the outcry that would come from these for-profit industries if national education ministries announced that they were abandoning assessment-driven school systems for a system based simply on teachers' grades derived from teacher-created tests? In many school systems this was the way it used to be, with teachers constructing their own tests and using the results from their tests to grade students. The for-profit companies discussed in this chapter have a political stake in supporting government policies that ensure the use of assessments produced by for-profit companies and maximizing the use of these assessments so that parental fears will enrich the shadow education system.

Conclusion: Ideology and the Education Business

Human capital ideology supports the educational policies that will maximize profits for the shadow education system. This creates a linkage between the public acceptance and support of human capital ideology and the for-profit interests of the shadow education system. In other words, the education industries will continue to be wedded to human capital economics even if it is wrong or promotes educational systems that might have a negative effect on what students learn and how they learn. Test-driven educational systems may continue to exist not because they are the "best," but because they are strongly supported by the education industry.

In addition, the education industry wants public support and acceptance of human capital ideology with its accompanying practices of using high-stakes testing to promote and sort students for careers and higher education, and to evaluate teachers and school administrators. Putting testing pressure on students means that parents will be willing to fork out extra money to the shadow education industry.

Consequently, the shadow education system and multinational testing corporations are interested in public acceptance of human capital ideology and the legitimization of assessment-driven school systems. The shadow education system would not be interested in the public questioning an ideology on which its profits depend. Nor would it be interested in the public questioning the very value of high-stakes testing. In this case, there is a symbiotic relationship between the shadow education system and human capital ideology.

As a growth industry and the second largest U.S. economic sector after health care, education businesses try to maximize their profits by supporting favorable government school policies and government funding. This means that the industry is involved in education politics at the local, state, and national levels. The education industry's lobbying efforts are made by trade associations such as the Education Industry Association, the Schools Division of the Association of American Publishers, and the Education Industry Forum. The most important federal legislation affecting the education industry is No Child Left Behind which promotes charter schools and the use of for-profit supplementary services. The Education Industry Association is very involved in representing for-profit companies during the reauthorization of No Child Left Behind. Also, investment bankers and law firms lobby federal and state governments to advance and protect education businesses.

Textbook publishing, a traditional education business, continues to be affected by state politics of textbook selection, particularly the selection process used by the Texas State Board of Education. However, traditional textbooks are now being challenged by open-source publishing as states try to reduce budgets. This new industry is interested in government support and the creation of new markets. This creates political conflicts over state laws and funding between the traditional publishers and open-source providers.

In the United States, both major political parties support the growth of charter schools. The charter school industry is primarily composed of for-profit and nonprofit educational management organizations. Both for-profit and nonprofit charter school management groups have a clear stake in supporting politicians and legislation favorable to the growth of charter schools.

And finally, there are the political concerns of the global shadow education system which has interests in promoting government policies that provide funding for for-profit education services. The shadow education industry is interested in government policies that promote high-stakes testing and the sorting of students for admission to elite and non-elite higher education institutions and for entrance into the work force. The use of high-stakes tests for promotion, graduation, and college admission increases parental anxieties about their children's futures which drives them to utilize supplementary education services. Of course, the multinational testing industry supports any government legislation which increases the use of their products.

Notes

1 This estimate was made by the BerkeryNoyes Investment Bankers, "Education." Retrieved from http://www.berkerynoyes.com/sector/education.aspx on February 10, 2010.
2 Seeking Alpha, "For-Profit Education Sector: Recession Proof." Retrieved from http://seekingalpha.com/article/117855-for-profit-education-sector-recession-proof on February 10, 2010.
3 Ibid.
4 Ibid.
5 For-profit Education Forum, "Home." Retrieved from http://www.iirusa.com/education/home.xml on February 10, 2010.
6 Education Industry Association & ESEA Organizing Principles (December 28, 2009). Retrieved from http://www.educationindustry.org/ on March 12, 2010.
7 Ibid.
8 Ibid.
9 U.S. Department of Education, "No Child Left Behind: Supplemental Educational Services Non-Regulatory Guidance" (January 14, 2009). Retrieved from http://find.ed.gov/search?q=supplemental+education+services&client=default_frontend&output=xml_no_dtd&proxystylesheet=default_

frontend&sa.x=18&sa.y=11&ie=UTF-8&ip=74.101.47.5&access=p&entqr
=3&entsp=a&oe=UTF-8&ud=1&sort=date%3AD%3AL%3Ad1 on March
17, 2010.

10 Education Industry Association, "SES/Public Policy." Retrieved from http://
www.educationindustry.org/tier.asp?sid=2 on March 2, 2010.

11 Ibid.

12 BerkeryNoyes Investment Bankers, "Education."

13 Ibid.

14 Ritzert & Leyton, "Higher/Postsecondary Education." Retrieved from http://
www.ritzert-leyton.com/prac_areas.htm on February 10, 2010.

15 Association of American Publishers, "More Gains in Book Sales for
November." Retrieved from http://www.publishers.org/main/PressCenter/
Archicves/2010_January/November10StatsRelease.htm on February 5, 2010.

16 Kathleen Kennedy Manzo, "California Faces a Curriculum Crisis: Major
Changes to State Policies Prompted by Budget Troubles," *Education Week*
(September 16, 2009). Retrieved from http://www.edweek.org/ew/articles/
2009/09/04/03califtexts_ep.h29.html?tkn=YSNF4%2FmhksSsT6yV3%2Bp7
JdKV2W1UWQZc3frq&print=1 on March 2, 2010.

17 Mariah Blake, "Revisionaries: How a Group of Texas Conservatives Is
Rewriting Your Kids' Textbooks," *Washington Monthly* (January/February
2010). Retrieved from http://www.washingtonmonthly.com/features/2010/
1001.blake.html on March 4, 2010.

18 Alexandra Stille, "Textbook Publishers Learn to Avoid Messing with Texas"
(June 29, 2002). *The New York Times on the Web* (June 29, 2002). Retrieved
from http://www.nytimes.com/ on July 6, 2002.

19 Blake, "Revisionaries."

20 Texas Curriculum: Developing 21st Century Learning Systems for Texas
Schoolchildren, "Texas Adoption Process: A Brief Overview." Retrieved
from http://www.texastextbooks.org/pdf/Brief_Overview_Adoption.pdf on
January 6, 2010.

21 Quoted in Transcript of Proceedings before the Commissioner of Education
and the State Textbook Committee, July 14–16, 1986 (Austin, TX: Kennedy
Reporting Service, 1986), p. 182.

22 Ibid., p. 183.

23 Mel Gabler's Educational Research Analysts: Public School Textbook
Reform through Textbook Reviews can be found at http://www.textbook
reviews.org/index.html?content=about.htm.

24 "About," Mel Gabler's Educational Research Analysts: Public School Textbook Reform through Textbook Reviews. Retrieved from http://www.
textbookreviews.org/index.html? content=about.htm on March 3, 2010.

25 Stille, "Textbook Publishers."

26 Ibid.

27 Ibid.

28 Ibid.

29 Ibid.

30 Ibid.

31 Ibid.

32 Terrence Stutz, "Texas Board of Education Chairman Don McLeroy a Step
Closer to Retaining Post," *Dallas Morning News* (May 21, 2009). Retrieved
from http://www.dallasnews.com/sharedcontent/dws/news/texassouthwest/
stories/DN-mcleroy_21tex.ART.State.Edition1.7654.html on March 5, 2010.

33 Blake, "Revisionaries."

34 Ibid.

35 "About," Peter Marshall Ministries. Retrieved from http://petermarshall ministries.com/about/rev_peter_marshall.cfm on March 2, 2010.
36 "Former Texas GOP Vice Chairman and WallBuilders President David Barton Endorses Gov. Perry for Re-election." Retrieved from http://www. rickperry.org/release/former-texas-gop-vice-chairman-and-wallbuilders-president-david-barton-endorses-gov-perry-re on March 5, 2010.
37 "About Us," WallBuilders. Retrieved from http://www.wallbuilders.com/ ABTOverview.asp on March 8, 2010.
38 "About," Peter Marshall Ministries.
39 Ibid.
40 Blake, "Revisionaries."
41 James C. McKinley, Jr., "Texas Conservatives Seek Deeper Stamp on Texts," *New York Times* (March 10, 2010). Retrieved from http://www.nytimes. com/2010/03/11/us/politics/11texas.html?ref=us on March 10, 2010.
42 Leslie Kaufman, "Darwin Foes Add Warming to Targets" (March 3, 2010). Retrieved from http://www.nytimes.com/2010/03/04/science/earth/04climate. html?ref=education on March 2, 2009.
43 Ibid.
44 James C. McKinley, Jr., "Texas Approves Curriculum Revised by Conservatives" (March 12, 2010). Retrieved from http://www.nytimes.com/ 2010/03/13/education/13texas.html?hp on March 12, 1010.
45 Manzo, "California Faces a Curriculum Crisis."
46 "News in Brief: Calif. Governor Sets Plan to Offer Open-Source Digital Texts," *Education Week* (May 20, 2009). Retrieved from http://www. edweek.org/ew/articles/2009/05/20/32brief-3.h28.html?tkn=QRYFmp 7iH2ybSN3rn0%2BuakaeTJSYB9F%2FKPhd&print=1 on February 24, 2010.
47 COSTP: California Open Source Textbook Project. Retrieved from http:// www.opensourcetext.org/ on February 26, 2010.
48 "About," Creative Commons. Retrieved from http://creativecommons.org/ about/ on March 5, 2010.
49 COSTP: California Open Source Textbook Project.
50 "People," California Open Source Textbook Project. Retrieved from http:// www.opensourcetext.org/people.htm on March 2, 2010.
51 Ibid.
52 "Project," California Open Source Textbook Project. Retrieved from http:// www.opensourcetext.org/project_updates.htm on March 1, 2010.
53 "World History Project," Wikibooks. Retrieved from http://en.wikibooks. org/wiki/COSTP_World_History_Project on March 1, 2010.
54 Chris Snyder, "Open Source Textbooks Challenge a Paradigm," *Wired* (September 1, 2008). Retrieved from http://www.wired.com/epicenter/2008/ 09/open-source-tex/ on March 1, 2010.
55 Motoko Rich, "Textbooks That Professors Can Rewrite Digitally" (February 22, 2010). Retrieved from http://www.nytimes.com/ on February 24, 2010.
56 Ibid.
57 "'Open-Source' Classroom Materials: Nation's Oldest Hispanic Rights Groups Urge Perry to Allow Public Review" (January 8, 2010). Retrieved from http://www.texasinsider.org/?p=20224 on March 8, 2010.
58 Ibid.
59 Ibid.
60 Greg DeKoenigsberg, "Open Source Textbooks a 'Threat' to Texas Education?" (January 2010). Retrieved from http://opensource.com/education/ 10/1/open-source-textbooks-threat-texas-education on March 1, 2010.

61 Public Law 107–110, 107th Congress, "An Act to Close the Achievement Gap with Accountability, Flexibility, and Choice, so that No Child Is Left Behind" (January 8, 2002), p. 70. Retrieved from http://www2.ed.gov/policy/elsec/leg/esea02/107-110.pdf on March 5, 2010.

62 "History," U.S. Charter Schools, Retrieved from http://www.uscharter schools.org/pub/uscs_docs/o/history.htm on March 11, 2010.

63 Public Law 107–110, 107th Congress, p. 364.

64 U.S. Department of Education, Office of Innovation and Improvement, *A Commitment to Quality: National Charter School Policy Forum Report* (Washington, DC: U.S. Department of Education, 2008), p. 1.

65 "A Cost Estimation Tool for Charter Schools," U.S. Charter Schools. Retrieved from http://www.uscharterschools.org/cs/n/view/cs_bmsg/6490 on March 12, 2010.

66 Alex Molnar, Gary Miron, and Jessica Urschel, "Profiles of For-Profit Educational Management Organizations Eleventh Annual Report" (September 2009). Retrieved from http://epicpolicy.org/publication/profiles-profit-emos-2008-09 on March 8, 2010.

67 Ibid., p. 3.

68 Ibid., pp. 1–2.

69 Ibid., p. 2.

70 Ibid., pp. 15–18.

71 K12, "Ron Packard." Retrieved from http://investors.k12.com/phoenix.zhtml?c=214389&p=irol-govBio&ID=170666 on March 6, 2010.

72 K12, "Partners." Retrieved from http://www.k12.com/partners/ on March 8, 2010.

73 "About," Imagine Schools. Retrieved from http://www.imagineschools.com/dynamic-about.aspx?id=996 on March 11, 2010.

74 Imagine Schools 2009 Annual Report. Retrieved from http://www.imagine schools.com/dynamic-learn.aspx?id=1044 on March 10, 2010.

75 "William 'Bill' Lager, IQ Innovations Inc." Retrieved from http://www.excelined.org/docs/2008EIAAchive/Bios/ Lager-bio.pdf on March 10, 2010.

76 "William Lager," CampaignMoney.Com. Retrieved from http://www.campaignmoney.com/political/contributions/william-lager.asp?cycle=08 on March 1, 2010.

77 IQity, "The E-learning Platform Overview." Retrieved from http://www.iq-ity.com/content/pdf/IQ_16page_BRO.pdf on March 9, 2010.

78 "David Brennan," White Hat Management. Retrieved from http://www.whitehatmgmt.com/brennan.html on March 10, 2010.

79 "Ed Harrison," White Hat Management. Retrieved from http://www.whitehatmgmt.com/harrison.html on March 10, 2010.

80 "Mark A. Rice," White Hat Management. Retrieved from http://www.whitehatmgmt.com/rice.html on March 10, 2010.

81 Gary Miron and Jessica Uschel, "Profiles of Nonprofit Education Management Organizations: 2008–2009." Retrieved from http://epicpolicy.org/publication/profiles-nonprofit-emos-2008-09 on March 10, 2010.

82 "About," Summit Academy Management. Retrieved from http://www.summitacademies.com/summit_academy_schools_about_us.php on March 11, 2010.

83 David P. Baker and Gerald K. LeTendre, *National Differences, Global Similarities: World Culture and the Future of Schooling* (Palo Alto, CA: Stanford University Press, 2005), pp. 54–60.

84 Ibid., p. 69.

85 Education Industry Association, "Code of Professional Conduct and Business Ethics for Supplemental Educational Services Providers Amended January 8, 2008." Retrieved from http://www.educationindustry.org/tier.asp?sid=2 on March 10, 2010.
86 "Careers in Education," Education Industry Association. Retrieved from http://www.educationindustry.org/tier.asp?sid=8 on March 18, 2010.
87 "Franchising: Is Sylvan for You?" Sylvan Learning. Retrieved from http://tutoring.sylvanlearning.com/franchising_is_sylvan_for_you.cfm on March 17, 2010.
88 "Franchising Opportunities," Sylvan Learning. Retrieved from http://tutoring.sylvanlearning.com/franchising_opportunities.cfm on March 17, 2010.
89 Ibid.
90 "Home," Sylvan Learning. Retrieved from http://tutoring.sylvanlearning.com/find_a_center.cfm?cid=PBM-MEC-search-google-ppc-brand_learn_ctr 0809&utm_source=google&utm_medium=ppc&utm_term=sylvan learning&utm_campaign=paid+search&CFID=16694361&CFTOKEN=252 16069 on March 17, 2010.
91 "Kumon Math & Reading Centers: Supplemental Education," *Entrepreneur.* Retrieved from http://www.entrepreneur.com/franchises/kumonmathandread ingcenters/282507-0.html on March 12, 2010.
92 "2010 Franchise 500 Rankings," *Entrepreneur.* Retrieved from http://www.entrepreneur.com/franchises/rankings/franchise500-115608/2010,-1.html on March 18, 2010.
93 "What is Kumon?" Kumon. Retrieved from http://www.kumon.ne.jp/english/index.html on March 18, 2010.
94 "Global Operations," Kaplan. Retrieved from http://www.kaplan.com/about-kaplan/global-operations on March 20, 2010.
95 Ibid.

Chapter 7

Politics of School Finance and the Economics of Education

"NJ governor wants local teachers union head who wrote memo joking about his death fired," Associate Press writer Angela Delli Santi titled her news article in the midst of the 2010 school finance crisis.[1] The prospect of layoffs, frozen salary scales, and increased class sizes sent chills down the spines of many New Jersey teachers, particularly the leaders of teachers unions. Republicans, as I discussed earlier in the book, have never been too fond of teachers unions. Teachers unions worried when New Jersey Republican Governor Chris Christie was elected in 2009 after they had campaigned against him. Would the financial crisis lead to retribution against the unions?

What sparked Governor Christie's anger was a prayer joking about his death that was placed in a memo by New Jersey's Bergen County teachers union head Joe Coppola:

> Dear Lord this year you have taken away my favorite actor, Patrick Swayze, my favorite actress, Farrah Fawcett, my favorite singer, Michael Jackson . . . I just wanted to let you know that Chris Christie is my favorite governor.[2]

The financial crisis added more strain to the relationship between the teachers union and Governor Christie which had already deteriorated during the fall 2009 campaign. In fact, the Governor refused to meet with the teachers unions. After the election, Governor Christie called for a freeze on teachers' salaries and urged local school districts, much to the horror of teachers, to vote against local school budgets if the local union did not agree to a freeze on salaries. Speaking at a business development event in Princeton, New Jersey, Governor Christie lamented, "I just don't see how citizens should want to support a budget where their teachers have not wanted to be part of the shared sacrifice."[3]

Does Money Matter?

While school districts worried about supporting their budgets some scholars wondered if money made any difference regarding student achievement. In most cases, scholars have not been able to pinpoint any direct effect of money on outcomes. Writing in the *Kappan*, W. Norton Grubb asserted, "The Money Myth is the contention that any education problem requires increased spending and, conversely, that reform is impossible without more funding ... Dollar bills do not educate children."[4]

Do groups like teachers unions, the PTA, the League of Women Voters, and other groups lobby Congress and state legislatures for more money primarily out of self-interest? Writing about the demands of these groups for greater funding to improve education, Paul T. Hill asserts, "The claim is best understood as a political statement, made in pursuit of interest groups' constant objective of getting more money for their clients."[5] With a cynical tone Hill titled a section of his essay, "We Don't Know How to Provide Effective Schools for All."[6] The key words in this title are "for All." Hill asserts that U.S. schools are preparing a majority of kids for higher education but the problem is the education of students from low-income families. Will more money solve the achievement gap?

In a commentary written for *Education Week*, Paul T. Hill and Marguerite Roza, after reviewing judicial efforts to provide extra money to educate kids from low-income families, point out that, "Critics noted that school finance lawsuits did little to benefit the poor students in whose names they were brought."[7] Why may this be true? They argue that urban school districts that got extra money misspent it on schools serving high-income students.

The reality is that the United States continues to increase funding for public education while politicians continually claim schools are failing. According to the National Center for Education Statistics' *The Condition of Education 2009*: "From 1989–90 through 2005–06, total elementary and secondary public school revenue increased 59 percent in constant dollars, from $348 billion to $554 billion."[8] According to this report, "Total expenditures per student in fall enrollment in public elementary and secondary schools rose 31 percent in constant dollars between 1989–90 and 2005–06, from $8,627 to $11,293."[9] It should be noted that during this time span expenditures on school debt per student increased the fastest (100 percent). While teachers' salaries increased during this period by 17 percent, the percentage of total school budgets spent on teachers' salaries actually declined by 5 percent.[10]

James Guthrie concurs that the United States spends a great deal of money on education but still is unable to close the achievement gap or improve scores on international tests. Writing about school finance, Guthrie opened his article with "A Modern Parable":

Once there existed a powerful, well-intentioned, and wealthy nation. The people and their representatives decided that the nation's children should learn more in school. To achieve this goal, for 50 years the nation continually spent more money on its schools, employed more people to work in the schools, and strove mightily to ensure that these resources were equitably distributed to all schools and all children ... Alas, little of this national effort seemed successful. Student achievement in mathematics and reading did not change much, and the gap between middle-class and poor children persisted. What was the powerful and wealthy nation to do?[11]

Guthrie concludes, "Added expenditures have purchased added personnel, not added pupil performance."[12]

Why hasn't more money made a difference? One reason suggested earlier is that urban schools spent the money on schools serving high-income parents. W. Norton Grubb argues that it was spent on incompetent teachers, weak after-school programs, teacher aides without clear plans, and low-quality professional development.[13] Guthrie argues that most of the money has gone on teacher salaries which increased in constant dollars by 26 percent from 1962 to 2004, in addition to extra money spent on fringe benefits.[14] It could be hypothesized that increased salaries would raise the quality of teachers. One statistical study suggested that this was the case.[15] In another study, it was concluded that increasing teacher pay for advanced education, for instance for teachers earning a master's or doctoral degree, would improve student achievement.[16] But there is little evidence, according to Guthrie, that this has happened when the relationship between the two is examined over time from the 1960s to the present.

In contrast to Guthrie, W. Norton Grubb despite his conclusion that a great deal of money is wasted in education argues that there are effective ways that financial resources can be used. After analyzing the data on the relationship between money and good schools, he concludes, "the most effective school resources prove to be . . . related to innovative teaching, staff development, planning time, teacher control and efficacy, and certain student support services."[17] Interestingly, Grubb argues that No Child Left Behind undermines this effective use of resources, particularly teacher control and efficacy, staff development, and planning time. He asserts that teacher control and efficacy are weakened by the over-reliance on standardized tests which results in rigid test-oriented teaching and professional development being focused on teaching a prescribed curriculum.

Why is money seen as the solution to educational problems? The answer is political and involves the intersection of the courts and the quest for educational equity. In the next section, I will consider the role of economic self-interest in school finance. This discussion will be followed by a consideration of the political background for inequity in school finance. I will then turn to the judicial story of the quest for equity in school finance beginning with the California Supreme Court case Serrano v. Priest (1971). By the twenty-first century court cases focused on the concept of "adequacy" in financing schools. These court cases involved the judiciary in determining education policies.

Economic Self-Interest and School Finance

The politics of school finance can include people trying to maximize their benefits from education while reducing their personal costs for paying for that education. In this situation, the ideal for an individual would be an educational system that increased the individual's political power and economic benefits with the cost being paid by other people. The attempt to achieve maximum benefits with little personal cost underpins many of the problems associated with inequality of educational spending.

Members of the educational community have an interest in increasing the money spent on education because this can result in increasing their personal economic benefits, including economic gains for teachers, administrators, educational bureaucrats, and knowledge brokers. Unlike other groups, educational workers do not necessarily seek to reduce their personal expenditure on education. For example, educators will often support tax increases (though the increases affect the taxes they themselves pay) because the money will eventually be returned in their paychecks.

Consider the recent decreases in corporate taxes and taxes on the wealthy and corporations while corporations were demanding better schools to meet the rigors of international economic competition. University of California economist Robert Reich argues that corporate donations to schools are a smoke screen for decreasing corporate support of schools through taxation. "It's a great irony that business is saying it is supporting education in the front door," Reich said in a 1991 interview for *Education Week*, "but [is] taking away money through the back door." Reich notes that the decline in corporate tax support of schools is occurring at the same time as corporations are demanding that schools provide an education to meet their labor needs. According to Reich, corporate donations increased by 1.7 percent in 1987 and 2.4 percent in 1988, while the corporate share of local property taxes declined from 45 percent to 16 percent between 1957 and 1987. "Corporate munificence is a high profile affair," Reich says. "Lobbying for huge tax breaks is conveniently, far less so."[18]

Reich's analysis is tied to a general theory of the internationalization of capital and labor. In his book *The Work of Nations*, he argues that the withdrawal of corporate support of public schools in the United States is part of a general withdrawal of support from the infrastructure of the country.[19] International corporations no longer feel an allegiance to a particular country, according to Reich, and, consequently, are primarily seeking production sites with the lowest taxes and labor costs. On the other hand, corporations do need an educated labor force.

Economist E.G. West provides an example of the economic self-interest of educators. West is concerned with the provision of free public education to all social classes, including the upper middle class and the rich. On the surface, there may be no reason to provide free education to those who can afford direct costs. West examines the development of free public schools in New York state during the nineteenth century. Originally, common schools were not free to all children. They were funded in part by the government and in part by parents, who paid rate bills according to the number of days their children attended. They provided a free education only to those children whose parents were too poor to pay the rate bills.

West asserts that rate bills created a problem for educators in gaining support for public schools from middle- and upper-income groups. Rate bills provided the opportunity for those with the means to decide to spend their money on private schools or pay the public school rate bill. Consequently, school officials campaigned for free public schooling hoping that middle- and upper-income groups would find public schools more attractive when faced with the decision to pay for private schooling or to utilize free public schooling.

The actions of the teachers and administrators fit into what West calls the economic theory of democracy. This theory suggests that people working in a government service want to influence government policy related to that service because their incomes depend on the policy. The average citizen has interests spread over most government services and cannot devote so much time to a single government issue, such as education. Those in the service of government tend to try to maximize their benefits on policies regarding their incomes. In West's words, the educator "may be prompted by the desire to help others and by the desire to help himself and his family . . . And what people do is a better guide than what they say."[20]

West believes that the interests of teachers and administrators in government service were enhanced by reducing the problem of salaries being dependent on the collection of rate bills and by the creation of a monopoly situation. The creation of free public schools made it more difficult for private schools to continue to exist. With rate bills there was still economic discretion for parents to choose private schooling. With compulsory taxation providing free schools, it became more difficult for private schools to compete for students. Middle- and upper-income parents were now faced with the choice of paying no tuition fees for public schools or paying private school fees.

Providing free public school education did cause parents to switch from private to public schooling. West found that the provision of free public schools resulted in a decline in the number of private schools. Few parents wanted to pay taxes to support free public schools and then pay again to send their children to private schools. West's figures from the office of the New York state superintendent show an increase in the number of students in private schools, from 48,451 in 1863 to 68,105 in 1867, when legislation was passed abolishing rate bills. In 1871, four years after the provision of free public schools in New York began, private school enrollment decreased to 49,691.[21]

Admittedly, the assumption that individuals want to maximize their gains from schooling while reducing their costs adds a cynical edge to an economic analysis of education. It suggests that educational rhetoric depends on economic interests. West argues that educators campaigned for free public schools promising reduced crime and poverty and increased political stability. There was no proof that these benefits would result from free schools. West states, "The suppliers of educational services to the government, the teachers and administrators, as we have seen, had produced their own organized platforms by the late 1840s; it was they indeed who were the leading instigators of the free school campaign."[22]

Therefore, one assumption of this chapter is that citizens desire to maximize benefits and reduce costs including those associated with education. Also, in some cases, educational rhetoric is a function of economic interests. The next section of the chapter will examine how citizens maximize their educational benefits to the disadvantage of other groups.

The Politics of Unequal Funding and School Finance

The complicated nature of the politics of school finance and the resulting inequalities in school spending are best described in Jean Anyon's *Ghetto Schooling: A Political Economy of Urban Educational Reform*.[23] As the phrase in the subtitle "political economy" suggests, school financing issues can only be understood in the context of its intersection with politics. The brilliance of Anyon's study lies in the exploration of the political forces that divided school districts according to income levels and the resulting inequalities in school spending. Based on a study of the historical development of the Newark, New Jersey schools, Anyon demonstrates the use of political power to create educational inequalities between wealthy suburban school districts and low-income city districts.

Originally, Newark's schools, Anyon reminds the reader, were national models of excellence. Then, during and after World War II, a combination of southern migration of low-income African Americans into Newark and the process of suburbanization changed the racial composition of the city. The suburbanization of America was aided by the political process. The 1956 National Defense Highway System made it possible for workers to travel longer distances from their suburban homes to city jobs. This was followed in 1962 by a federal program that subsidized the construction of manufacturing plants and the purchase of new equipment, which in turn made it possible for businesses to move out of cities into suburban areas at the expense of the taxpayer. The result of suburbanization and the movement of businesses was a disproportionate growth of low-income families and a decline in employment opportunities in cities.

The growing political power of suburban communities in state legislatures added to the plight of low-income city communities. A series of U.S. court decisions in the 1960s resulted in the reapportionment of state legislative districts based on population. By the 1970s, this reapportionment favored suburban districts. "Thus," Anyon wrote, "dominance in the legislature bypassed the cities and was allocated to suburban representatives . . . One result of the cities' political isolation from state power . . . was continued dependence on local property taxes for educational and other municipal spending."[24] With the erosion of the tax base in low-income districts, the reliance on local property taxes meant a decline in their educational services and buildings.

The importance of political power was most evident in suburban resistance to attempts to equalize spending between state school districts. In 1990, the New Jersey Supreme Court ordered the state legislature to develop a plan for equalizing spending between rich and poor school districts. In response, the state legislature passed the Quality Education Act which increased state monies to poorer school districts. However, this increase in state funding meant an increase in state income taxes which were primarily paid by residents of suburban areas. The result was the doubling of state income taxes in some suburban communities to finance the equalization plan.

The increase in state income taxes for suburban residents resulted in a political revolt against the equalization plan. According to Anyon, the New Jersey Republican senate minority leader John Dorsey proclaimed that the equalization plan required "working-class people in middle-class communities who drive around in Fords to buy Mercedes for people in the poorest cities because they don't have cars."[25] A Democratic assemblyman from wealthy Monmouth County referred to the equalization legislation as the act of "almost a socialist state" and declared, according to Anyon, "This is New Jersey; this is not Moscow in 1950."[26] The result of the suburban taxpayer revolt was new legislation that eluded attempts at equalization. The new law reduced state education aid from $1.15 billion to $800 million. Political power overruled judicial intent.

Anyon's study highlights the reality of political power in shaping the financing of schools. Political calls for protection of local control of schools and for reliance on local property taxes are, in reality, often efforts to protect the educational advantages of wealthy suburban school districts. The resulting financial disparities between school districts resulted in a number of court cases. The next two sections deal with judicial involvement in school equity issues.

Judicial Involvement in School Finance: Equity

Jean Anyon's study highlights the types of political forces that resulted in financial inequities between school districts. The attempt to correct these inequities, as exemplified by Anyon's discussion of New Jersey, can be traced back to the civil rights movement of the 1950s and 1970s and two scholarly groups whose publications highlighted the disparities in school finance, namely Arthur Wise's *Rich Schools, Poor Schools* (1968) and *Private Wealth and Public Education* (1970) by John Coons, William Clune, and Stephen Sugarman.[27]

Coons and Sugarman were the lawyers in the first major school equity case, Serrano v. Priest (1971). This case was adjudicated by the California Supreme Court which found that California's method of financing schools contributed to inequality of educational opportunity. The case involved the two sons of John Serrano, who lived in a poor, mainly Mexican American community in Los Angeles. The local school experienced increasing class sizes and a resulting shortage of textbooks and supplies. Local school authorities told Serrano that the financial situation in the school would not improve, and the only option for the Serrano family was to move to another school district. The California Supreme Court decision states, "Plaintiff contends that the school financing system classifies on the basis of wealth. We find this proposition irrefutable. . . ."[28]

In court, John Coons and Stephen Sugarman argued that the only means of overcoming inequality of educational funding is through some form of voucher system in which the family is allowed to exercise educational choice. Under one type of voucher proposal, intended to overcome problems associated with different educational needs, all children receive a voucher of equal value. In addition, grants based on needs are made to each family. Larger grants then go to the poorest families, with a progressive reduction in the grant to zero for families of average income.[29]

The traditional reliance on local property taxes for school financing became an issue in the Serrano case. The California Supreme Court concluded in the case that property taxes are often regressive forms of taxation. In other words, property taxes can be a greater burden for middle- and low-income families than for wealthy families. When a regressive property tax is combined with the process of school districting, extreme inequalities result, in both the payment of taxes and the distribution of revenues to schools. Low-income families pay higher rates and receive less revenue for their efforts.

Eventually, a school finance case involving equity, Rodriguez v. San Antonio Independent School District (1973), reached the U.S. Supreme Court. In this case, the U.S. Supreme Court refused to consider the issue of school finance, declaring, "The consideration and initiation of fundamental reforms with respect to state taxation and education are matters reserved for the legislative processes of the various states."[30] This meant that changes in educational financing would have to be the work of state courts and legislatures.

A result of these and similar cases was courts increasing the amount of state aid. As school finance scholar James Guthrie noted, "The cumulative result [of these cases] was a substantially greater level of interdistrict spending equality than had ever existed in the nation's history."[31] This heightened role of states in financing schools would eventually lead to a financial meltdown for local school districts when state budget crises occurred after 2008.

Judicial Involvement in School Finance: Adequacy

Judicial concern about educational "adequacy" surfaced with the implementation of learning standards and the heavy use of standardized tests in the 1990s and their eventual embodiment in No Child Left Behind. Did schools have adequate resources to accomplish state learning standards and prepare students to successfully take required standardized tests? As I suggested above, there is little firm evidence that can demonstrate a relationship between availability of financial resources and improvement in test scores. However, advocates for low-income students persisted in their efforts to convince state courts and legislatures to provide more financial aid so that all schools would be able to provide an "adequate" education. Courts did respond and what has been called the "high-water mark" for plaintiffs seeking greater equity by using the argument for "adequacy" in preparing students to meet state education standards occurred in 2005 when Kansas courts ordered the state legislature to provide an extra $750 million in aid to local schools.[32] After that case court battles in other states began to face increased questioning about the notion of adequacy. In several states (Oklahoma, Indiana, Nebraska, Colorado, Oregon, and Kentucky) courts threw the issue back to the state legislature claiming it was a political question and not one for the courts. In some states (Texas, Alaska, and Massachusetts), courts ruled that school funding was adequate.[33]

Writing in *Education Week*, Alfred Lindseth, a lawyer who specializes in school finance litigation and participated in "adequacy" lawsuits in New York, Connecticut, Florida, Georgia, Minnesota, Missouri, and North Dakota, outlined the problems facing lawsuits based on adequacy concerns.

1. Schools alone cannot fix the problem. Courts are beginning to realize that schools alone are not responsible for much of what plagues American education.
2. Increased spending is not the answer. Prior to 2005, most courts took it for granted that insufficient funding was the primary problem, and that increased appropriations were therefore the appropriate remedy.
3. Court remedies have not been effective.[34]

In his most telling statement, Lindseth wrote, "One can search the literature in vain for any peer-reviewed or other credible studies showing that such remedies have resulted in significantly improved student achievement in those states in which they have been implemented."[35]

Federal, State, and Local Spending on Education

Judicial decisions combined with federal initiatives to help children from low-income families resulted in high-income and low-income school districts spending more per pupil than middle-income school districts. It could be argued that the middle class lost out as students from low-income families benefited from the civil rights movement—politicians claiming that schools could end poverty, and national leaders worrying about the effect of the achievement gap between the rich and poor on America's ability to compete in global trade. In addition, despite the struggles over equity in financing schools, the rich continued to spend more on schooling. *The Condition of Education 2009* concludes, "Current expenditures per student in 2005–06 were highest in high-poverty districts ($10,458) and in low-poverty districts ($10,447) and were lowest in middle-poverty districts ($8,630)."[36] The report divided school districts into five income levels: low, middle low, middle, middle high, and high. During the school year 2007–08, districts labeled low-income spent $10,447 per pupil (in 2007 dollars) while high-income school districts spent $10,458 per pupil. In contrast, the per pupil expenditures for middle low, middle, and middle high income school districts were $9,089, $8,630, and $9,140 respectively.

While children of middle-income parents were having less spent on their public education than children from low- and high-income families, there was a major shift in revenue sources from the local to the state and federal governments. Judicial cases and federal legislation resulted in this shift. In

1989–90, the federal government provided 6.1 percent of the revenue for public elementary and secondary schools while states provided 47.1 percent and local property taxes 35.9 percent. An additional 10.9 percent came from other sources. In 2005–06, the federal percentage increased by 3 percent to 9.1 percent while the state percentage declined by 0.06 percent. During the same period the dependence on local property taxes declined by 1.7 percent to 34.2 percent.[37] What emerges from these figures is a slightly increasing role of the federal government in financing public schools.

Interestingly, the National Center for Education Statistics reports that states with a more conservative voter base are receiving more federal education monies than states with more liberal voters. The Center reports:

> In 2005–06, the percentage of revenue from federal sources was highest in Mississippi (21 percent) and Louisiana (18 percent) and lowest in New Jersey (4 percent) and Connecticut (5 percent). Revenue receipts from federal sources increased 43 percent in constant dollars from 2004–05 to 2005–06 in both Mississippi and Louisiana.[38]

Twenty-one states received the majority of education revenues from state governments, including Hawaii with only one school district receiving 90 percent from the state government. Among all the states, Nevada (67 percent) had the highest revenue from local sources.[39]

Financial Crisis: How Should Educational Monies Be Distributed?

Another way of looking at the distribution of educational monies is to examine what happens during a financial crisis. What is eliminated from school budgets when there isn't enough money? What political conflicts are triggered by budget cuts? Teacher and administrator associations tend to resist anything related to layoffs and salary cuts. Parents complain about cutting the school year or school week. Republicans often see the teacher and administrator unions as enemies while Democrats count on their support. What does a politician do when a state runs out of money?

Across the country large public demonstrations accompanied the announcement of school cuts as California sank deeper into debt. Wanting to save jobs and maintain class sizes, the Los Angeles teachers union agreed to a shortened school calendar which resulted in a loss of seven pay days for district teachers. The administrators union accepted the decision to cut pay by shortening the school calendar. Los Angeles School Superintendent Raymond Cortines said, "I appreciate the understanding of the district's teachers and the sacrifices they are making in instructional time and salary."[40] Up the coast in Santa Cruz, California, the school board contemplated shortening the school year. Reporter Blair Stenvick wrote, "Teachers Union President Barry Kirschen, said shortening the school year may be the district's only option. 'Without adequate funding, we can't keep the doors open.'"[41]

While teachers worried and in some cases struggled with politicians over pay cuts and job losses, some parents were upset at suggestions that money could be saved by reducing the length of the school week. Who would watch their children on days when they weren't in school? In Illinois, the suggestion of reducing the school week pitted Republicans against Democrats. Springfield, Illinois Superintendent Mark Janesky suggested reducing the school transportation budget, "What if its buses were parked one day? What if kids were in school just four days . . . [It] would save $100,000 a year."[42] Republican state representative Bill Black sponsored legislation, which passed the Illinois state legislature, to allow school districts to shorten their school week with the off days being Friday or Monday. Democratic state representative Karen Yarbrough voted against the legislation. She said, "Parents simply are not ready for this, I want to expand school. This is going the wrong direction."[43] Democratic Mayor Richard Daley of Chicago opposed the shortened week because parents would have to struggle to find extra child care.

Would shortening the school year really save money? "People get really excited about it and think they're going to cut their costs by 20 percent because they're dropping one day, but it doesn't work that way," said Mike Griffith, a senior policy advisor of the Education Commission of the States. "You're still going to have to heat the building. You're still going to have to purchase the textbooks and the computers."[44] However, Griffith suggested that it was easier to shorten the school week than fire teachers.

How about closing schools to save money? This proposition leads to another political hornet's nest when parents suddenly find out that one of the schools being closed is one attended by their children. In April 2010, the DeKalb County, Georgia school board announced school closings as their answer to the budget crisis. Several board members voted against school closings and called for increasing taxes. Board member Eugene Walker declared, "I'm not going to vote for any proposal that does not include a millage increase. I feel if we adopt the budget that is being proposed, it will have a severe and very adverse impact on our capability to teach our kids."[45] Other school board members urged tax increases over school closings. One parent, Latasha Walker, proposed trimming money spent on administrators and lawsuits. "My daughter's school is not on the list, but it seemed to be a coincidence that the majority of recommended schools were African-American," she said. "I'm bothered by the fact that any schools on the north or south side are even up for closure."[46]

These are all proposals for cutting costs during financially troubling times. Can the above actions be an indication of what politicians, administrators, teachers, and the public consider important in schools? Is the choice of cutting one item over another from the school budget an indication of what is considered valuable in education? It is difficult to answer these questions because of the complicated nature of school budget decisions and the lack of clear public expressions of concern from the various stakeholders. One could ask: What else can school districts cut beside big ticket items like salaries and plant costs?

Are stakeholder decisions influenced by personal self-interest? They probably do play an important role. Teachers and their unions are most likely interested in protecting their salaries and jobs. The same is true of administrators. Parents are probably not too keen on budget cuts that shorten the school week or year and force them to worry about what to do with their kids if they work. Most likely parents and teachers are not interested in larger classes. Many property owners and business people are against increased taxes and therefore they favor budget cuts.

Educational Administrators

As budget cuts came crashing down on school districts the American Association of School Administrators quickly surveyed its membership in 2008 and 2009 about the effects on their districts and their feelings about spending priorities. One thing they noticed in their surveys was that between 2008 and 2009 the number of respondents indicating that their districts were inadequately funded increased from 67 percent to 75 percent, with 21 percent of respondents indicating that they would have to engage in short-term borrowing to meet payrolls and accounts payable.[47]

The reader can get some sense of the economic priorities of school administrators from the results when they were asked to rank projects that could be funded under the American Recovery and Reinvestment Act of 2009. The following is a list of their spending priorities ranked from high to low. The percentages indicate the numbers of respondents who selected the item as high priority, priority, and low priority.

1. High priority
   a. Classroom technology (57 percent)
   b. School modernization/repair (54 percent)
   c. Safety/security measures (40 percent)
   d. Connectivity (39 percent)
   e. Professional development (37 percent)
2. Priority
   a. Classroom equipment/supplies (48 percent)

   b. Software (48 percent)
   c. Supportive technology for students with needs (48 percent)
   d. Professional development (47 percent)
   e. Textbooks (44 percent)
3. Low priority
   a. Health equipment (67 percent)
   b. Start a new career/technical program (66 percent)
   c. Art education equipment/supplies (65 percent)
   d. Physical education equipment/supplies (64 percent)
   e. Music education equipment/supplies (57 percent)[48]

   How should this list of priorities be interpreted? According to this list, administrators seem to favor spending money on hardware (including connectivity), buildings, safety, and professional development. They don't seem to want to spend much money on health and gym equipment and career, art, and music education. The choice of professional development is difficult to interpret because the content of the professional development is not specified. This list then favors items that might be related to human capital education in contrast to an arts-based education. There is no way of knowing if this is just personal preference or the reality of problems in implementing human capital education.
   In approving school budgets, what do school boards favor? In response to the economic downturn, the report found school boards making the following decisions:

1. Most frequent budget cuts
   i.   Increasing class size more than tripled from 13 percent in 2008–09 to 44 percent in 2009–10
   ii. Schools laying off personnel quadrupled from 11 percent in 2008–09 to 44 percent in 2009–10
2. Least frequent budget cuts
   i.   Schools cutting academic programs (such as academic intervention and Saturday classes) more than tripled from 7 percent in 2008–09 to 22 percent in 2009–10
   ii. Schools deferring maintenance increased from 21 percent in 2008–09 to 33 percent in 2009–10
   iii. The percentage of schools cutting extracurricular activities almost tripled from 10 percent in 2008–09 to 28 percent in 2009–10.[49]

   The above list of administrative priorities does not necessarily represent the economic preferences of school boards. Personnel costs are often the biggest budget item. An increase in class sizes is a method of cutting personnel. This could also be the reason for deferring maintenance since this budget item doesn't directly impact the size of the teaching staff or academic instruction.

Teachers

Of course, teachers are also an economic interest group concerned with higher pay and benefits. Politically, teacher union representatives negotiate with local school boards for better pay and benefits and lobby state and federal governments for increased school funding. The political techniques used by the unions are exemplified by their reactions to the educational cuts resulting from the financial crisis beginning in 2008. The American Federation of Teachers (AFT) posted on its website: "Urgent! Call Now!"[50] Below this call to arms was an image of a telephone. Who were teachers to call? They were to call their Senators demanding passage of the American Recovery and Reinvestment Act:

> Tell your Senators to act now by passing a meaningful jobs bill that will bring needed relief to our communities where unemployment is at nearly 10 percent. Failure to preserve and create jobs endangers our economic progress, putting at risk any sustainable recovery.[51]

It is important to recognize that the AFT is committed to support the general organized labor movement besides worrying about teachers' salaries. The union exhorted its membership to write their Congressional representatives using a form letter posted on its website that opened: "I'm writing to ask that you act now to pass a meaningful jobs bill . . . I urge you to include these points as you develop the final jobs bill."[52] The form letter mixed pleas for increased funding of Medicaid, supplemental unemployment insurance, expansion of COBRA health care benefits, and additional food assistance with concerns about school funding: "Rebuild America's schools, roads and energy systems. Funds must be included in the jobs bill that will put people to work to fix our schools, invest in transportation, green technology and energy efficiency."[53]

In contrast to the AFT, the National Education Association (NEA) uses more Internet tools to rally its members and create a sense of community. The NEA uses the social website Facebook to unite its members and create a sense of community struggle among teachers. The Facebook site is called "Speak Up For Education and Kids."[54] On the Facebook site there are YouTube videos urging teachers to pressure Congress to provide added funding for teacher jobs. One video is titled "The Issue is JOBS" while another is titled "Ask Congress to Appreciate Teachers by Saving Jobs."[55] The use of Facebook also makes available a social networking tool that allows for easy dialogue between union members.

Despite the more technologically sophisticated methods of the NEA, both unions rely on traditional political pressure to try to persuade law-makers to back funding that would save teaching jobs. What is important to note about these efforts is that members are primarily being urged to lobby Congress for funds rather than state governments. The economic crisis which busted state budgets resulted in union leaders seeing federal aid to state education budgets as the major hope for protecting teaching jobs. One might argue that the economic crisis strengthened the educational governance role of the federal government.

Framework for Understanding the Politics of School Finance

My goal in these concluding sections of the chapter is to give the reader a basic framework for thinking about future educational finance issues. This framework is reflected in the preceding discussions in this chapter. The framework I am suggesting contains three basic economic questions regarding the financing of education. The remainder of the chapter will consider these questions.

- Who should pay?
- How should educational monies be distributed?
- How much money should be spent on education?

Who Should Pay?

Answers to the first question most often consider public benefits. If there are no public benefits, then arguing that all people including those without children should support public schools is difficult. Economists make a distinction between private and public benefits. Private benefits from education include increased personal income; personal satisfaction gained through learning new skills and acquiring new knowledge; and increased political and social power. Private benefits can be used as a justification for personal investment in education. In other words, one could argue that all people should pay directly for education because it is an investment that yields an economic return in the form of higher lifetime wages. Public benefits include economic growth, political stability, efficient use of labor, and reduction in crime.

To understand the role of public benefits in the debate about the financial support of schooling, consider the arguments of nineteenth-century common school crusader Horace Mann. Mann provided the basic justification for public support of schools in the United States. In campaigning for public support of the common school ideal, Mann needed to convince all adults that they should support public schools even if they had no children or sent their children to private schools. If schooling provided only private benefits, such as increased income or personal satisfaction, there might be little justification for all members of the community having to pay for the support of a common school. Purely private benefits from schooling would support the argument that users should bear the expenses of public schools.

Mann made economic benefits the center of his argument that all adults should support public schooling. He argued that property values depended on the quality of the surrounding community and on improvements made in that community. In addition, a present owner of property was merely a trustee of wealth inherited from a previous owner. This meant that personal wealth was dependent on the wealth of the community and the wealth of previous generations.

If schooling increases the skills and abilities of one individual, Mann argued, then all individuals in the community would benefit and all future generations would benefit. According to this reasoning, even if an individual had no children or sent his or her children to private schools, he or she still benefited economically from common schools because an educated generation increased the value of the individual's property. Therefore, the public benefits of schooling justified taxing all members of the community to provide financial support for schools. Mann wrote, about successive generations of citizens of Massachusetts, "The property of this Commonwealth is pledged for the education of all its youth, up to such point as will save them from poverty and vice and prepare them for the adequate performance of their social and civil duties."[56]

Mann's arguments remain the major justification for general support of public schooling. In this argument, the wealth of a community depends on the level of crime and poverty, the fulfillment of political obligations by its citizens, and the skills and knowledge of its workers.

While efforts have been made to use education to eliminate crime and poverty, there is still no proof that it can effectively do so. Despite this lack of documentation, educators continue to claim these as public benefits from education. In the twentieth century, the major public benefit claimed for public schooling was the improvement of the work force or, in the language of the twentieth and twenty-first centuries, the development of human capital.

Working within Mann's theory, twentieth-century economist Theodore Schultz elaborated on human capital as a major public benefit of education. Schultz defined human capital as that form of capital that is an integral part of a person and enhances the capabilities of individuals to produce. As a form of capital, human capital lends itself to investment. These potential investments include health facilities and services, the migration of individuals to adjust to changing job opportunities, study programs for adults, on-the-job training, and formally organized education.[57]

Schultz admitted, however, that deciding the amount each factor contributes to the improvement of human capital is difficult. Despite this difficulty, Schultz tried to decide the relationship between education and economic growth. He argued that if one compared increases in labor and capital invested in the U.S. economy between 1919 and 1957 with the 2.1 percent per annum economic growth during that period, then the economic growth could not be explained by inputs from the quantity of labor and capital. In other words, whereas the number of hours of labor and capital increased each year by 1 percent, the output of the system increased by 3.1 percent. For Schultz, part of the unexplained 2.1 percent annual increase was the result of improvement in human capital, which in turn was a consequence of increased education levels.[58]

Regarding public benefits, Schultz was concerned about the economic payoff of investment in education. Using three different estimates, he concluded, "The increase in the education per person of the labor force that occurred between 1929 and 1957 explains between 36 and 70 percent of the otherwise unexplained increase in earnings per laborer, depending on which of the estimates of the rate of return that is applied."[59] Even at the lower figure of 36 percent, education made a significant contribution to increasing national income.

In the tradition of Horace Mann, Schultz concluded that the modern state had nothing to lose and everything to gain by pouring money into education. Schultz's optimism about the importance of education in economic development continued after the 1960s:

> Education has become a major source of economic growth in winning the abundance that is to be had by developing a modern agriculture and industry. Having this abundance simply would not be possible if people were predominantly illiterate and unskilled.[60]

Other studies seemed to confirm Schultz's optimism about the economic benefits of education. Economist Edward Denison concluded that education accounted for a fifth of the increase in national income in the United States between 1929 and 1957, and studies of underdeveloped countries seemed to confirm that investment in education resulted in economic growth.[61]

The preceding arguments justify requiring all citizens to pay for support of public schools. In addition, Horace Mann's argument that individual wealth is dependent on the general wealth of the community, which in turn is dependent on the educational level of community members, leads to an argument that the wealthy should pay higher taxes to support schools. The one problem with this argument, as discussed previously, is that the wealthy are able to protect the educational benefits of their children by living in high-income school districts.

How Should Educational Monies Be Distributed?

A major political issue is public financing of private schools. Since the nineteenth century, many religious schools, particularly Catholic schools, have sought some form of government aid by arguing that private schools produce public benefits similar to public schools. Private school parents often argue that they must pay twice to support the educational system. First, they pay taxes to support public schools, and, second, they pay tuition fees to send their children to private schools. In addition, private school parents argue that by paying tuition fees for private schools they reduce public school expenditures.

On the other hand, common school advocates argue, as Mann did, for the importance of all children attending a public school. Part of the public benefit of attendance at a common school was the creation of common moral and political values.[62] In addition, government financial support of private schools continues to raise the issue of separation of church and state. Besides the issue of government support of privately controlled education, there is the explosive political issue of inequality of educational funding.

In recent years, the issues of government aid to private schools and inequality of educational funding have been linked to proposals for vouchers and tuition tax credits. Under a voucher system, a voucher worth a particular sum of money would be given to parents to spend on their child's education. Tuition tax credit plans, alternatively, would allow parents to credit educational expenses to their income taxes. Both plans offer the possibilities of government funding of private schools and erasing differences in educational expenditures. For instance, vouchers or tax credits could be given to parents who send their children to private schools, and an equivalent amount of money could be provided to all children.

Economist Milton Friedman first made the link between vouchers and ending inequality in educational expenditures. His arguments for the use of vouchers provided an early justification for the choice plans supported by the Reagan and Bush administrations. Government support of education, he argues, can be justified by the necessity of maintaining a stable and democratic society, and the maintenance of these public benefits requires that each person receive "a minimum amount of schooling of a specified kind."[63]

Unlike Mann, Friedman believes that public benefits justify government financing of education, but they do not justify "the actual administration of educational institutions by the government, the 'nationalization,' as it were, of the bulk of the 'education industry.'" He proposes government subsidization of education by giving parents vouchers "redeemable for a specified maximum sum per child per year if spent on 'approved' educational services."[64] Through a system of vouchers, parents would purchase education for their children from private institutions. Public benefits would be guaranteed by the government regulating private schools to ensure that schools met certain minimum standards and had certain minimum content.

An important reason Friedman gives for a voucher system is the inequality in financing public schools. Although Mann dreamed of the rich and poor being mixed in the same school buildings, the reality is a district system with rich and poor school districts. The district system allows the wealthy to live in school districts where more money is spent per pupil than in districts with low-income families. The option to move into school districts that spend more per pupil is not usually available to low-income families because they cannot afford housing in the wealthier district. The existence of the district system, as I discussed previously, is one major source of inequality of educational opportunity.

Friedman argues that these disparities result in schools that create social class divisions in education: "Under present arrangements, stratification of residential areas effectively restricts the intermingling of children from decidedly different backgrounds."[65] Further, parents can still send their children to private schools. Except for parochial education, Friedman argues, only a few can afford private schooling, which results in further stratification.

Friedman gives the example of a low-income African American family in an inner city trying to obtain a high-quality education for their gifted child. The district system makes it almost impossible for the family to send the child to a school outside the inner city. Friedman argues that because good schools are in high-income neighborhoods, it is difficult for a poor family to save extra money for a child's education and afford the expense of moving to a wealthy suburb.

Friedman's voucher proposal for solving disparities in educational finance, while widely debated, was never implemented, resulting in a continued divide between rich and poor school districts, with the only substantial changes resulting from the previously discussed involvement of the judiciary.

How Should Money for Education Be Collected?

The ideal situation for most taxpayers is to pay a minimum of taxes, while having a maximum amount spent on the education of their children. The traditional reliance on local property taxes for the support of schooling provided this type of opportunity. As the California Supreme Court found in Serrano v. Priest, property taxes are often regressive forms of taxation. In other words, property taxes can be a greater burden for middle- and low-income families than for wealthy families. In the Serrano case, the California Supreme Court gave an example of this situation: "Baldwin Park citizens, who paid a school tax of $5.48 per $100 of assessed valuation, can spend less than half as much on education as Beverly Hills residents, whom they taxed at a rate of $2.38 per $100."[66]

Most corporations resist increased corporate taxes to support education and favor reliance on lotteries and sales taxes. Corporate resistance to taxation for schools is described in Ira Shor's book *Culture Wars: School and Society in the Conservative Restoration, 1969–1984*. Shor argues that business leaders in the early 1980s, while campaigning for state school reform, saw to it that increased taxes would fall primarily on the shoulders of the poor and the lower middle class. "Once public acceptance of the crisis and of official solutions emerged," Shor writes, "it was time to present the bill. Regressive taxes were identified as the source of funds to finance school excellence."[67]

Shor argues that strong resistance to increased taxes was overcome by claims that the failure of the public schools was a major cause of economic decline. As a result, tax increase plans that avoided significant increases in corporate taxes and relied on regressive funding, particularly sales taxes and lotteries, which primarily affect the poor and lower middle class, spread from state to state. In Shor's words,

> This strategy generated new revenues from the bottom in hard times, while protecting key constituencies at the top military-industrial complex, high-tech corporate profits, the rich and their tax loopholes, tax abatements for corporate construction in local areas, the oil depletion allowance, etc.[68]

Shor accuses business interests of having adopted a Machiavellian attitude in the early 1980s, when, rather than pay increased taxes, business interests gave their support directly to schools through grants, partnerships, and direct aid. Shor writes,

> Businesses in the third phase plan were called upon to "do their part," by getting more involved in schools, adopting poor districts like orphans, donating over-age equipment, offering excess supplies and furniture, and by lending experts to short staffed departments. All this generosity was tax-deductible.[69]

Problems associated with the use of property taxes are exacerbated when tax abatements are granted to corporations. Professor of Education Michael Apple commented, "Companies are caught in a contradictory situation. They want more spent on education but prefer that it not come out of their own pockets."[70]

Examples of the effect of tax abatements exist across the country. For example:

- Corpus Christi, Texas, lost $900,000 in tax support because of breaks given to local companies. On the other hand, local companies donated $250,000 to the school system. Consequently, corporations reduced their support of the schools by $650,000, while projecting an image of increasing financial support.
- In Wichita, Kansas, local companies reduced their tax support of schools through concessions by $1.6 million, while donating $1.1 million.[71]

Tax concessions at the state level proved the biggest aid to business. The issue of state tax concessions will increase in importance as state governments assume a greater role in school finance issues. For example:

- Florida granted $500 million in concessions to businesses through breaks in state sales taxes, fuel costs, and machinery. These concessions overshadowed the $32 million given to schools.
- In Washington, tax concessions to businesses have come under increasing attack by the state teachers unions. A particular concern was the concessions given to the Boeing Corporation, which received breaks on sales taxes totaling $900 million.[72]

Businesses can win these tax concessions by threatening to leave a local area or state or by demanding breaks before locating in a given area. They defend their tax exemptions as necessary for remaining competitive. Nevertheless, in compensating for these tax reductions by making contributions to the schools, they can exert greater control over education. Corporate contributions can be made for specific educational programs and, therefore, shape local school practices.

Tax concessions to businesses represent only one part of the current protest over collection of taxes to support schools. During the 1980s, changes in local, state, and federal taxes resulted in a major redistribution of the tax burden. According to economist Robert Reich, the federal tax burden for the top fifth of taxpayers dropped from 27.3 to 25.8 percent, while the rate for the bottom fifth increased from 8.4 to 9.7 percent. Reich found that the combined federal, state, and local taxes on the top 1 percent of American earners had declined from 39.6 percent in 1966 to 26.8 percent at the end of the 1980s. This was followed by further lowering of tax rates for the wealthy during the administration of President George W. Bush from 2000 to 2008.[73]

Those objecting to decreases in taxes on businesses and the wealthy, and who are concerned about equalizing school financing, face major problems in political organization. Obviously, workers in the educational system have the greatest interest in increasing taxes on businesses and the wealthy. Teachers unions now play an active role in trying to change tax structures. On the other hand, school board members and administrators in wealthy school districts resist any changes that might threaten their privileged positions. Consequently, educators from these districts are often at odds with educators who advocate equalization of funding. Those who have the most to gain—taxpayers and parents in low-wealth school districts—are poorly organized to deal with complex tax and school finance issues in state legislatures.[74]

Clearly, the methods of collecting taxes for schools and equalization of funding will continue to be two of the major educational issues in the twenty-first century. The conflict generated by these two issues will frequently pit business against teachers unions and the poor against the wealthy. All will be seeking to maximize their educational and economic advantages.

How Much Money Should Be Spent on Education?

Any society will have some limit on its resources; therefore, no society can provide maximum amounts for all of its government agencies. Obviously, most government agencies would like to maximize their revenues. Under political pressure, Congress and state legislatures must decide how to distribute money among human services, defense, law enforcement, and many other government functions.

Political philosopher Amy Gutmann provides guidelines for considering this problem. Concerned about the amount of resources that a democratic state should devote to schooling as opposed to other social ends, she argues there are four possible guiding principles. The first principle, maximization, would result in the government spending as much money on education as necessary for maximizing the life chances of all children. The second principle, equalization, involves the government spending enough money to raise the life chances of the disadvantaged child to the level of those of the most advantaged child. Meritocracy, the third principle, would distribute educational money according to ability and desire to learn. Gutmann adopts a fourth principle, the democratic threshold principle, only after rejecting the other three principles.[75]

Gutmann argues that the principle of maximization holds a moral ransom over society. In fact, it suggests that citizens should give up everything they value for the sake of education. The problem is that some claims for improving life chances might be trivial. In fact, operating under this principle, it would be difficult to establish any criteria for denying educational expenses. Consequently, it is difficult, if not impossible, to fund schools according to this principle.

Gutmann also rejects the principle of equalizing the chances of less advantaged children with those of more advantaged children because of the possible increase of government intrusion in daily lives: "To equalize educational opportunity, the state would have to intrude so far into family life as to violate the equally important liberal ideal of family autonomy."[76] In addition, she argues that equalization requires eliminating all differences in cultural, intellectual, and emotional dispositions—something that she believes is neither possible nor desirable.

Gutmann finds the argument for meritocracy completely undemocratic because it does not provide average and below-average students with an education adequate for democratic citizenship. Overall, Gutmann finds it difficult to dismiss the meritocratic principle. Nevertheless, as she points out, enough money to provide an adequate training in citizenship could be spent on all children while extra money is being spent on children with greater intellectual ability. Still, Gutmann argues that the principle must be tempered by democratic principles. In other words, within a democratic framework, a meritocracy should not mean that more money should be distributed to those with greater intellectual abilities, but that the population may decide to make that type of distribution.

The democratic threshold principle, according to Gutmann, allows for this type of flexibility. It allows for unequal distribution of educational money but only after enough money is provided to educate all children for democratic citizenship. Following in the tradition of Horace Mann, Gutmann believes that the major public benefit from education is the training of democratic citizens. Recognizing the difficulty of determining this standard for the distribution of money, she nevertheless feels that it should be the principle. Working under this principle, citizens or their elected representatives would decide how much money to appropriate for education.

Of course, citizens and elected representatives might not function according to the democratic threshold principle. Gutmann sees the principle as a moral guide for decision-making. Her principles take on a different meaning when cast into the real world of educational politics. For instance, let us consider each of her principles according to the assumption that people want to maximize their educational benefits while reducing their costs.

Within the framework of these assumptions, one could argue that the maximization principle might be supported by all people with children. However, this would mean that they would have to sacrifice other social goods for maximum spending on education. The only group that might favor the maximization principle would be educators, who would greatly benefit from maximum spending on education.

The equalization principle might be supported by a variety of groups. Parents of children with special needs would be interested in schools giving their children an equal chance. Dominated racial and ethnic groups might be concerned with maximizing their children's life chances. Of course, low-income families would have an important stake in any equalization plan. Obviously, parents with intellectually talented children would tend to support plans for distributing money according to the principle of meritocracy. Because of a variety of factors, including the cultural environment of the family, the role of peer groups, and biases within the school and in standardized tests, students identified as academically talented tend to come from upper-income families. Consequently, it is these families, as opposed to low-income families, who would tend to support the meritocracy principle.

Identifying groups that might support the democratic threshold principle is difficult. It could be argued that all people support the idea of schools preparing all children for democratic citizenship. Nevertheless, the idea of democratic citizenship is vague. Unions might want schools to prepare children for an industrial democracy, while conservatives might have a more law-and-order idea of citizenship. I would argue that because of the difficulty in defining good citizenship (Gutmann has her own definition) the democratic threshold principle is unworkable.

The most important of Gutmann's principles for understanding the distribution of money for education are equalization and meritocracy. When social concerns about the poor are at the top of the agenda, as they have been since the 1960s, the equalization principle becomes most important. When the emphasis is on educating more engineers and scientists, as in the 1950s and 1980s, the meritocracy principle becomes important.

School Finance in a Global Context

When considered in a global context those arguing that money is not the solution to problems in U.S. education might be right. It is clear from international comparisons that the United States is not stingy in funding its schools. It is the world's leading country in educational expenditures. OECD's *Education at a Glance 2009: OECD Indicators* reports that the United States spent more per pupil from primary through higher education than any other country. As reported in 2009, the United States spent more than $13,000 per student annually while the average for OECD countries (member nations are the wealthiest in the world) was $8,857 annually.[77] In 2005, the Organization for Economic Cooperation and Development (OECD) reported that the United States (7.1 percent) followed Denmark (7.4 percent) and Korea (7.2 percent) in the total share of gross domestic product devoted to educational spending.[78]

U.S. expenditure on education remains near the top of the list when expenditures for primary, secondary, and higher education are separated out. Global comparisons of spending on primary education show the United States comes second after Luxembourg which spends about $14,000 annually for each primary student and about $18,000 for each secondary student. The United States spends more than $9,000 annually on each primary school student and about $10,000 on each secondary student. The United States leads other nations in spending on higher education, at the rate of $25,109 annually per student in public institutions as compared to the average for OECD countries of a little more than $12,000 annually per student.[79]

Where the U.S. lags behind other nations is in salaries for secondary school teachers with fifteen or more years of experience. This may be a crucial issue if one assumes that experience results in a better teacher and that high teacher salaries result in the retention of experienced teachers. Luxembourg leads OECD nations with an average annual salary for secondary teachers of $90,000, followed by Switzerland (+$60,000) and Germany (about $59,000). The average for U.S. teachers is a little over $50,000.[80]

In summary, the "money myth" about improving U.S. education might be correct since the U.S. is a leading world spender on schooling. Those criticizing the quality of U.S. schools certainly can't point at the lack of spending as the source of the problem. About the only thing that can be pointed at is the relatively low salaries paid to experienced teachers when compared to some other OECD countries. Of course, given the rhetoric about schooling discussed in Chapter 2, politicians may be wrong about the so-called failure of American public schools. American schools may be a success compared to other nations considering the large enrollment of children of immigrant populations who have a great deal of linguistic diversity. One thing is for sure—the United States can't be criticized for the amount it spends on education when compared with other OECD countries.

The Economics of Schooling in the Global Labor Market

A chief characteristic of the emerging new world order in the twenty-first century is the internationalization of the labor force. Workers, corporate leaders, and companies increasingly move from country to country in search of higher wages or, for companies, in search of a cheap labor supply. As companies move, their management with their spouses and children also move. The internationalization of the labor force is affecting education in many ways.

It was President Bill Clinton's Secretary of Labor Robert Reich who in the 1990s articulated U.S. policies regarding schooling and the global labor supply.[81] His analysis was based on human capital economics which assumes that education is a key factor in economic growth and finding high-paying jobs in the global economy. I will consider Reich's arguments regarding schooling and global labor supply in the context of recent reports from OECD.

Reich labeled the upper strata of the new international force "symbolic analysts." He argued that this group of global workers are losing their allegiance to any particular nation and are withdrawing support from national infrastructures, including public schools. Secondly, Reich claims symbolic analysts require an education that emphasizes higher order thinking and technical skills. Thirdly, the international quality of the labor force is resulting in demands for multicultural forms of education in most developed nations of the world. Specifically, occupations that are typical of symbolic analysts are lawyers, investment bankers, computer experts, corporate managers, engineers, scientists, software developers, advertising executives, media experts, writers, journalists, and college professors. It is this group of occupations that is benefiting, according to Reich, from the redistribution of incomes. The remaining occupations are classified by Reich as production, service, farmers and miners, and miscellaneous, including government workers and teachers.[82]

Wielding the most economic power and seeking to maximize educational benefits, the education of symbolic analysts has topped the educational reform agenda since the 1980s. This was reflected in calls for more academic requirements for high school graduation and a stress on higher order thinking skills. Reich states, "The formal education of an incipient symbolic analyst thus entails refining four basic skills: abstraction, system thinking, experimentation, and collaboration."[83]

Of course, symbolic analysts, who understand the wage structure of the present international economy, want their children to enter similar occupations. The key, of course, to entering these occupations is the right education. Nevertheless, while symbolic analysts are seeking a good education for their children, they are attempting to withdraw financial support from the nation's infrastructure. As mentioned previously, support of the infrastructure through paying taxes has declined significantly for upper-income groups. As their tax contributions decline, symbolic analysts demand more educational benefits for their children.

Several options exist for educating the children of symbolic analysts. One option is for symbolic analysts to abandon public schooling completely by sending their children to private schools and reducing the taxes they pay for the support of public schools. Certainly, any form of voucher or tuition tax credit that would help this process would be welcomed by symbolic analysts. Another option is for symbolic analysts to live in privileged suburban communities, where public schools are clearly designed to provide the best education necessary for entering upper-income occupations. If the symbolic analyst cannot live in a privileged suburban community, then the next option is a choice plan. By being able to select from a wide variety of offerings, a choice plan would allow symbolic analysts to send their children to the best schools in their area. In addition to concerns about educating symbolic analysts there are worries about the integration into the U.S. labor market of immigrant service and production workers.[84]

Reich's analysis of the global labor market impacted President Clinton's administration regarding the educating of workers for the global economy and added another element to the ongoing emphasis on human capital economics that stretched into the twenty-first century. An assumption was that gearing the school system to prepare students for the global economy would ensure that most American school graduates would get the highest-paying jobs in the global economy, namely as symbolic analysts.

In OECD countries tertiary or higher education does result in higher personal income. However, the value of a higher education varies between countries and according to gender. According to OECD's 2009 *Education at a Glance*: "Tertiary education brings substantial rewards in most countries and the present value of the gross earnings premium for males exceeds USD 300 000 in Italy and the United States over the working life."[85] Continued labor market discrimination against women is reflected in the finding that returns on investment in higher education are lower for females, except—and this is where differences in social organization, labor market needs, and laws come into play—"in Australia, Denmark, Korea, Norway, Spain and Turkey where the returns on the overall investment are higher for females than for males."[86] Variations in the economic value of higher education indicate the effect of local economic circumstances on the value of personal investment in higher education. OECD reports,

> Tertiary education brings substantial rewards in the Czech Republic, Hungary, Ireland, Italy, Poland, Portugal and the United States where an investment generates over USD 100,000 indicating strong incentives to continue education. The present value of the gross earnings premium exceeds USD 300,000 in Italy and the United States. The rewards for tertiary education are substantially lower in Denmark, France, New Zealand, Norway and Sweden where returns are USD 40,000 or below.[87]

The importance of particular national economic conditions is also reflected in the income for graduates from each level of education. In general, the more education an individual receives the higher her or his income. But if you want to receive maximum income gains from education as compared to the local population then you should go to Brazil, where post-secondary education provides males and females with about twice the relative income of the local population as compared to twelve other

OECD countries. The United States is tenth on the list of benefits in relative income from post-secondary education.[88]

In summary, arguments regarding investment in education as the key to income improvement must be tempered by the reality of local economic circumstances. OECD statistics indicate the variation in the economic impact of schooling. Supposedly, according to current rhetoric, education will improve the ability of workers to compete in a global economy. However, it might be the case that workers are primarily competing for jobs in local rather than global labor markets. There is also the issue of global migration of workers and "brain drain" from some countries of highly educated workers. What is the effect of "brain drain" into the United States on the incomes of American graduates of higher education? I will consider the issue of "brain migration" in the next chapter.

Conclusion

The economics of schooling adds an important perspective to the politics of education. It is an analytical tool that raises important questions about who benefits and who pays. Educational spending should be scrutinized according to public and private benefits. Since the 1990s, the major direction of school reform may have been for the benefit of those entering upper-income occupations.

Every educational proposal needs to be examined according to who pays. As discussed in this chapter, the recent pattern is for the wealthy and corporations to pay less for the support of public schools, and for middle- and lower-income groups to pay more for the support of public schools. In addition, every educational proposal should be considered for the economic benefits it provides for educational workers. Admittedly, this type of examination places the actions of educators in a cynical light, but one must remember that educators are people, and, like many people, they want to increase their economic benefits.

There is an opinion among some educators that more money will not improve American schools. Other factors might be more important such as teacher efficacy and control, advanced degrees for teachers, and teacher development. Equity and adequacy lawsuits have increased the funding to school districts serving low-income families. However, judicial decisions have not helped middle-income families since schools serving high- and low-income families spend more per student than those serving the 60 percent of U.S. families considered as middle-income.

In reflecting on the unfolding of education politics, the reader should keep in mind the previously mentioned questions: Who should pay? How should educational monies be distributed? How much money should be spent on education? The reader should also question the relationship between more investment in education and solutions to economic problems, such as income growth. OECD statistics indicate that the economic value of education varies with local circumstances.

In the next chapter I will consider American education politics in the framework of global education policies and I will again touch on some of these economic issues. Certainly general global educational issues include questions of who should pay, how the money should be distributed, and who benefits.

Notes

1 Angela Delli Santi, "NJ governor wants local teachers union head who wrote memo joking about his death fired" (April 12, 2010). Retrieved from *Los Angeles Times* http://www/latimes.com/news/nationworld/nation/wire/sns-ap-us-nj-governor-union-memo,0,4852373.story on April 12, 2010.
2 Ibid.
3 Ibid.
4 W. Norton Grubb, "Correcting the Money Myth: Re-Thinking School Resources," *Kappan* (December 2009/January 2010), pp. 51–52.
5 Paul T. Hill, "Spending Money When It Is Not Clear What Works," *Peabody Journal of Education* (2008), p. 238.
6 Ibid., p. 241.
7 Paul T. Hill and Marguerite Roza, "The End of School Finance As We Know It," *Education Week* (April 30, 2008), p. 36.
8 National Center for Education Statistics, *The Condition of Education 2009* (Washington, DC: U.S. Department of Education, 2009), p. 80.
9 Ibid., p. 82.
10 Ibid.
11 James Guthrie, "Next Needed Steps in the Evolution of American Education Finance and Policy: Attenuating a Judicially Imposed Policy Distraction, Activating a Balanced Portfolio of K-12 School Reforms, Advancing Rationality as a Goal in Pursuing Productivity, Advocating Change in a Responsible and Effective Manner," *Peabody Journal of Education* (2008), p. 260.
12 Ibid., p. 261.
13 Grubb, "Correcting the Money Myth," pp. 52–53.
14 Guthrie, "Next Needed Steps," p. 265.
15 Robert C. Knoeppel, Deborah A. Verstegen, and James S. Rinehart, "What Is the Relationship between Resources and Student Achievement? A Canonical Analysis," *Journal of Education Finance* (Fall 2007), pp. 183–202.
16 G. Kennedy Greene, Luis A. Huerta, and Craig Richards, "Getting Real: A Different Perspective on the Relationship between School Resources and Student Outcomes," *Journal of School Finance* (Summer 2007), pp. 49–68.
17 W. Norton Grubb, "When Money Might Matter: Using NELS88 to Examine the Weak Effects of School Funding," *Journal of School Finance* (Spring 2006), p. 373.
18 Quoted in Jonathan Weisman, "Business's Words, Actions to Improve Education at Odds, Economist Argues," *Education Week* (March 13, 1991), pp. 1, 26.
19 Robert Reich, *The Work of Nations: Preparing Ourselves for 21st Century Capitalism* (New York: Alfred A. Knopf, 1991).
20 E.G. West, "The Political Economy of Public School Legislation," in *Studies*

in Education, No. 4 (Menlo Park, CA: Institute of Humane Studies, 1977), p. 19. This article was originally published under the same title in the October 1967 issue of the *Journal of Law and Economics*.

21 Ibid., p. 25.
22 Ibid., p. 20.
23 Jean Anyon, *Ghetto Schooling: A Political Economy of Urban Educational Reform* (New York: Teachers College Press, 1997).
24 Ibid., p. 104.
25 Ibid., p. 142.
26 Ibid., pp. 142–143.
27 Arthur Wise, *Rich Schools, Poor Schools* (Chicago: University of Chicago Press, 1968); and John Coons, William Clune, and Stephen Sugarman, *Private Wealth and Public Education* (Cambridge, MA: Harvard University Press, 1970).
28 Joel Spring, *American Education: An Introduction to Social and Political Aspects* (White Plains, NY: Longman, 1978), p. 227.
29 John E. Coons and Stephen D. Sugarman, *Education by Choice: The Case for Family Control* (Berkeley: University of California Press, 1978).
30 Spring, *American Education*, p. 228.
31 Guthrie, "Next Needed Steps," p. 272.
32 Alfred A. Lindseth, "A Reversal of Fortunes: Why the Courts Have Cooled to Adequacy Lawsuits" (September 12, 2007). Retrieved from http://www.edweek.org/ew/articles/2007/09/12/03lindseth.h27.html?tkn=SOZFiRyC1Ift i05uh4lcu3IDXdgRItt7q0w4&print=1 on April 22, 2010.
33 Ibid.
34 Ibid.
35 Ibid.
36 National Center for Education Statistics, *The Condition of Education 2009*, p. 86.
37 Ibid., p. 218.
38 Ibid., p. 80.
39 Ibid.
40 Jason Song, "Teachers Agree to Shorten LAUSD School Year" (April 11, 2010). Retrieved from *Los Angeles Times* http://www/latimes.comlatimes.com/news/local/la-me-lausd11-2010apr11,0,6136114.story.
41 Blair Stenvick, "Local Public Schools Suffer from Budget Cuts" (April 8, 2010). Retrieved from City on a Hill Press http://www.cityonahillpress.com/2010/04/08/local-public-schools-suffer-from-budget-cuts/ on April 10, 2010.
42 John O'Conner, "Ill. Lawmakers May Let Schools Adopt 4-Day Week" (April 12, 2010). Retrieved from *Business Week* http://www.businessweek.com/ap/financialnews/D9F1NSK03.htm on April 20, 2010.
43 Ibid.
44 Ibid.
45 Megan Matteucci, "DeKalb Adopts Budget with School Closings" (April 12, 2010). Retrieved from *Atlanta Journal-Constitution* http://www.ajc.com/news/dekalb/dekalb-adopts-budget-with-456408.html?printArticle=y on April 17, 2010.
46 Ibid.
47 Robert S. McCord and Noelle M. Ellerson, *Looking Back, Looking Forward: How the Economic Downturn Continues to Impact School Districts* (Arlington, VA: American Association of Administrators, 2009), pp. 2–3.
48 Ibid., p. 3.

49 Ibid., p. 4.
50 American Federation of Teachers, "It's about Jobs: Take Action Now!" Retrieved from http://www.aft.org/click2call/jobs_senate.cfm on April 30, 2010.
51 Ibid.
52 Ibid.
53 American Federation of Teachers, "It's about Jobs: Take Action Now!"
54 National Education Association, "Speak Up For Education and Kids." Facebook website. Retrieved from http://www.facebook.com/speakupforkids on May 7, 2010.
55 National Education Association, Facebook Videos, "The Issue is JOBS" and "Ask Congress to Appreciate Teachers by Saving Jobs." Retrieved from http://www.youtube.com/watch?v=yAEQQfDqf_s and http://www.youtube.com/watch?v=Q9D5MZH3S8o&feature=channel respectively on May 7, 2010.
56 Horace Mann, "Tenth Annual Report," in *The Republic and the School*, edited by Lawrence Cremin (1846; reprint, New York: Teachers College Press, 1957), p. 77.
57 Theodore W. Schultz, "Investment in Human Capital," in *Economics of Education*, edited by M. Blaug (Harmondsworth, UK: Penguin, 1968), pp. 22–24.
58 Theodore W. Schultz, "Education and Economic Growth," in *Social Forces Influencing American Education*, edited by Nelson Henry (Chicago: University of Chicago Press, 1961), pp. 48–51.
59 Ibid., p. 82.
60 Theodore W. Schultz, *Investment in Human Capital: The Role of Education and of Research* (New York: Free Press, 1971), p. 56.
61 Ibid., p. 69.
62 See Joel Spring, *The American School 1642–1990*, 2nd edn. (White Plains, NY: Longman, 1990), pp. 73–115.
63 Milton Friedman, *Capitalism and Freedom* (Chicago: University of Chicago Press, 1962), p. 86.
64 Ibid., p. 89.
65 Ibid., p. 92.
66 "Poorer New York School Districts Seek More Aid," *The New York Times* (May 6, 1991), pp. A1, B4.
67 Ira Shor, *Culture Wars: School and Society in the Conservative Restoration, 1969–1984* (Boston: Routledge & Kegan Paul, 1986), p. 152.
68 Ibid.
69 Ibid.
70 William Celis III, "Educators Complain Business Tax Breaks Are Costing Schools," *The New York Times* (May 22, 1991), p. A1.
71 Ibid., p. A23.
72 Ibid.
73 Reich, *The Work of Nations*, pp. 199–200.
74 Walter Garms, James Guthrie, and Lawrence Pierce, *School Finance: The Economics and Politics of Public Education* (Englewood Cliffs, NJ: Prentice Hall, 1978), p. 343.
75 Amy Gutmann, *Democratic Education* (Princeton, NJ: Princeton University Press, 1987), pp. 127–171.
76 Ibid., p. 132.
77 Organization for Economic Cooperation and Development, *Education at a Glance 2009: OECD Indicators* (Paris: OECD Publishing, 2009), p. 188.

78 National Center for Education Statistics, *The Condition of Education 2009*, p. 228.
79 Ibid., p. 192.
80 Ibid., p. 388.
81 Reich, *The Work of Nations*.
82 Ibid., pp. 175–197.
83 Ibid., p. 229.
84 Ibid., pp. 208–226.
85 OECD, *Education at a Glance 2009*, p. 153.
86 Ibid.
87 Ibid., p. 157.
88 Ibid., p. 139.

Chapter 8

Global Education Politics and the United States[*]

The complex interlinking of political groups in global and national education politics is illustrated by a session at the 2010 Annual Meeting of the American Educational Research Association (AERA) titled: "International Benchmarking: Current Contributions and Future Directions for Policymakers and Researchers."[1] I am using this AERA session to illustrate the interconnections of global education politics and national politics. My intention is to show how this AERA session and its context are illustrative of the global political interconnections driving educational policy-making between the following:

- Global intergovernmental organizations: Organization for Economic Cooperation and Development (OECD) and the World Bank
- NGOs: global nongovernment organizations
- National governments' sponsorship of global interconnections
- National governments' response to global education policies
- Global education associations
- Education business

There are other political forces than those listed above which I will discuss later in the chapter. After this illustration of the complexity of global education decision-making, I will discuss each political player in detail.

Benchmarking Global Standards and Tests

As mentioned previously in this book, President Barack Obama campaigned for national standards and tests that would be benchmarked against global standards and tests. By 2010, the U.S. Office of Education

---

[*] Some sections of this chapter have been taken from Joel Spring, *Globalization of Education: An Introduction* (New York: Routledge, 2009). These sections have been reorganized and expanded to emphasize the political structure of global schooling and its relationship to American educational politics.

was engaged in global benchmarking of tests used to measure student progress in achieving state standards. Global benchmarking of U.S. state curriculum standards and tests moves the determination of what knowledge is most worth teaching into an international arena.

The global benchmarking standards identified at this AERA session by U.S. Department of Education representative Valena Plisko are three global tests: PISA (Program for International Student Assessment), PIRLS (Progress in International Reading Literacy), and TIMSS (Trends in International Mathematics and Science Study).[2] In a brochure distributed by the National Center for Education Statistics of the U.S. Office of Education, "U.S. Participation in International Assessments," the above three tests are listed as global benchmarking standards along with the Program for the International Assessment of Adult Competencies (PIAAC).[3] Within the global context of AERA and among the session's presenters there was an unquestioning assumption that the standards to be used in benchmarking U.S. tests would be those of a global inter-governmental organization, the Organization for Economic Cooperation and Development (OECD), and a global nongovernment association, the International Association for the Evaluation of Educational Achievement.

The global context of global benchmarking efforts was highlighted at the 2010 AERA session by Robin Horn of the World Bank: "The World Bank's Benchmarking Education Systems for Results: Emerging Lessons in Building International Benchmarking System."[4] As I discuss later in this chapter, the World Bank is a major player in global education politics.

The two other presentations also involved global standardization. One presentation, "Studies in International Benchmarking," was made by Gary Phillips of the American Institutes for Research, where he is Vice President for Assessment. While the American Institutes for Research is a non-government and nonprofit global organization its staff is dependent on outside funding. The organization lists as a client the U.S. Department of Education. The organization claims: "AIR [American Institutes for Research] is one of the largest behavioral and social science research organizations in the world."[5] This organization clearly believes it is in the business of determining on a global scale what students should know: "Education Assessment and Evaluation: AIR's educational assessment work in developing countries helps governments determine what students should know and be able to do in relation to standards and curriculum."[6]

Adding another aspect to this global maze of education groups was a presentation by Michael Feuer: "International Benchmarking and the Rhetoric of Reform: From Research to Policy and Back." Feuer is the executive director of the Division of Behavioral and Social Sciences and Education at the National Research Council (NRC) of the National Academies. The National Academies is an umbrella organization for the National Academy of Engineering, the National Academy of Sciences, and the Institute for Medicine. The stated goal of the NRC's Board on Testing and Assessment is as follows:

> The Board on Testing and Assessment was created to assist policy-makers and the public by providing scientific expertise around critical issues of testing and assessment in education, the workplace, and the armed services. BOTA's fundamental role is to raise questions about —and provide guidance for judging—the technical qualities of tests and assessments and the intended and unintended consequences of their use.[7]

In addition to the above presenters was the discussant Felice Levine, executive director of AERA. AERA has an important role in the arena of global education politics. It is an international organization that provides for the global interchange and dissemination of education research and ideas. In addition to her role at AERA, Felice Levine serves as Interim Secretary General of the World Education Research Association (WERA). Officially established in 2009, the organization held its second official meeting the day after the ending of the 2010 AERA meeting. WERA's membership consists of twenty-seven education associations ranging from the All India Association of Educational Research to the Turkish Educational Research Association. Special sessions and receptions indicated the global presence of AERA. The 2010 AERA annual meeting was cosponsored by Beijing Normal University, East China Normal University, and Ambow Education Group. Ambow Education Group represents another player in global education politics, namely the education business. The Ambow Education Group advertises itself as follows:

> Ambow Education Group is a national provider of personalized educational and career enhancement services in China. With roots in the Silicon Valley, we have developed industry-leading, proprietary technologies that enable us to provide students with the highest quality of learning and educational services.[8]

How did PISA, PIRLS, and TIMSS become the benchmarking standards for American schools? My suspicion is that many parents, teachers, and school staff know little about the origin of these tests or how they became global standards. I cannot find any dissent to the use of the tests for benchmarking U.S. assessment standards. Why? One would think that the content of tests that indirectly shape what is taught in American schools would be part of a public discussion about state and national standards for American schools.

In summary, the above identification of participants at the 2010 annual AERA benchmarking session illustrates the complex interrelations in global education policy. The global benchmarking standards of PISA, PIRLS, and TIMSS are linked, as I discuss in the next section, to the intergovernmental organization OECD. The World Bank plays an important role in determining education standards in developing countries. The global sharing of education ideas takes place in organizations like AERA and WERA. Global nongovernment groups like the American Institutes for Research are political players in world education. Ambow is only one of many global for-profit education businesses that influence education policies. The participation of national governments in global education discussions is illustrated by the role of the U.S. Office of Education and U.S. National Research Council.

An important question related to global benchmarking of U.S. standards and tests is: What are the political forces behind making PISA, PIRLS, and TIMSS global education standards? In the next section, I will suggest the possible reasons for these tests holding power over global schools.

Global Academic Olympics: OECD and the International Association for the Evaluation of Educational Achievement (IEA)

PISA and TIMSS tests have a direct impact on the politics of national education systems. Writing about world education culture, David Baker and Gerald LeTendre assert that,

> After the first set of TIMSS results became public, the United States went into a kind of soul searching . . . The release of the more recent international study on OECD nations called PISA led Germany into a national education crisis. Around the world, countries are using the results of international tests as a kind of Academic Olympiad, serving as a referendum on their school system's performance.[9]

The potential global influence of PISA is vast since the participating member nations and partners represent, according to OECD, 90 percent of the world's economy.[10] OECD promotes PISA as an important element in the global knowledge economy: "PISA seeks to measure how well young adults, at age 15 and therefore approaching the end of compulsory schooling, are prepared to meet the challenges of today's knowledge societies—what PISA refers to as 'literacy'."[11]

The important thing to note about these tests is that they are supposed to address the needs of the so-called global knowledge economy. In other words, they reflect an internationalized version of human capital education designed to educate workers and promote economic growth. These goals for global schooling, it can be argued, primarily favor businesses interested in a steady stream of employees educated to work but not to be critical of economic and political conditions. Of course, like the United States, many in the global population accept the human capital argument and rush to school hoping for better employment.

The use of human capital arguments to justify international assessments can be tied to the overall mission of OECD. In describing the knowledge and skills tested, OECD's *PISA 2003 Assessment Framework* states:

> These are defined not primarily in terms of a common denominator of national school curricula but in terms of what skills are deemed to be *essential for future life* . . . They [national curricula] focus even less on more general competencies, developed across the curriculum, to solve problems and apply ideas and understanding to situations *encountered in life* [author's emphasis].[12]

In other words, PISA is creating global standards for the knowledge required to function in what OECD defines as the everyday life of a global economy. By shifting the emphasis from national curricula to global needs, PISA is defining educational standards for a global economy.

While OECD is responsible for PISA, the organization also works with the International Association for the Evaluation of Educational Achievement (IEA) in the development and implementation of TIMSS. Both PISA and TIMSS are considered tests that reflect the needs of the global economy and consequently serve dominant economic interests. This service to economic interests is the very basis for the original creation of OECD.

At the 2007 UNESCO Ministerial Round Table on Education and Economic Development, the OECD Secretary-General Angel Gurría stated the position of the organization on the linkage between education and economic growth.

> In a highly competitive globalized economy, knowledge, skills and know-how are key factors for productivity, economic growth and better living conditions . . . Our estimates show that adding one extra year to the average years of schooling increases GDP per capita by 4 to 6 per cent. Two main paths of transmission can explain this result: First, education builds human capital and enables workers to be more productive. Second, education increases countries' capacity to innovate—an indispensable prerequisite for growth and competitiveness in today's global knowledge economy.[13]

A similar message appeared in the 2007 OECD book *Human Capital*: "In *developed* economies, the value of knowledge and information in all their forms is becoming ever more apparent, a trend that is being facilitated by the rapid spread of high-speed information technology [author's emphasis]."[14]

OECD's 1961 founding document highlights its economic goals and its service to business interests. The document gives as the goal of OECD: "to achieve the highest sustainable economic growth and employment and a rising standard of living in Member countries, while maintaining financial stability, and thus to contribute to the development of the world economy."[15] From its original membership of twenty nations it has expanded to thirty-one of the richest nations of the world.[16] In addition, OECD provides expertise and exchanges ideas with more than 100 other countries including the least developed countries in Africa.[17] To promote economic growth in member nations and other nations, OECD focuses on the collection and dissemination of data including economic and education statistics on providing global benchmarks for schooling. The organization claims that:

> For more than 40 years, the OECD has been one of the world's largest and most reliable sources of comparable statistics, and economic and social data. As well as collecting data, the OECD monitors trends, analyses and forecasts economic developments and researches social changes or evolving patterns in trade, environment, agriculture, technology, taxation and more.[18]

OECD claims the following activities provide benefits to member and cooperating nations:

- Develops and reviews policies to enhance the efficiency and the effectiveness of education provisions and the equity with which their benefits are shared;
- Collects detailed statistical information on education systems, including measures of the competence levels of individuals;
- Reviews and analyzes policies related to aid provided by OECD members for expansion of education and training in developing nations.[19]

OECD's involvement in testing was made possible by the early work of IEA which demonstrated the possibility of making international comparisons of test scores. IEA was officially founded in 1967 by educators who had been working with UNESCO since 1958 to identify effective educational methods that could be shared between nations. According to the organization's official history, the original group of psychometricians, educational psychologists, and sociologists thought of education as a global enterprise that could be evaluated by national comparisons of test scores. They "viewed the world as a natural educational laboratory, where different school systems experiment in different ways to obtain optimal results in the education of their youth."[20] They assumed that educational goals were similar between nations but that the methods of achieving those goals were different. International testing, it was believed, would reveal to the world community the best educational practices.

Initially working with UNESCO, this original group of educators tried to prove that large-scale cross-cultural testing was possible when between 1959 and 1962 they tested 13-year-olds in twelve countries in mathematics, reading comprehension, geography, science, and non-verbal ability. The results of this project showed, according to an IEA statement, that "it is possible to construct common tests and questionnaires that 'work' cross-culturally. Furthermore, the study revealed that the effects of language differences can be minimized through the careful translation of instruments."[21]

Besides demonstrating the possibility of global testing programs, IEA claimed to have an effect on the curriculum of participating nations. After a 1970 seminar on Curriculum Development and Evaluation involving twenty-three countries, IEA officials asserted: "this seminar had a major influence on curriculum development in at least two-thirds of the countries that attended."[22] Through the years IEA has conducted a number of international testing programs and studies, including First International Mathematics Study (FIMS), Second International Mathematics Study (SIMS), International Science Study (ISS), Preprimary Education (PPP), Computers in Education Study (COMPED), Information Technology in Education (ITE), Civic Education Study (CIVED), and Languages in Education Study (LES).

In 1995, IEA worked with OECD to collect data for the Third International Mathematics and Science Study (TIMSS). IEA officials called the 1995 TIMSS "the largest and most ambitious study of comparative education undertaken."[23] And they claimed that "It was made possible by virtue of IEA experience and expertise, developed through the years of consecutive studies, which saw research vision combining with practical needs as defined by educational policy-makers."[24]

Today, IEA's stated goal is to have its tests and results used as benchmarks by nations, such as the United States, to judge the effectiveness of national school systems. In fact, the mission statement given below includes the creation of a global network of educational evaluators.

IEA Mission Statement

Through its comparative research and assessment projects, IEA aims to:

- Provide international benchmarks that may assist policy-makers in identifying the comparative strength and weaknesses of their educational systems

- Provide high-quality data that will increase policy-makers' understanding of key school- and non-school-based factors that influence teaching and learning
- Provide high-quality data which will serve as a resource for identifying areas of concern and action, and for preparing and evaluating educational reforms
- Develop and improve educational systems' capacity to engage in national strategies for educational monitoring and improvement
- Contribute to development of the world-wide community of researchers in educational evaluation[25]

In summary, international assessments promote global uniformity of curricula, the service of education to economic interests, and human capital economics. Business leaders in OECD might consider schooling for the knowledge economy as a means of ensuring compliant workers who contribute to economic growth and, consequently, corporate profits. In the context of global education politics those promoting these international assessments might be servants of economic power.

In what has been referred to as an international Academic Olympiad, international tests are used to measure the quality of national school systems. Politicians in countries undergoing testing might be held accountable for the success or failure of their school systems based on international comparisons of test scores. When test scores are comparatively high, politicians can brag about the success of their educational leadership. When test scores are comparatively low, politicians might be criticized and they might engage in educational reforms to raise scores on these tests. A consequence of this reform effort might be to align national education curricula with the tests, with a resulting uniformity of global school systems.

The World Bank: Human Capital in Developing Nations

I was startled by the admission of Robin Horn of the World Bank at the AERA benchmarking session that OECD countries needed to pay attention to education in developing nations because they would be their future source of labor. With declining birth rates, Horn argued, OECD countries would become increasingly dependent on foreign workers from developing nations. Therefore, the World Bank's educational endeavors in developing countries serve the economic interests of the richest nations. In 2010, the World Bank described its work:

The Bank is the world's largest external education financier to the developing world and has further increased this support as a result of the financial crisis. In the previous five years, the Bank averaged about

$2 billion per year in loans, credits, and grants to support education. In FY09, new financing for education totaled an unprecedented $3.4 billion, and projected lending is expected to again reach record highs in FY10. In FY09, $1.6 billion was for zero-interest International Development Association (IDA) credits and grants to bolster education in the world's poorest countries.[26]

Founded in 1944, the World Bank provides educational loans to developing nations based on the human capital idea that educational investment is the key to economic growth.[27] Improving schools became a World Bank goal in 1968 when the then president of the Bank, Robert McNamara, announced, "Our aim here will be to provide assistance where it will contribute most to economic development. This will mean emphasis on educational planning, the starting point for the whole process of educational improvement."[28] McNamara went on to explain that it would mean an expansion of the World Bank's educational activities. The World Bank continues to present its educational goals in the framework of economic development: "Education is central to development . . . It is one of the most powerful instruments for reducing poverty and inequality and lays a foundation for sustained economic growth."[29]

The World Bank includes the International Bank for Reconstruction and Development (IBRD), which lends money to governments of middle- and low-income countries, and the International Development Association (IDA), which provides interest-free loans and grants to governments of the poorest nations. The World Bank is also part of the World Bank Group which includes three other organizations which provide technical assistance to developing nations, guarantee against losses for investors in developing nations, and arbitrate investment disputes.[30]

Each division of the World Bank is owned by member countries. In 2007, 185 member countries owned IBRD and 166 member countries owned IDA. Voting power in the World Bank is based on the number of shares owned by member countries. The five largest shareholders of the World Bank are the United States, Japan, Germany, France, and the United Kingdom. Money for loans through IBRD (middle- and low-income countries) is primarily raised through the world's financial markets. In contrast, loan money from IDA (poorest countries) comes primarily from the richest member countries.[31] The countries contributing the most to IDA are the United States, Japan, Germany, the United Kingdom, and France.[32] Countries eligible to receive loans from IBRD (middle- and low-income countries) in 2006 ranged from the Republic of Korea, with an annual per capita income of $15,810, to the Philippines, with an annual per capita income of $1,250. Those eligible for IDA (poorest countries) ranged from the Maldives, with an annual per capita income of $2,390, to Burundi, with an annual per capita income of $100.[33]

As the leading global investor in education in developing nations, the World Bank is linked through extensive networks to other worldwide organizations. Through these networks the Bank is a major participant in global educational discourses.[34] World culture theorists consider the World Bank to be a major contributor to the development of a global culture.[35] Critics see the World Bank's agenda as serving wealthy nations and multinational organizations.[36] The Bank's worldwide networks influence local education practices.[37]

Similar to OECD, the World Bank operates its education programs in the framework of human capital theory. Discussions about human capital and the knowledge economy occur on the networks linking the World Bank to governments, global intergovernmental and nongovernmental organizations, and multinational corporations. In its book *Constructing Knowledge Societies*, the World Bank declares, "The ability of a society to produce, select, adapt, commercialize, and use knowledge is critical for sustained economic growth and improved living standards."[38] The book asserts, "Knowledge has become the most important factor in economic development."[39] The World Bank describes its education assistance as helping countries adapt their entire education systems to the new challenges of the "learning" economy in "two complementary ways . . . Formation of a strong human capital base . . . [and] Construction of an effective national innovation system."[40] The creation of a national innovation system for assisting schools to adapt to the knowledge economy creates a global network. The World Bank describes this network: "A national innovation system is a well-articulated network of firms, research centers, universities, and think tanks that work together to take advantage of the growing stock of global knowledge, assimilate and adapt it to local needs, and create new technology."[41] In other words, the World Bank members consider its networks as sustaining a devotion to human capital education.

United Nations and the World Bank: Global Networks

A goal of this section is to illustrate the complicated global networks linking organizations and people in the formulation of global education policies. These networks play an important role in creating common educational policies between the world's nations. The global network that I will describe in this section links groups associated with the World Bank to those connected to the United Nations and its agency the United Nations Educational, Scientific and Cultural Organization (UNESCO). UNESCO is another major intergovernmental organization influencing global education politics. However, unlike the World Bank, UNESCO's educational mission as displayed on its website is "Building peace in the minds of people."[42] Specifically, UNESCO fosters global instruction in human rights and peace education, as represented by its global website "Cyberschoolbus" which offers curriculum and teaching units on Peace Education, Poverty, Schools Demining Schools, Human Rights, Cities of the World, World Hunger, Indigenous People, Rights at Work, Ethnic Discrimination and Racial Discrimination.[43] Therefore the UNESCO global curriculum is focused on social justice issues as compared to human capital education. Both organizations do share a common objective of promoting education as a solution to world poverty.

The World Bank and the United Nations are formally tied together by a 1947 agreement making the World Bank an independent specialized agency of the United Nations and an observer in the United Nations General Assembly.[44] The World Bank supports the United Nations' Millennium Goals and Targets which were endorsed by 189 countries at the 2000 United Nations Millennium Assembly. The Millennium Goals directly addressing education issues are:

- Goal 2 Achieve Universal Primary Education: Ensure that by 2015, children everywhere, boys and girls, will be able to complete a full course of primary schooling.
- Goal 3 Promote Gender Equality and Empower Women: Eliminate gender disparity in primary and secondary education, preferably by 2005, and at all levels of education no later than 2015.[45]

These two Millennium Goals were part of the Education for All program of the United Nations Educational, Scientific and Cultural Organization (UNESCO) which had established as two of its global goals the provision of free and compulsory primary education for all and the achieving of gender parity by 2005 and gender equality by 2015.[46] Highlighting the intertwined activities of the World Bank and United Nations agencies is the fact that these two goals were a product of the 1990 World Conference on Education for All convened by the World Bank, UNESCO, the United Nations Children's Fund (UNICEF), the United Nations Population Fund (UNFPA), and the United Nations Development Program (UNDP). This World Conference was attended by representatives from 155 governments.[47]

The Education for All program is coordinated with another series of organizations and networks cited by UNESCO as:

- International Bureau of Education (IBE), Geneva, Switzerland.
- International Institute for Educational Planning (IIEP), Paris, France and Buenos Aires, Argentina.
- UNESCO Institute for Lifelong Learning (UIL), Hamburg, Germany.
- Institute for Information Technologies in Education (IITE), Moscow, Russian Federation.

- International Institute for Higher Education in Latin America and the Caribbean (IESALC), Caracas, Venezuela.
- International Institute for Capacity-Building in Africa (IICBA), Addis Ababa, Ethiopia.
- European Centre for Higher Education (CEPES), Bucharest, Romania.
- International Centre for Technical and Vocational Education and Training (UNEVOC), Bonn, Germany.
- UNESCO Institute for Statistics (UIS), Montreal, Canada.[48]

These global networks are linked to nongovernment organizations (NGOs) through what UNESCO calls the Collective Consultation of Non-Governmental Organizations on EFA (CCNGO/EFA). UNESCO describes this Collective as follows:

It connects UNESCO and several hundred NGOs, networks and coalitions around the world through a coordination group composed of eight NGO representatives (five regional focal points, two international focal points and one representative of the UNESCO/NGO Liaison Committee), and a list serve for information sharing.[49]

Millennium Goals, Global Networks, and Human Capital Education

The Millennium Goals of universal primary education and gender equality in schools complement the World Bank's emphasis on human capital education in developing nations. From the perspective of the leaders of the World Bank, the United Nations' Millennium Goals provide a focus on human development as one aspect of general economic development. The concept of human development dovetails into the human capital framework. The original United Nations Millennium Declaration lists the issues related to human development. While this list mentions the goals of universal education and gender equality in education it also calls for the elimination of poverty; reducing maternal and infant mortality rates; halting the spread of HIV/AIDS and malaria; and improving the lives of slum dwellers. These development goals aid human capital education in achieving economic growth and employment in the global economy. Also, the Millennium Declaration contains goals directly related to human capital education and knowledge economy concerns: "To develop and implement strategies that give young people everywhere a real chance to find decent and productive work" and "To ensure that the benefits of new technologies, especially information and communication technologies . . . are available to all."[50]

Officially, the World Bank makes this connection between Millennium Goals and human development and the building of global networks:

The Millennium Development Goals commit the international community to an expanded vision of development, one that vigorously promotes human development as the key to sustaining social and economic progress in all countries, and recognizes the importance of creating a global partnership for development. The goals have been commonly accepted as a framework for measuring development progress.[51]

In addressing Millennium Goal 2, to achieve universal primary education by 2015, the World Bank focuses on the human capital and knowledge economy aspects of education:

Education is the foundation of all societies and globally competitive economies. It is the basis for reducing poverty and inequality, improving health, enabling the use of new technologies, and creating and spreading knowledge. In an increasingly complex, knowledge-dependent world, primary education, as the gateway to higher levels of education, must be the first priority.[52]

Goal 3, eliminating gender disparity in primary and secondary education, is tied to human development: "When a country educates its girls, its mortality rates usually fall, fertility rates decline, and the health and education prospects of the next generation improve."[53] Equal educational opportunities for women are also linked to the role of women in economic development: "Low education levels and responsibilities for household work prevent women from finding productive employment or participating in public decision-making."[54]

In summary, the network between the United Nations, the World Bank, and other global organizations highlights the forces shaping education in developing nations. Unlike the human rights and peace education goals of UNESCO, the United Nations' Millennium Goals are tied to general ideology of human capital and education for the knowledge economy. It is these developing nations that may be the source of labor for OECD countries with their declining birth rates and the increasing global migration of workers. In the next section, I will discuss how OECD countries, including the United States, benefit from global brain migration.

Brain Gain and Brain Drain: Human Capital and Multiculturalism

The expansion of schooling in developing countries has contributed to a "brain drain" and a "brain gain" for OECD countries. In other words, the World Bank's loans for education in developing countries have benefited OECD countries by providing them with a supply of educated workers.

Also, global migration has become a major education issue for the United States and other OECD countries. Today the majority of students in New York public schools are first or second generation immigrants.[55] Global migration has pushed multicultural education to the top of the agenda for many OECD nations and the World Bank. One vision of the global economy is a world of nomads; workers moving around the globe and having to adapt to multicultural workplaces. In this context, the knowledge economy becomes a world of migrant workers including corporate leaders, managers, technical operatives and professionals, and skilled and unskilled laborers.

In recent years, OECD nations have turned to foreign workers to compensate for a shortage of workers resulting from declining birth rates. OECD asserts that each woman must have 2.1 children to maintain a nation's population. Since the 1970s, the birth rate in OECD countries has fallen below that rate. For example, in Austria, Germany, Italy, and South Korea the birth rate has declined to an average of 1.3 children per woman. With declines in birth rates, OECD nations fill the labor shortages with immigrant labor or by contracting foreign workers. The result is increasing tensions between the families of immigrant and contracted workers and local populations. Adding to the problem of declining birth rates is increasing longevity. As people live longer in OECD nations there is greater dependence of retirees on a shrinking labor force. One of OECD's responses is: "Part of the answer is getting women working."[56] The other is to rely on migrant labor from developing countries.

Consequently, OECD members are very concerned about education increasing social cohesion to reduce conflicts between immigrant communities and the local populations. OECD policy-makers give special emphasis to the social capital aspects of human capital. OECD defines social capital as "networks together with shared norms, values and understandings that facilitate co-operation within and among groups."[57] The organization divides social capital into three main categories. The first category is the *bonds* that link people to a shared identity through family, close friends, and culture. The second category is the *bridges* that link people to those who do not share a common identity. The last category is the *linkages* that connect people to those up and down the social scale or, in other words, those from different social classes.

The problem with the first category is that *bonds* through a shared identity might be so strong that it hinders making *bridges* to others. This, the OECD claims, is a problem with some immigrant communities in member nations. Consequently, schools need to ensure an education that builds these bridges to others and linkages that reduce conflict between social classes. OECD warns that: "Companies and organizations can also suffer if they have the wrong sort of social capital—relationships between colleagues that are too inward-looking and fail to take account of what's going on in the wider world."

World Bank leaders have a similar concern about reducing social tensions in multicultural settings. The Bank's *Lifelong Learning in the Global Knowledge Economy* contains a section with the descriptive title: "Equipping Learners with the Skills and Competencies They Need to Succeed in a Knowledge Economy." One of the listed competencies is the ability to work in multicultural settings:

> *Functioning in socially heterogeneous groups:* Being able to interact effectively with other people, including those from different backgrounds; recognizing the social embeddedness of individuals; creating social capital; and being able to relate well to others, cooperate, and manage and resolve conflict.[58]

As wealthier countries worry about multicultural education they are benefited by brain drain and brain gain. Migration is both international and national. Migrations of populations within a country primarily involve population movement from rural to urban areas. The tendency is for newly graduated rural youth to migrate to urban areas searching for better-paying work. A 2008 United Nations report predicted that, "During 2008, the population of the world will become, for the first time in human history, primarily urban, and is likely to continue to urbanize substantially over the coming decades."[59] The report also claimed that, "The shift of population from relatively low-productivity rural areas to higher productivity urban areas has been a major aspect if not a driver of economic progress."[60]

The report also noted that the rural to urban migrants tend to be young and tend to be better educated and have more skills than the rest of the rural population. In other words, there is a brain drain from rural to urban centers. In addition, as noted above, in developing countries the poor constitute half the urban population. This has strained social services including the provision of public education. Many of the rural to urban migrant poor have been forced "to invade and settle ('squat') on marginal lands, such as under bridges, on floodplains or on steep slopes."[61]

In addition to rural to urban migration, international global migration has increased and it appears will continue to increase. The largest migration patterns are from poorer to wealthier nations. While wealthier nations have only 16 percent of the world's workers they have over 60 percent of global migrants.[62] The Report of the Global Commission on International Migration declared,

> International migration has risen to the top of the global policy agenda . . . In every part of the world, there is now an understanding that the

economic, social and cultural benefits of international migration must be more effectively realized, and that the negative consequences of cross–border movement could be better addressed.[63]

Migrants are defined by the United Nations as people outside their country of birth or citizenship for twelve months or more. In a world of 190+ sovereign nation states, each of which issues passports and regulates who can cross its borders and stay in its sovereign territory, the United Nations' Population Division estimated there were 175 million migrants in 2000, including 65 million or 37 percent in "less developed" nations, which are those outside Europe and North America, Australia/New Zealand, Japan, and the ex-USSR "where it is presented as a separate area." The number of migrants in less-developed countries was stable in the 1990s, but the developing countries' share of the world's migrant stock fell with their rising population.[64]

The United Nations' Population Division reports that "Between 1960 and 2005 the number of international migrants in the world more than doubled, passing from an estimated 75 million in 1960 to almost 191 million in 2005, *an increase of 116 million over 45 years* [author's emphasis]."[65] Prior to 1985, the number of international migrants in developing nations about equaled that in developed nations. After 1985, the number of international migrants to developed nations increased at a rapid rate while the number in developing nations remained about the same. Currently, the economic causes of migration are resulting in the rapid growth of migrant populations in developed nations. In 2005, only 7 percent of the migrant population were refugees. The United Nations estimates that: "In 1960, 57 per cent of all migrants lived in the less developed regions but by 2005, just 37 per cent did so."[66]

The benefits and problems reaped by wealthier nations are evident when global migration patterns are broken down by country. A small number of countries host 75 percent of the world's international migrants. In 2005, the United States had 20.2 percent of total global migrants, which is the world's highest national percentage. It should be noted that for the United States this was an increase of more than 5 percent since 1990.[67] The following is a list of the top eleven countries hosting the highest percentages of the world's migrant population.

Percentage of Global Migrants Hosted by a Nation in 2005

United States	20.2
Russian Federation	6.4
Germany	5.3
Ukraine	3.6
France	3.4

Saudi Arabia	3.3
Canada	3.2
India	3.0
United Kingdom	2.8
Spain	2.5
Australia	2.2[68]

The high percentage of global migrants in the Russian Federation and Ukraine is a result of the 1991 disintegration of the Union of Soviet Socialist Republics (USSR). This is an example of how political changes can affect citizenship. The high percentage in these two countries is a result of the reclassification of citizens after the dissolving of the USSR. Prior to 1991, there were large numbers of internal migrants who moved from former parts of the USSR to what is now the Russian Federation and Ukraine. After 1991 these formerly internal migrants were reclassified as international migrants.[69]

What countries are the sources of the world's migrants? OECD has provided statistics for the sources of immigration into OECD European countries and into OECD countries outside of Europe. I will remind readers that OECD members include thirty-one of the richest nations in the world. Migration to OECD nations is often, but not always, a result of migrants seeking better economic opportunities. Many of the immigrants to European OECD nations are from poorer nations of the European Union, namely Poland and Romania.[70]

The statistics for sources of immigration outside of OECD Europe provide a broader view of migration from developing to developed nations. However there are exceptions in the list below. Some citizens of the United Kingdom and the United States are retirees living abroad or people who want to relocate to other countries.

Ten Top Sources for Immigration to OECD Countries Outside of Europe, 2005 (From Largest Source to Smallest Source)

- China
- Mexico
- Philippines
- India
- United Kingdom
- Korea
- United States
- Vietnam
- Russian Federation
- Cuba[71]

One aspect of international migration is the brain drain of skilled and educated workers from poorer countries and brain gain in wealthier nations. The term "brain drain" was first used in the United Kingdom to describe the influx of Indian scientists and engineers.[72] In this situation, the United Kingdom had a brain gain while India lost educated workers. Now there is also a focus on "brain circulation" where skilled and professional workers move between wealthy nations or return to their homeland after migrating to another country. The Report of the Global Commission on International Migration provided a justification for dropping "brain drain" in favor of "brain circulation":

> Given the changing pattern of international migration, the notion of "brain drain" is a somewhat outmoded one, implying as it does that a migrant who leaves her or his own country will never go back there. In the current era, there is a need to capitalize upon the growth of human mobility by promoting the notion of "brain circulation", in which migrants return to their own country on a regular or occasional basis, sharing the benefits of the skills and resources they have acquired while living and working abroad.[73]

Brain circulation is aided by national efforts to bring back educated workers lost in the brain drain. In China, returning knowledge workers are called "turtles," as explained in a 2007 issue of *China Daily*: "Enticed by more opportunities in a blossoming economy, many overseas Chinese—or 'turtles'—are swimming home."[74] The Chinese government is offering special benefits to encourage turtles. Malaysia has developed a national strategy to bring scientists home.[75]

There is a great deal of debate about the effect of the movement of highly educated populations on the knowledge economies of nations. For instance, what is the long-term impact of the fact that "many Central American and island nations in the Caribbean had more than 50 percent of their university–educated citizens living abroad in 2000."[76] Nearly 40 percent of tertiary-educated adults have left Turkey and Morocco while Africa has lost 30 percent of its skilled professionals.[77]

The problem of brain drain appears serious when you consider the statistics for other nations. In 2000, the number of post-secondary-educated citizens emigrating from Guyana, Grenada, and Jamaica was 89, 85.1, and 85.1 percent respectively. The numbers emigrating from these countries are small because of their small populations. However, the problem is more serious for these countries when considered as a percentage of the total population. Sub-Saharan Africa, a region struggling with poverty, health problems, and wars, has lost its educated population: Ghana (46.9 percent), Mozambique (45.1 percent), Sierra Leone (52.5 percent), Kenya (38.4 percent), Uganda (35.6 percent), Angola (33.0 percent), and Somalia (32.7 percent). The same pattern is occurring in developing countries in Asia, such as Lao Peoples Democratic Republic (37.4 percent), Sri Lanka (29.7 percent), Vietnam (27.1 percent), Afghanistan (23.3 percent), and Cambodia (18.3 percent).[78]

A loss of such high percentages of educated workers from developing countries to wealthier nations has devastating effects on health and education services. In part, this is a result of losses to the tax base as high-paid professional workers migrate overseas.[79] For instance, 85 percent of Filipino nurses work overseas, with many having migrated to the United Kingdom, Saudi Arabia, Ireland, and Singapore. Over half the graduates of Ghana's medical schools left the country within five years of graduation. Only 360 doctors out of 1,200 doctors educated in Zimbabwe in the 1990s remained in 2001. And 21,000 doctors have left Nigeria to practice in the United States. Similar examples of the loss of medical personnel can be found for other developing countries.[80]

Another way of considering the brain drain is to look at the percentage of educated immigrants in a particular country, such as the United States. For instance, 83 percent of those over 25 years old migrating from Nigeria to the United States had some form of post-secondary education. Other examples are: India (80 percent), Indonesia (75 percent), Egypt (78 percent), Sri Lanka (72 percent), and Pakistan (67 percent).[81]

Also, if a country invests money in educating a worker and that worker migrates to another country, then the country that provided the original education loses its investment. For example, training an Indian worker as a data-processing specialist in 2001 cost the Indian government about $15,000 to $20,000. If that worker migrates to another country then India loses the cost of the training plus the worker's potential contribution to the Indian economy, estimated at $2 billion.[82] This fact is important when one considers that in the 1970s, 31 percent of the graduates of one of India's most prestigious schools, Indian Institute of Technology Mumbai, migrated overseas. The overseas migration rate for graduates from India's most prestigious medical school, All India Institute for Medical Sciences, was 56 percent between 1956 and 1980 and 49 percent in the 1990s.[83] This represents a tremendous loss of talent and educational investment for India.

Some researchers claim positive effects for countries experiencing brain drain. One positive effect for nations losing educated people to wealthier nations is the remittances sent home, with some of these remittances being used for education and health care.[84] Also, some researchers are suggesting that migration results in demands for greater government spending on education (brain gain) by populations in less developed countries wanting to migrate.[85] These researchers believe that this can result in a "net brain gain [for countries losing educated workers], that is, a brain gain that is larger than the brain drain; and a net brain gain raises welfare and growth."[86]

The argument that there is a net brain gain as a result of pressures for expanded educational opportunities might only apply to larger nations. The net brain gain argument does not apply to small developing countries that have difficulty maintaining their educational systems because of the loss of educational workers. Also, in a 2004 study for the World Bank, Schiff concludes that previous studies were overly optimistic about the positive effects of brain drain on countries experiencing the loss of educated workers. He concludes: "the brain drain on welfare and growth is likely to be significantly greater, than reported."[87] Frustrated by the difficulty of determining the economic consequences of brain circulation, Vinokur argues that the debate over "who wins, who loses and how much" in brain circulation is "irresolvable—analytically and empirically."[88]

In summary, aided by OECD and the World Bank, wealthier nations benefit from the expansion of human capital schooling in developing countries. Combined with the effects of human capital schooling on rural populations, the result in many cases is to educate people to leave their lands. The educational ideology of human capital education for the knowledge economy serves the economic interests of wealthier nations and multinational corporations.

The Global Education Business

Human capital education, such as that in the United States, benefits multinational education corporations by relying on standardization of the curriculum and massive use of standardized tests. Standardization of the curriculum makes it easier for multinational publishers to match their textbooks to what is taught in the classroom. A reliance on standardized testing for promotion, secondary school graduation, teacher evaluations, and college entrance has caused the growth of a global shadow education system composed of for-profit test preparation and cramming schools. I discussed the growth of the U.S. shadow education industry in Chapter 6, as exemplified by Sylvan Learning Centers, Kumon Learning Centers, and Kaplan.

The globalization of English as the language of commerce has been a boon to test makers, the shadow education industry, and publishers of English as a Second Language textbooks. In other words, the global education industry has a stake in keeping alive the rhetoric of human capital education and the use of English as the language of global commerce.

Educate, Inc. exemplifies the new global education corporation with its entanglement in politics, universities, and private financiers. "Thank You For Your Interest in the Premier Brands in the Education Industry!" is emblazoned on the website of Educate, Inc.[89] It is an example of the growth of the for-profit education industry. Linked to a complex network of business and financial institutions, the corporate structure of Educate,

Inc. is similar to that of other for-profit schools and knowledge industries. After the 2007 purchase of Sylvan Learning Centers from Laureate Education Inc., Educate, Inc. could boast of ownership of Hooked on Phonics, Catapult Learning, Educate Online, and Progressus Therapy. Educate, Inc. markets its products in Europe under the Schülerhilfe brand.[90] Exemplifying the complex financial arrangements of education companies, Educate, Inc. is owned by Edge Acquisition, LLC with Citigroup Capital Partners and Sterling Capital Partners as investors.[91] The chairman of Edge Acquisition, R. Christopher Hoehn-Saric, is also a trustee of Johns Hopkins University.[92] The interplay of politics and education is evident on the Board of Directors of Educate, Inc. One director, Raul Yzaguirre, is a professor at Arizona State University, the director of the Mexican American advocacy group LaRaza, and was co-chair of the 2008 Hillary Rodham Clinton Presidential campaign.[93] Another director, Douglas Becker, is Chairman and CEO of Laureate Education Inc. along with being director of Baltimore Gas and Electric Company and director of For Inspiration and Recognition of Science and Technology.[94] Director Cheryl Gordon Krongard is a regent of the University System of Maryland and director of US Airways Group Inc.[95] Other directors of Educate, Inc. have similar ties to industry, investment companies, and higher education.

For-profits are undergoing a period of global expansion. For instance, Laureate Education Inc. has a presence in fifteen countries serving 240,000 students, with ownership in the United States of Walden University and twenty-three other universities in Asia, Europe, and the Americas.[96] Laureate Education Inc. claims to potential investors that the global market for for-profit higher education is increasing because of the worldwide expansion of the middle class, expanding youth populations in Latin America and Asia, the need for educated human capital and, most importantly, the difficulties faced by governments in financing public higher education.[97] In 2007, the company announced:

> Laureate International Universities, one of the world's largest networks of private higher education institutions, and the University of Liverpool today announced the expansion of a unique partnership to leverage programs and expertise to create the next generation of international programs for students worldwide.[98]

In September 2007, Laureate made a dramatic move to capture the Asian market when Douglas Becker, its Chairman and Chief Executive Officer, announced that he and his family were moving to Hong Kong to ensure the expansion of the company and to establish Asian headquarters. In an example of the international financing of for-profit education, Becker and an investor group engineered a $3.8 billion private-equity buyout of the company in June 2007. The international investor group included Harvard University, Citigroup, Microsoft co-founder Paul Allen, global philanthropist George Soros, Kohlberg Kravis Roberts & Co. (KKR), S.A.C. Capital Management, LLC, SPG Partners, Bregal Investments, Caisse de depot et placement du Quebec, Sterling Capital, Makena Capital, Torreal S.A., and Brenthurst Funds. In reporting the move, a *Chronicle of Higher Education* article commented, "Mr. Becker devised the transformation of Laureate into an internationally focused higher-education company from its roots as a tutoring business called Sylvan Learning Systems."[99]

There are information and publishing companies that benefit from global uniformity of schooling. These so-called global knowledge companies include Bertelsmann, HCIRN, Holtzbrinck Publishers, Informa, Pearson Education, Reed Elsevier, the McGraw-Hill Companies, and Thomson.[100] All of these companies include publishing and vast information systems. For instance, Bertelsmann, which identifies itself as "media worldwide," is composed of six corporate divisions including media groups RTL, Aravato, DirectGroup, and BMG. It also owns Random House book publishers and a magazine and newspaper conglomerate called G+J.[101] HCIRN stands for Human-Computer Interaction Resource Network and it is comprised of, among other products, Kluwer Academic Publishers.[102]

The global publishing and information conglomerates are vast. With home headquarters in Stuttgart, Germany, Holtzbrinck Publishers describes its company as: "active in more than 80 countries and publishes works in both print and electronic media, providing information, disseminating knowledge, and serving the needs of educational, professional, and general readership markets."[103] In the United States alone, the company owns Audio Renaissance, Bedford/St. Martin's, Farrar, Straus & Giroux, Henry Holt and Company, Palgrave Macmillan, Picador, St. Martin's Press, Tor Books, W.H. Freeman, Bedford, Freeman and Worth Publishing Group, and Worth Publishers.[104] Informa, which advertises that it provides "Specialist Information for Global Markets," owns an array of publishers including Taylor & Francis Group comprised of Routledge, Garland Science, and Psychology Press.[105]

As I mentioned at the end of Chapter 6, global test producers, such as Pearson, McGraw-Hill, and Educational Testing Services, benefit from educational systems that rely on standardized tests for promotion, graduation, and college entrance, and on English as the global language of commerce. Their tests also serve to drive the growth of test preparation centers in the shadow education industry.

Pearson exemplifies the complex corporate structure of these global test producers. Headquartered in England, Pearson boasts that it "is an international media company with world-leading publishing and data services for education, business information and consumer publishing."[106] With 29,000 employees working in sixty countries, Pearson lists its valuable assets as the Financial Times, Penguin, Dorling Kindersley, Scott Foresman, Prentice Hall, Addison Wesley, and Longman. The company's website declares: "From our roots as the world's largest book publisher, we've grown to provide a range of related services: testing and learning software for students of all ages; data for financial institutions; public information systems for government departments."[107] Pearson Education North Asia has offices in China, Korea, Japan, and Taiwan and offers pre-K to adult English Language Teaching (ELT) resources, including Longman dictionaries, companion websites, and teaching tools. Pearson Education Indochina, which includes Cambodia, Laos, Myanmar, Thailand, and Vietnam and Pearson Education India, offers pre-K and 1–12 ELT, materials for higher education, and professional/technical print and online resources. In India, the company sells sixty locally produced books for schools and colleges.

Pearson markets its international computer-based tests through its Pearson VUE division. According to the company's official history in 1994 Virtual University Enterprises (VUE) was established by three pioneers in the field of electronic tests, including the developer of the first electronic system, E. Clarke Porter. Pearson purchased VUE in 2000. In 2006, Pearson acquired Promissor, a provider of knowledge measurement services, which certifies professionals in a variety of fields. Focusing on the certification of professionals, Pearson VUE serves 162 countries with 4,400 Pearson VUE Testing Centers. "Today," according to its company description,

> Pearson VUE, Pearson's computer-based testing business unit, serves the Information Technology industry and the professional certification, licensor, and regulatory markets. From operational centers in the United States, the United Kingdom, India, Japan, and China, the business provides a variety of services to the electronic testing market.[108]

The range of computer-based tests offered by Pearson is astonishing and it is beyond the scope of this book to list all the tests. However, Pearson VUE provides the following categories of online tests: Academic/Admissions; Driving Tests; Employment, Human Resources & Safety; Financial Services, Health, Medicine; Information Technology (IT); Insurance; Legal Services; Real Estate, Appraisers & Inspectors; and State Regulated.[109] On December 17, 2007, Pearson VUE announced that it had signed a contract with the Association for Financial Professions to provide test development to be delivered globally in over 230 Pearson Professional Centers by its Pearson VUE Authorized Test Centers.[110] On the same date it announced renewal of its contract with Kaplan Test Prep for delivery of the "Ultimate Practice Test" for another Pearson VUE test—the Graduate Management Admission Test.[111]

Another major test producer, the McGraw-Hill Companies, boldly displays its global economic philosophy on its company website:

McGraw-Hill aligns with three enduring global needs
- the need for Capital
- the need for Knowledge
- the need for Transparency

"These are the foundations necessary to foster economic growth and to allow individuals, markets and societies to reach their full potential."[112]

In the 1990s McGraw-Hill began focusing on three global markets— education, financial services, and media. With headquarters in New York City and offices in ten Asia-Pacific, eleven Latin American, and eight European countries, McGraw-Hill is a major player in global publishing and information services. Like other global conglomerates, McGraw-Hill is involved in a range of activities including magazines, broadcasting, television, investor education, research services, network information solutions, databases, geospatial tools, and, of course, education publishing.[113] Education publishing is broken down into a number of divisions including McGraw-Hill Education International with education offices and individual websites for Asia, Australia, Europe, Spain, Latin America, Canada, the United Kingdom, and India. The company is also involved in testing programs through its CTB/McGraw-Hill division.[114]

Educational Testing Services (ETS) is benefiting from English being the language of global commerce and the increasing requirement by national school systems that their students learn English. Global English language testing is resulting in the standardization of commercial English as contrasted to the various forms of English used in particular cultures or nations, such as India, Nigeria, and the United States. A global business English allows for communication across cultures in the world's workplaces. Focused primarily on work situations it may result in teaching a limited vocabulary. The trend to a global business English was reflected on a sign I saw in Shanghai which read "Learn the English words your bosses want to hear!"

Until 2000, ETS primarily focused on the U.S. testing market. In 2000, businessman Kurt Landgraf became president and CEO, turning a non-profit organization into one that looks like a for-profit with earnings of more than $800 million a year. As part of Landgraf's planning, the company expanded into 180 countries. "Our mission is not just a U.S.-oriented mission but a global mission," Landgraf is quoted as saying in a magazine article. "We can offer educational systems to the world, but to do that, you have to take a *lesson from the commercial world* [author's emphasis]."[115] The official corporate description of ETS's global marketing is:

ETS's Global Division and its subsidiaries fulfill ETS's mission in markets around the world. We assist businesses, educational institutions, governments, ministries of education, professional organizations, and test takers by designing, developing and delivering ETS's standard and customized measurement products and services which include assessments, preparation materials and technical assistance.[116]

An important role of the Global Division is standardizing English as a global language. Almost all of its products are for English language learners. The Division markets the widely used Test of English as a Foreign Language (TOEFL), Test of English for International Communication (TOEIC), and Test of Spoken English (TSE). TOEFL has long served as an assessment tool for determining the English language ability of foreign students seeking admission into U.S. universities. In 2002, ETS opened a Beijing office and began marketing TOEIC along with TOEFL. In addition, the Global Division offers TOEFL Practice Online which indirectly serves as a teaching tool for English instruction. In March, 2007 ETS proudly announced that the service had been extended to its Chinese market. The Test of English for Distance Education (TEDE) is used worldwide to determine if a student has enough skills in English to participate in online courses conducted in English. Criterion is a web-based Online Writing Evaluation which promises to evaluate student writing skills in seconds. In 2007 ETS's Criterion won highest honors from the Global Learning Consortium. In addition to all these tests associated with global English, ETS offers ProofWriter, an online tool that provides immediate feedback on grammar and editing issues for English language essays.[117]

In another major step in the global standardization of English, ETS and G2nd Systems signed an agreement in 2007 for G2nd Systems to join ETS's Preferred Vendor Network and to use TOEIC. G2nd Systems is promoting an intercultural form of English for use in the global workplace. "G2nd Systems defines the way people use non-culture-specific English in workplace environments as intercultural English, which is not the same as any national version of English that naturally includes cultural presumptions, idioms and local ways of communicating ideas," explains Lorelei Carobolante, CEO of G2nd Systems, in a news release from ETS.

TOEIC test scores indicate how well people can communicate in English with others in today's globally diverse workplace. G2nd Systems recognizes that measuring proficiency in English speaking and writing capabilities allows business professionals, teams and organizations to implement focused language strategies that will improve organizational effectiveness, customer satisfaction and employee productivity.[118]

A for-profit corporation, G2nd advertises itself as "Global Collaborative Business Environments across multiple cultures at the same time!" and a "Global Second Language Approach." The corporate announcement of its affiliation with ETS states: "Today, over 5,000 corporations in more than 60 countries use the TOEIC test, and 4.5 million people take the test every year."[119] G2nd Systems offers instruction in an intercultural form of English as opposed to the Englishes of particular countries, such as India, Britain, or the United States. Referring to "Intercultural English— A New Global Tool," the company explains, "Intercultural English developed in response to the new dynamics emerging in today's global business environment, characterized by multiple cultures operating in a collaborative structure to execute projects that are often geographically dispersed."[120] Highlighting the supposedly culturally neutral form of English taught by the organization, it claims: "Intercultural English is a communication tool rather than a national version of any language, and *this tool is as vital as mathematics or computer literacy in facilitating normal business processes* [author's emphasis]."[121]

In summary, the global education business benefits from human capital education systems that rely on standardization of the curriculum, standardized testing, and the teaching of commercial English. Believing that the future employment of their children depends on them attending a prestigious institution of higher education or graduating from secondary school, parents rush to enroll them in for-profit tutorial or test preparation schools in the shadow education system. Publishers and testing corporations sell their products to national school systems adopting the human capital model of standardization. In other words, the education businesses have a financial stake in an ideology that promises better jobs and economic growth if school systems adopt uniform curricula and rely on standardized testing.

Conclusion: The Global Cloud

What I call the global cloud is the Internet and information technology which facilitate contact and information sharing between political forces shaping global education systems. Through e-mail, the World Wide Web, and social networking sites, global organizations and citizens are linked to intergovernmental and nongovernmental organizations affecting education; professional education organizations; education businesses; national and local governments; and school systems. It is over the Internet that OECD and IEA can broadcast the test results that spark the Academic

Olympiad and worry education ministers if their nation's test scores fall. It is over the Internet that education statistics are broadcast from groups such as OECD, professional education organizations, the United Nations, the World Bank, and national governments. Search engines propel the user through libraries of global information locating documents, journals, books, reports, surveys, and websites supplying more information. The Internet allows education businesses to market online degrees, courses, services, and learning modules. It is within the global cloud that particular educational ideologies are supported and criticized.

Global dominance of human capital ideology over education policies could occur for a number of reasons. There are educational ideologies competing for attention in the global arena. Many of these educational ideologies stress differing versions of social justice education, including human rights education, peace education, and environmental education. There are also various forms of progressive education seeking global attention with the most famous being associated with the educational methods of John Dewey and Paulo Freire. These forms of progressive education advocate reconstruction of society to ensure democracy and social and economic justice.[122]

One can assume that global and national businesses feel threatened by education policies that emphasize instruction in social and economic justice. Graduates of schools teaching social and economic justice might be more likely to criticize business and economic systems that foster financial inequalities. The economic interests of business enterprises are served by a human capital education which promises to supply educated and uncritical workers who can accept a life of global migration and working in multicultural settings.

National ministers of education and their staffs might favor human capital education because the ideology attracts important political and financial support by promising economic prosperity. Important inter-governmental and nongovernmental organizations may favor human capital arguments because it serves the economic interests of their members; this is particularly true for OECD and the World Bank. Education businesses flourish in school systems operating under human capital education policies because schools must rely on testing products and the policies motivate parents to use the shadow education system to aid their children to achieve academic and economic success. Education businesses associated with publishing favor standardized curricula because it makes it easier to tailor textbooks to meet the needs of national markets. The publishing industry is also aided in the same manner by the growing standardization of global curricula. The promotion of English as the language of global commerce—"Learn the English words your bosses want to hear!"—helps the shadow education industry, textbook companies, and purveyors of online instruction and software.

Many political leaders of wealthy nations support the World Bank's efforts to introduce human capital education systems into developing nations because wealthier nations are increasingly dependent on the migration from developing nations of skilled and knowledgeable workers. Developing nations, which have a long history of exploitation by dominant global powers, might be better served by social justice forms of education, particularly those associated with the reconstruction of economic and political systems. Human capital education might not advance the economic interests of the ordinary citizen if a national government is authoritarian and is controlled by economic groups interested in accruing more wealth at the expense of the rest of the population.

In summary, U.S. educational policies are nested in a global network that is increasingly being used to benchmark U.S. tests and curriculum standards; can spark criticisms of schools through the Academic Olympiad of international comparison of test results; links education policy leaders to those in other countries; and provides global contacts between professionals. Publishers and producers of textbooks, tests, software, and online education for U.S. schools are part of the operations of the global education industry. American schools must accommodate the growing global circulation of workers. And, of course, American schools press an English acquisition agenda as in the national interest and as part of the global use of English as the language of commerce. One wonders what would have happened to U.S. language policies if Spanish had become the language of world commerce. After all, during the eighteenth and nineteenth centuries there were many conscious efforts to make Russian, French, Spanish, Esperanto, and English the global language.[123]

The global nesting of the U.S. school system contributes to arguments that the quality of U.S. schools is the key to international economic competition. Human capital ideology has displaced other traditional concerns of American schools, such as education for democracy, progressive education, civil rights education, environmental education, and education to maintain culture and the arts. As U.S. schools become embedded in global education policies they may become further out of the control of the majority of parents. I wonder how many U.S. parents can identify the workings of OECD, the World Bank, and international education businesses. How many parents know the content of global benchmarking tests such as PISA, PIRLS, and TIMSS? Are American schools now out of the reach of political control by the typical parent?

Notes

1 "International Benchmarking: Current Contributions and Future Directions for Policymakers and Researchers," Session held at the 2010 Annual Meeting of the American Educational Research Association, Denver, Colorado, May 1, 2010.

2 Valena Plisko, "The U.S. Department of Education's Role in International Surveys and Benchmarking," PowerPoint handout at "International Benchmarking: Current Contributions and Future Directions for Policymakers and Researchers."

3 National Center for Education Statistics, "U.S. Participation in International Assessments." Retrieved from http://nces.ed.gov/surveys/international on May 17, 2010.

4 Ibid.

5 American Institutes for Research, "About." Retrieved from http://www.air.org/about/ on May 17, 2010.

6 American Institutes for Research, "International Development." Retrieved from http://www.air.org/focus-area/international-development/?id=21 on May 17, 2010.

7 The National Academies, "Board on Testing and Assessment." Retrieved from http://www7.nationalacademies.org/BOTA/ on May 17, 2010.

8 Ambow Education Group, "About Us." Retrieved from http://www.ambow.com.cn/en/about_technology.html on May 18, 2010.

9 David Baker and Gerald LeTendre, *National Differences, Global Similarities: World Culture and the Future of Schooling* (Palo Alto, CA: Stanford University Press, 2005), p. 150.

10 OECD, *PISA—The OECD Programme for International Student Assessment* (Paris: OECD, 2007), p. 4.

11 Ibid., p. 6.

12 OECD, *The Pisa 2003 Assessment Framework—Mathematics, Reading, Science and Problem Solving, Knowledge and Skills* (Paris: OECD, 2003), p. 14.

13 OECD Directorate for Education, "UNESCO Ministerial Round Table on Education and Economic Development: Keynote Speech by Angel Gurría, OECD Secretary-General, Paris, 19 October 2007." Retrieved from http://www.oecd.org/document/19/0,3343,en_2649_33723_1_1_1_1,00.html on November 13, 2007.

14 Brian Keeley, *Human Capital: How What You Know Shapes Your Life* (Paris: OECD Publishing, 2007), p. 14.

15 OECD, *Internationalization of Higher Education* (Paris: OECD, 1996), p. 2.

16 OECD, "OECD Member Countries." Retrieved from http://www.oecd.org/document/58/0,3343,en_2649_201185_1889402_1_1_1_1,00.html on May 17, 2010. OECD states:

> Twenty countries originally signed the Convention on the Organisation for Economic Co-operation and Development on 14 December 1960. Since then eleven countries have become members of the Organisation. The Member countries of the Organisation and the dates on which they deposited their instruments of ratification are:
>
> AUSTRALIA: 7 June 1971
> AUSTRIA: 29 September 1961
> BELGIUM: 13 September 1961

CANADA: 10 April 1961
CHILE: 7 May 2010
CZECH REPUBLIC: 21 December 1995
DENMARK: 30 May 1961
FINLAND: 28 January 1969
FRANCE: 7 August 1961
GERMANY: 27 September 1961
GREECE: 27 September 1961
HUNGARY: 7 May 1996
ICELAND: 5 June 1961
IRELAND: 17 August 1961
ITALY: 29 March 1962
JAPAN: 28 April 1964
KOREA: 12 December 1996
LUXEMBOURG: 7 December 1961
MEXICO: 18 May 1994
NETHERLANDS: 13 November 1961
NEW ZEALAND: 29 May 1973
NORWAY: 4 July 1961
POLAND: 22 November 1996
PORTUGAL: 4 August 1961
SLOVAK REPUBLIC: 14 December 2000
SPAIN: 3 August 1961
SWEDEN: 28 September 1961
SWITZERLAND: 28 September 1961
TURKEY: 2 August 1961
UNITED KINGDOM: 2 May 1961
UNITED STATES: 12 April 1961

17 OECD, "About the OECD." Retrieved from http://www.oecd.org on November 7, 2007.
18 Ibid.
19 Ibid.
20 International Association for the Evaluation of Educational Achievement, "Brief History of IEA." Retrieved from http://www.iea.nl/brief_history_iea.html on January 28, 2008.
21 Ibid.
22 Ibid.
23 Ibid.
24 Ibid.
25 International Association for the Evaluation of Educational Achievement, "Mission Statement." Retrieved from http://www.ies.nl/mission_statement.html on January 28, 2008.
26 World Bank, "Education." Retrieved from http://web.worldbank.org/WBSITE/EXTERNAL/TOPICS/EXTEDUCATION/0,,contentMDK:20040939~menuPK:282393~pagePK:148956~piPK:216618~theSitePK:282386,00.html on May 17, 2010.
27 Joel Spring, *Education and the Rise of the Global Economy* (Mahwah, NJ: Lawrence Erlbaum, 1998), pp. 179–182; and World Bank, *A Guide to the World Bank*, 2nd edn. (Washington, DC: World Bank, 2007).
28 Michael Goldman, *Imperial Nature: The World Bank and Struggles for Social Justice* (New Haven: Yale University Press, 2005), p. 69.

29 World Bank, "About Us: Organization: Boards of Directors." Retrieved from http://www.worldbank.org, para. 1, on July 17, 2007.
30 The three other members of the World Bank Group are the International Finance Corporation, the Multilateral Investment Guarantee Agency, and the International Centre for Settlement of Investment Disputes.
31 World Bank, A *Guide to the World Bank*, pp. 9–19.
32 Ibid., pp. 18–19.
33 Ibid., pp. 14–16.
34 Spring, *Education and the Rise of the Global Economy*, pp. 159–189; World Bank, A *Guide to the World Bank*.
35 See Collete Chabbott, "Development INGOS," in *Constructing World Culture: International Nongovernment Organizations Since 1875*, edited by John Boli and George Thomas (Palo Alto, CA: Stanford University Press, 1999), pp. 222–248; and Leslie Sklair, "Sociology of the Global System," in *The Globalization Reader*, edited by Frank Lechner and John Boli (Malden, MA: Blackwell Publishing, 2004), pp. 70–76.
36 For example, Goldman, *Imperial Nature*; and Richard Peet, *Unholy Trinity: The IMF, World Bank and WTO* (London: Zed Books, 2003).
37 See Manuel Castells, *The Rise of the Network Society* (Oxford: Blackwell, 2000), pp. 77–147, 216–247.
38 World Bank, *Constructing Knowledge Societies: New Challenges for Tertiary Education* (Washington, DC: World Bank, 2002).
39 Ibid., p. 7.
40 World Bank Education, "Education for the Knowledge Economy." Retrieved from http://web.worldbank.org/wBSTIE/EXTERNAL/TOPICS/ EXTEDUCATION/0,,contentMDX:20161496~menuPK:540092~pagePK: 148956~piPK:216618~theSitePK:282386,00.html on October 10, 2007.
41 Ibid.
42 UNESCO, "Building peace in the minds of people." Retrieved from http:// www.unesco.org/new/en/unesco/ on May 18, 2010.
43 Cyberschoolbus, "Curriculum." Retrieved from http://cyberschoolbus.un. org/ on May 18, 2010.
44 Ibid., p. 43.
45 United Nations, "Millennium Development Goals." Retrieved from http:// www.un.org/millenniumgoals/education.shtml on May 18, 2010.
46 UNESCO, "Education for all (EFA) International Coordination: The Six EFA Goals and MDGs." Retrieved from http://portal.unesco.org/education/ en/ev.phpURL_ID=53844&URL_DO=DO_TOPIC&URL_SECTION=201 .html on October 5, 2007.
47 UNESCO, "Education for All (EFA) International Coordination: The EFA Movement." Retrieved from http://portal.unesco.org/education/en/ ev.phpURL_ID=54370&URL_DO=DO_TOPIC&URL_SECTION=201. html on October 5, 2007.
48 UNESCO, "Education for All (EFA) International Coordination: Mechanisms Involving International Organizations." Retrieved from http:// portal.unesco.org/education/en/ev.php-URL_ID=47539&URL_DO=DO_ TOPIC&URL_SECTION=201.html on October 5, 2007.
49 UNESCO, "Education for All (EFA) International Coordination: Collective Consultation of NGOs." Retrieved from http://portal.unesco.org/ education/en/ev.php-URL_ID=47477&URL_DO=DO_TOPIC&URL_ SECTION=201&reload=114567740 on October 5, 2007.
50 The Millennium Assembly of the United Nations, "United Nations Millennium Declaration." Retrieved from http://www.un.org/millennium/ on May 18, 2010.

51 World Bank, "Millennium Development Goals." Retrieved from http://ddp-ext.worldbank.org/ext/GMIS/gdmis.do?siteId=2&menuId=LNAV01HOM E1 on May 18, 2010.
52 World Bank, "Millennium Development Goals: Goal 2." Retrieved from http://ddp-ext.worldbank.org/ext/GMIS/gdmis.do?siteId=2&goalId=6& menuId=LNAV01GOAL2 on May 18, 2010.
53 World Bank, "Millennium Development Goals: Goal 3." Retrieved from http://ddp-ext.worldbank.org/ext/GMIS/gdmis.do?siteId=2&goalId= 7&menuId=LNAV01GOAL3 on May 18, 2010.
54 Ibid.
55 See Philip Kasinitz, John Mollenkopf, Mary Waters, and Jennifer Holdaway, *Inheriting the City: The Children of Immigrants Come of Age* (Cambridge, MA: Harvard University Press, 2008).
56 Brian Keeley, *Human Capital: How What You Know Shapes Your Life* (Paris: OECD Publishing, 2007), p. 45.
57 Ibid., p. 103.
58 Ibid., p. 22.
59 United Nations, Department of Economic and Social Affairs, Population Division, *United Nations Expert Group Meeting on Population Distribution, Urbanization, Internal Migration and Development New York, 21–23 January 2008* (New York: United Nations, 2008), p. 3.
60 Ibid., p. 3.
61 Ibid., pp. 5–9.
62 See Phillip Martin, "Migrants in the Global Labor Market"; and John Parker, "International Migration Data Collection." Both papers were prepared for the policy analysis and research program of the Global Commission on International Migration and were utilized in the Report of the Global Commission on International Migration, *Migration in an Interconnected World: New Directions for Action* (Geneva: Global Commission on International Migration, 2005).
63 Report of the Global Commission on International Migration, p. vii.
64 Martin, "Migrants in the Global Labor Market," p. 7.
65 United Nations, Department of Economic and Social Affairs, Population Division, *Trends in Total Migrant Stock: The 2005 Revision* (New York: United Nations Population Division, 2006), p. 1.
66 Ibid., p. 2.
67 Ibid., p. 3.
68 Ibid.
69 Ibid., p. 2.
70 OECD, *International Migration Outlook: Annual Report 2007 Edition* (Paris: OECD, 2007), p. 39.
71 Ibid., p. 38.
72 Annie Vinokur, "Brain Migration Revisited," *Globalisation, Societies and Education*, 4(1) (2006), pp. 7–24.
73 Report of the Global Commission on International Migration, p. 31.
74 R. Jiaojiao, "The Turning Tide," *China Daily* (May 30, 2007), p. 20.
75 Susan Robertson, "Editorial: Brain Drain, Brain Gain and Brain Circulation," *Globalisation, Societies and Education*, 4(1) (2006), pp. 1–5.
76 Caglar Ozden and Maurice Schiff, "Overview," in *International Migration, Remittances and the Brain Drain*, edited by Caglar Ozden and Maurice Schiff (Washington, DC: World Bank, 2006), p. 11.
77 Robertson, "Editorial: Brain Drain, Brain Gain and Brain Circulation," pp. 1–5.

78 Frederic Docquier and Abdeslam Marfouk, "International Migration by Educational Attainment, 1990–2000," in *International Migration, Remittances and the Brain Drain*, pp. 175–185.
79 See Devesh Kapur and John McHale, *Give Us Your Best and Brightest: The Global Hunt for Talent and Its Impact on the Developing World* (Washington, DC: Center for Global Development, 2005).
80 Ibid., pp. 25–29.
81 Ibid., p. 17.
82 Vinokur, "Brain Migration Revisited."
83 Kapur and McHale, *Give Us Your Best and Brightest*, pp. 21–22.
84 Richard Adams, "Remittances and Poverty in Guatemala," in *International Migration, Remittances and the Brain Drain*, pp. 53–80; and Jorge Mora and J. Edward Taylor, "Determinants of Migration, Destination, and Sector Choice: Disentangling Individual, Household, and Community Effects," in *International Migration, Remittances and the Brain Drain*, pp. 21–52.
85 O. Stark, "Rethinking the Brain Drain," *World Development*, 32(1) (2004), pp. 15–22.
86 Maurice Schiff, "Brain Gain: Claims about Its Size and Impact on Welfare and Growth Are Greatly Exaggerated," in *International Migration, Remittances and the Brain Drain*, p. 202.
87 Ibid., p. 203.
88 Vinokur, "Brain Migration Revisited," p. 20.
89 Educate, Inc., "About Us." Retrieved from http://www.educateinc.com/aboutus.html on July 15, 2007.
90 Ibid.
91 Ibid.
92 Ibid.
93 Ibid.
94 Ibid.
95 Ibid.
96 Laureate Education Inc., "About Laureate." Retrieved from http://www.laureate-inc.com on July 12, 2007.
97 Laureate Education Inc., "Global Post-Secondary Education Market." Retrieved from http://www.laureate-inc.com/GPSEM.php on July 15, 2007.
98 Laureate Education Inc., "Investors Relations: News and Information. University of Liverpool and Laureate International Universities Announce Expanded International Collaboration." Retrieved from http://phx.corporate-ir.net/phoenix.zhtml?c=91846&p=irol-newsArticle&ID=993862 & highlight= on July 12, 2007.
99 Goldie Blumenstyk, "The Chronicle Index of For-Profit Higher Education," *Chronicle of Higher Education* (August 17, 2007). Retrieved from http://chronicle.com/weekly/v54/i11/fptest.htm on January 18, 2007.
100 Bertelsmann, "Corporate Divisions." Retrieved from http://www.bertelsmann.com on July 8, 2007; HCIRN, "Human–Computer Interaction Resource Network." Retrieved from http://www.hcirn.com on July 13, 2007; HCIRN, "Kluwer Academic Publishers." Retrieved from http://www.hcirn.com/res/kap.php on July 13, 2007; Informa, "About." Retrieved from http://www.informa.com on July 14, 2007; Informa, "Divisions: Taylor and Francis." Retrieved from http://www.informa.com/corporate/divisions/academic_scientific/taylor_francis.htm on July 14, 2007; Holtzbrinck Publishers, "Who We Are." Retrieved from http://www.holtzbrinckus.com/about/about_who.asp on July 13, 2007; Pearson Education, "About Pearson Education." Retrieved from http://www.pearsoned.com on July 16,

2007; Reed Elsevier, "About Us." Retrieved from http://www.reed-elsevier.com on July 17, 2007; McGraw-Hill Companies, "Education. Financial Services. Information & Media." Retrieved from http://www.mcgraw-hill.com on July 13, 2007; Thomson, "About Scientific." Retrieved from http:// scientific.thomson.com/aboutus on July 13, 2007.

101 Bertelsmann: Media Worldwide, "One Company—Six Divisions." Retrieved from http://www.bertelsmann.com/bertelsnann_corp/wms41/brn/ index.php?ci=99&language=2 on January 6, 2008.

102 HCIRN, "Kluwer Academic Publishers." Retrieved from http://www.hcirn.com/res/kap.php on July 13, 2007.

103 Verlagsgruppe Georg Von Holtzbrinck, "The Company." Retrieved from http://www.holtzbrinck.com/artikle/778433&s=en on January 7, 2008.

104 Holtzbrinck Publishers, "Employment Opportunities." Retrieved from http://www.holtzbrinckusa-jobs.com on January 7, 2008.

105 Informa, "Divisions: Taylor and Francis."

106 Pearson, "Live and Learn." Retrieved from http://www.pearson.com on January 7, 2008.

107 Pearson, "About Us." Retrieved from http://www.pearson.com/index.cfm?pageid=2 on January 7, 2008.

108 Pearson Vue, "About Pearson VUE: Company History." Retrieved from http://www.pearsonvue.com/about/history on January 9, 2008.

109 Pearson Vue, "Welcome to the New Pearson Vue." Retrieved from http://www.pearsonvue.com on January 9, 2008.

110 Pearson Vue, "Pearson VUE Renews Global Test Delivery Contract with Association for Financial Professionals." Retrieved from http://www.pearsonvue.com/about/release/07_12_17_afp.asp on January 9, 2008.

111 Pearson Vue, "Kaplan Test Prep and Admissions and Pearson VUE Renew Exclusive Agreement to Deliver GMAT Ultimate Practice Test." Retrieved from http://www.pearsonvue.com/about/release/07_12_17_Kaplan.asp on January 9, 2008.

112 McGraw-Hill Companies, "About Us, Overview." Retrieved from http://www.mcgraw-hill.com/about us/overview.shtml on January 8, 2008.

113 McGraw-Hill Companies, "Information & Media, Overview." Retrieved from http://www.mcgraw-hill.com/ims/default.shtml on January 8, 2008.

114 McGraw-Hill Companies, "Education, Overview." Retrieved from http://www.mcgraw-hill.com/edu/default.shtml on January 8, 2008.

115 Thomas Wailgum, "Testing 1, 2, 3: Kurt Landgraf of ETS Has All the Right Answers," Continental (January, 2008), p. 59.

116 ETS (2007), "ETS Global." Retrieved from http://www.ets.org/portal/site/ets/menuitrn.435c0bd0ae7015d9510c3921509/?vgnextoid=d04b253b164f4010VgnVCM10000022f95190RCRD on July 12, 2007.

117 ETS, "ETS Global." Retrieved from http://www.ets.org on January 7, 2008.

118 ETS, "News: G2nd Systems Group Named ETS Preferred Vendor." Retrieved from http://www.ets.org/portal/site/ets/menuitem.c988ba0e5dd572bada20bc47c3921509/?vgnextoid=aacabafbdc86110VgnVCM10000022f9510RCRD&vgnextchannel= on January 8, 2008.

119 G2ndSystems, "News & Press Releases." Retrieved from http://www.g2nd.com/public_systems?News%20and%20Press%20Releases.thm on January 8, 2008.

120 G2ndSystems, "Intercultural English—A New Global Tool." Retrieved from http://www.g2nd.com/public_systems/courses/Intercultural%20 English %20A%20New%20Global%20Tool.htm on January 8, 2008.

121 Ibid.

122 See Joel Spring, *Globalization of Education: An Introduction* (New York: Routledge, 2009), for a discussion of the global competing educational ideologies.
123 For a discussion of global language competition see Joel Spring, *How Educational Ideologies Are Shaping Global Society: Intergovernmental Organizations, NGOS, and the Decline of the Nation-State* (Mahwah, NJ: Lawrence Erlbaum, 2005), pp. 168–174.

Chapter 9

Political Control of Education in a Democratic Society
Proposal for Amendment to U.S. Constitution

In Chapter 1 I listed questions to aid the reader in analyzing educational politics and policies. These questions included ones about citizens' decisions regarding representation at all levels of government and direct votes on referenda. Presumably there is a relationship between what a voter knows and the quality of their decisions at the voting booth and in trying to influence representatives. I have rephrased some of the questions asked in Chapter 1 so that they directly pertain to preparing citizens to make knowledgeable political decisions:

• What knowledge is important to teach so that citizens can make knowledgeable political decisions?
• What are the best instructional methods for preparing students to make knowledgeable political decisions?

Freedom of ideas is a key factor in answering the first question. As I have discussed throughout this book, politicians and special interest groups want the schools to teach ideas that support their ideological positions and support their continued power. In other words, the politics of education can be considered a struggle for the minds of future voters. In a democratic society school systems should be structured so that no single citizen or group is able to control what is taught in schools. In other words, freedom of ideas is an essential component of democratic school-ing. Of course, freedom of ideas in school must be limited by potential threats to public security. This educational freedom with limitations is exemplified in the Convention on the Rights of the Child adopted in 1989 by the General Assembly of the United Nations. Article 13, Section 1 of the Convention states:

> The child shall have the right to freedom of expression; this right shall include freedom to seek, receive and impart information and ideas of all kinds, regardless of frontiers, either orally, in writing or in print, in the form of art, or through other media of the child's choice.[1]

The limitations on this freedom are given in Section 2 of Article 13:

The exercise of this right may be subject to certain restrictions, but these shall be such as are provided by law and are necessary:

a. For respect of the rights or reputations of others; or
b. For the protection of national security or public order (*ordre public*), or of public health or morals.[2]

In recent years protecting freedom of ideas and exercising democratic control of the curriculum have become problematic because of federal requirements that states create curriculum standards and standardized tests for all public schools. In addition, there is a continuing effort to create national standards and tests that will be benchmarked to international tests. This process of state, national, and global benchmarking undermines democratic control of what is taught in U.S. public schools by removing decision-making from the control of the ordinary citizen. How does the ordinary U.S. voter participate in determining the content of global tests like PISA, PIRLS, and TIMSS?

By prescribing what knowledge is to be taught, curriculum standards can undermine students' "freedom to seek, receive and impart information and ideas of all kinds, regardless of frontiers, either orally, in writing or in print, in the form of art, or through other media of the child's choice." If teachers teach to the test, these freedoms are further restricted. If teachers use packaged or scripted lessons then both the teacher and student are restricted in their "freedom to seek, receive and impart information and ideas of all kinds."

In the dominant paradigm of human capital education, the dissemination of knowledge is linked to giving individuals credentials for entry into the labor market. Does this mean simply teaching behaviors, skills, and knowledge for the workplace? What about the critical thinking and political knowledge needed for active citizenship in a democratic society? Could the emphasis on preparing students for the global knowledge economy undermine education for a democratic society?

For a free society to exist, I would argue, the free dissemination of ideas and information is required. For equal opportunity to exist, schooling must not be used to give some individuals a privileged position in the labor market, while reducing the ability of other individuals to compete. There are certain elements in the current political structure that inhibit the free flow of ideas and information through schools and allow certain individuals to gain privileges over others. Included in these elements is the effect of globalization on national systems of schooling. In summary, these elements include:

1. The problem of majoritarian control
2. The power of special interest groups
3. The political use of schools
4. The economics of education
5. Global changes in the nation-state

The Problem of Majority Rule

Majoritarian control of American education does not exist. However, the idea continues to influence those wanting democratic control of the schools. Under majoritarian control, a majority of the people determine what knowledge is of most worth. The problem with majority control is that minority viewpoints regarding politics, culture, and social organization are excluded from the curriculum. Thus the parameters of political dialogue are narrowed, and political learning is reduced to consensus values.

Rather than being arenas for the free exchange of political ideas, the public schools are institutions for the imposition of values and ideas that do not offend most people. Horace Mann, the father of the American common school, predicted this outcome. Mann argued that political controversy, including controversial ideas, had to be excluded from common schools because including them would cause warring public factions to destroy the schools.[3]

Ironically, therefore, democratic, or majoritarian, control of public schools limits the free political dialogue that is necessary for the maintenance of a free society. Thus, democratic control of public schools could be said to contain the seeds of destruction of a democratic society.

On the other hand, some people argue that the limitation of political dialogue by democratically controlled schools creates political and social stability. From this perspective, narrowing the parameters of political dialogue reduces the possibility of political conflict. Some people might argue that this places necessary curbs on the potential for democratic societies to create excessive political activity.

There are sharp differences in concepts of citizenship. Some people believe that a wide-ranging political dialogue is necessary for maintaining a democratic society. Others believe that limiting such dialogue is essential for political stability. One side wants the schools to produce active citizens who have the intellectual tools to participate in democratic control. The other side wants citizens who are educated to obey the law and assume the responsibilities of government. One group emphasizes an active concept of citizenship; the other, a passive concept.

Political philosopher Amy Gutmann believes that the free flow of ideas in public schools is essential for the maintenance of a democratic society. Consequently, she argues for the principle of nonrepression as a guiding standard for public schools in the United States: "The principle of nonrepression prevents the state, and any group within it, from using education to restrict rational deliberation of competing conceptions of the good life and the good society."[4]

I agree with the importance of nonrepression for a democratic society. However, I do not agree with Gutmann's proposal for ensuring non-repression in U.S. schools. She believes that teachers' professionalism is important for maintaining nonrepression in schools. She wants teachers to assume a professional responsibility to maintain the principle of nonrepression and cultivate democratic deliberation in the classroom.

How does one ensure that teachers will assume the professional responsibility of upholding the principle of nonrepression in schools? Gutmann's answer is teachers unions. She writes, "The principle of nonrepression defines the democratic purpose of teachers' unions: to pressure democratic communities to create the conditions under which teachers can cultivate [a] critical reflection on democratic culture."[5] In fact, she considers upholding the principle of nonrepression as the democratic concept of professionalism in American schools.

I would like for teachers and teachers unions to uphold a principle of nonrepression but the reality is that teachers do not have that type of power under the current political system. Freedom of expression in the classroom is limited by the power of school administrators; curricula mandated by state governments and school boards; pressures from special interest groups; activities of politicians; standardized testing; and mandated textbooks. Teachers unions do sometimes attempt to protect classroom activities, but their primary concern is with wages and working conditions.

How can Gutmann's principle of nonrepression be incorporated into the public school system? One way to ensure freedom of ideas in school is through an amendment to the U.S. Constitution. This amendment could give courts the power to protect the exercise of the principle of nonrepression. However, it would appear that restrictions on freedom of ideas in schools will increase, and schools will continue to function as ideological managers.

The Power of Special Interest Groups

Despite discussions of majoritarian control, this book demonstrates that public schools are battlegrounds for groups seeking to have knowledge serve their interests. Important are the continual attempts by business interests to shape the schools to meet their economic needs. Since the late twentieth century, business interests have assumed ever greater control of state educational policies. The educational goal of preparing citizens for participation in a democracy has been replaced by preparation for employment.

In keeping with an economic system based on the pursuit of profit, business interests are primarily concerned that public schools serve their needs. But business groups are often preoccupied with short-range goals, and one of their overriding concerns is to reduce employment costs to increase profits. The short-range economic goals of business cause constant changes in educational policies. One needs only to contrast the major goals of schooling in the 1970s with those of the early twenty-first century. The 1960s War on Poverty was replaced by demands for education to prepare students to compete in the global economy.

Economic predictions about future employment needs are unreliable. The Vietnam War in the 1960s, the energy crisis of the 1970s, international competition in the late twentieth and early twenty-first centuries, and the economic crash in 2008 are some of the unforeseen factors that have shaped the U.S. labor market. It is difficult for economists to predict future events and include them in long-range economic forecasting.

Therefore, educational goals derived from projected economic needs could actually have a negative impact on students. Consider a situation that might have occurred for many students in the 1950s and early 1960s: A student enters the first grade in 1955 at a time when business is proclaiming a shortage of scientists and engineers. The student remains in school, including college, for approximately sixteen years. However, economic conditions change dramatically during this time. The student graduates from college in 1971, near the end of the Vietnam War and the beginning of the energy crisis, just when the demand for scientists and engineers is at its lowest. Consequently, the student cannot find a job.[6]

A student's future career can be damaged not only by educational goals derived from predicted labor market needs but also by the desire of business interests to reduce labor costs. If labor costs follow the law of supply and demand, then business has to be interested in maintaining a large labor supply to keep wages and salaries down. In fact, business is in the most advantageous position regarding labor costs when there is an oversupply of workers in needed job categories.

When business interests claim that there is a shortage of trained workers in a particular job category, it may be because they are being forced to pay higher salaries. In other words, business interests, feeling the impact of increasing wage costs, might declare a shortage of workers in order to ultimately reduce those costs. The public schools might respond by training more workers, and the labor market might be flooded with workers trained for that particular job category, which in turn might cause salaries and labor costs to decrease.

It is difficult to determine to what degree the declared shortage of scientists and engineers in the 1950s and 1980s was the result of business feeling the pressure of increased labor costs. One could hypothesize the following scenario. In the 1950s, business interests, in reaction to increasing costs for engineers and scientists, put pressure on the schools to increase training in those areas. As a result, the labor market was flooded with scientists and engineers by the late 1960s, which drove down salaries and labor costs. Consequently, business stopped pressuring the schools for training in those areas, and, because of reduced salaries and employment problems, fewer students chose to enter those fields. As a result, by the early 1980s the supply of engineers and scientists was low, and business, beginning to experience rising labor costs in those areas, again pressured the schools to emphasize science and mathematics.

Of course, business is not the only interest group seeking to have the schools serve its needs. Powerful interest groups other than business influence education policy, such as teachers unions, civil rights groups, politically conservative and right-wing religious organizations, and a whole host of other organizations. Protecting the schools from these pressures is as difficult as ensuring the principle of nonrepression. One possible solution is to make public schooling, through a constitutional amendment, the fourth branch of government, with the same protection from outside influences that is given to the Supreme Court and the Federal Reserve Bank.

Obviously, no branch of government can be completely free of outside influences. The Supreme Court is politicized by the process by which its members are appointed. The administration in power fills vacant seats on the Supreme Court with justices attuned to the administration's political philosophy. The same is true of the Federal Reserve. While complete freedom from outside influences is impossible, a structure could be created that would minimize the influence of special interest groups. In addition, this new branch of government could be organized to protect and support the free expression of ideas.

Like the proposal for an amendment to ensure the principle of nonrepression, making public schools a fourth branch of government does not seem very likely. The reality is that business and other interest groups want to keep the school doors open to outside pressures. In the present climate, it appears most likely that public schools will continue to serve the interests of those with the most power or groups actively pursuing a particular education agenda.

The Political Use of Schools

The education system is in constant change as a result of pressures from elected politicians and educational politicians. Continual change creates unknown costs that never seem justified by the results. Education, despite endless new programs, has not eliminated poverty, solved problems of national defense, ended unemployment, or resolved any of the other social problems foisted on the schools. Some might argue that because of the constant state of change, the schools never have sufficient time to solve any single economic or social problem. The goals of the system change so swiftly that nothing is ever given a chance to work. On the other hand, it could be argued that schools cannot solve major social and economic problems. From this perspective, it is not that the schools fail, but that they truly do not have the power to reform society and save the economic system.

Measuring the economic costs of changes in education is a complex job. At the federal level, one has to consider the actual costs of developing and implementing new programs, along with the money spent on the programs themselves. The same is true at state and local levels. Each change in national and state educational goals breeds a new crop of administrators in state departments of education and the central offices of local school systems.

There are also the costs of financing the research programs that usually accompany each new direction in national and state education policies. One cost is the funding of the great army of educational researchers who inhabit colleges of education around the country and whose professional lives depend on each swing of the policy pendulum. It would certainly be interesting to do a cost effectiveness study to see whether educational research has improved student learning. For instance, has all the money spent on reading research since the 1950s produced any improvement in students' reading skills?

Often, educators are the last to admit that schools cannot solve the world's problems. It is in the interests of educators and educational researchers to accept and promote the idea of schooling being a panacea for society's problems. By doing so, educators can demand more financial support and can enhance their feelings of self-worth.

One difficult solution is limiting educators' perspectives on what schools can accomplish. In addition, politicians and the public must be convinced that schools are not a panacea for social and economic problems. The propensity of politicians constantly to turn to schools as politically safe solutions to social and economic problems makes it difficult to change images of schools as a means of social improvement. Educators will probably continue to boast about the social power of schooling. Consequently, schools will continually be tied to policy goals.

Education Amendment to U.S. Constitution

In recent years I have advocated an education amendment to the U.S. Constitution.[7] This is hardly a radical idea since most national constitutions written after World War II contain an educational rights article. When the U.S. Constitution was written, schooling was not a major concern. Consequently, education has never been considered a right in the United States. As a result, the issue of inequality of educational opportunity has never been completely resolved, particularly in school finance cases. The United States Constitution provides no way of rectifying the problem of equal educational opportunity without the addition of an amendment guaranteeing an equal right to an education. Without any guaranteed right to education, federal and state governments cannot be required to ensure equal resources for education. This was the decision of the U.S. Supreme Court in its famous 1973 decision, Rodriguez v. San Antonio Independent School District. As I discussed in Chapter 7, state courts and legislatures throughout the United States have engaged in struggles over providing equal financing of public school students.

The unequal funding of education is particularly problematic in a society that considers schooling a means for ensuring equality of opportunity. At the time of the writing of the U.S. Constitution, the ideology of equality of opportunity through schooling was not dominant. If it had been, the writers of the Constitution might have added an Article providing for the right to equal education.

There are several dimensions to ensuring equality of educational opportunity. First is family wealth. Any constitutional provision must recognize the ability of wealthy families to purchase superior educational advantages for their children. The second issue is the child's access to adequate nutrition, shelter, particularly for homeless children, and medical care. These are necessary conditions for receiving an adequate education. Thirdly, there is the issue of making higher education free to all.

At best the constitutional right to education can only ensure equal access to educational institutions regardless of a child's economic circumstances. Realistically, even with provisions for financial aid and protection of children's welfare, complete equality of educational opportunity cannot be achieved. There are so many variables, including differences in peer groups, access to cultural institutions, the culture of families, and even geographical location, such as rural versus urban living. Therefore, the best that can be hoped for is maximizing the chance of achieving equality of educational opportunity. There is also the issue of school financing regarding how much money should be spent on schooling.

The following constitutional provision would help increase the chances for achieving equality of educational opportunity and provide some guidelines for how much should be spent on education:

1. Everyone has the right to receive an education.
2. Primary, secondary, and higher education shall be free.
3. Primary and secondary education shall be compulsory until the age of 16. The government will ensure through financial assistance, scholarships, or other means that no one is denied an education or

access to an educational institution because of lack of financial resources including resources for food, shelter, and medical care.

4. Except in time of war, total government funds allocated for education should always exceed the total of government funds allocated for the military, weapons research, and other forms of defense spending.

In addition to concerns about equality of educational opportunity, there is the relationship between Gutmann's nonrepression of ideas in the classroom and the functioning of a democratic society. With so many groups trying to ensure that their brands of the truth are disseminated through schools it is very difficult to maintain freedom of ideas in the classroom, particularly for teachers. Therefore, I would argue, an important part of any educational amendment would be protection of the freedom of teachers to choose the methods and classroom materials to fulfill the requirements of their school's curricula guidelines. In addition, as already noted regarding the Convention on the Rights of the Child, such an amendment should include protection of students' freedom of expression including the "freedom to seek, receive and impart information and ideas of all kinds, regardless of frontiers."

There should also be the right of parents to exert some control over what their children are taught. This is particularly important regarding political and religious values. Freedom of ideas requires a diversity of ideas to think about, otherwise freedom of thought is meaningless. Family values are important for maintaining this diversity. Some public school advocates want parental values to be overridden in favor of teaching children ideas that are determined by the governance structure of schools. It is important from this standpoint that parental cultural values are recognized by the educational system.

The Establishment Clause of the First Amendment to the U.S. Constitution has made it difficult to provide public financing of religious-based schools. However, Article 18 of the Universal Declaration of Human Rights provides the right to have religious beliefs reflected in "teaching" while at the same time recognizing the right to change religions. Article 18 states:

Everyone has the right to freedom of thought, conscience and religion; this right includes freedom *to change* his religion or belief, and freedom, either alone or in community with others and in public or private, to manifest his religion or belief in *teaching*, practice, worship and observance [author's emphasis].[8]

A model for recognizing parental religious values in school choice is the 1950 European Convention which was incorporated into the Treaty for the European Union. Currently, the European Union includes within its jurisdiction a variety of religions including Christianity and Islam. The Convention declares, "the State shall respect the right of parents to ensure such education and teaching in conformity with their own religious and philosophical convictions."[9]

To ensure freedom for the teacher in the classroom, protect the right of students to freedom of expression and the right to explore any source of knowledge that does not endanger public safety, and the right of parents to choose an education for their children that reflects their cultural and religious or philosophical values, I would propose the following additions to be included in my proposed constitutional amendment:

1. Teachers in all government-operated schools will have the academic freedom to choose the methods of instruction and class materials to implement curriculum requirements.
2. Teachers in government-operated schools will protect the right of their students to freedom of expression and the right to knowledge that does not threaten public safety.
3. The right to an education includes the right to a secular or religious education financed by the government. No student will be forced to receive a religious education.
4. The duty and right to an education includes the right of parents to choose a government-financed school based on their philosophical convictions and cultural values as long as that school does not advocate or teach anything that violates rights granted in the Universal Declaration of Human Rights. The exercise of this right is dependent on enough parents making the same choice based on philosophical convictions and/or cultural values to make it financially feasible for the government to operate the school.
5. The right of the parents to choose a government-financed school based on their philosophical convictions and/or cultural values includes the right for their philosophical convictions and/or cultural values to be reflected in the content and methods of instruction.

Language rights are an important issue in the United States given its multilingual population. Frequently, language rights are ignored or suppressed in the interest of making English the dominant language. Language rights are an important educational issue. Educational equality is difficult when classroom instruction is presented in a language that is different from the family language of the student. In this circumstance, the student is at a disadvantage compared to pupils whose home language is the same as the language of instruction. There is also the issue of minority language rights. Destruction of a language can contribute to the destruction of a culture. Therefore, minority languages should be recognized and supported by the school. On the other hand, students from minority language families need to learn the dominant language of their country if they are going to have equal political and economic opportunities.

To rectify the rapid disappearance of many of the world's languages, Tove Skutnabb-Kangas proposes "A Universal Covenant of Linguistic Human Rights":

> Everybody has the right to identify with their mother tongue(s) and to have this identification accepted and respected by others, to learn the mother tongue(s) fully, orally (when physiologically possible) and in writing, to education mainly through the medium of their mother tongue(s), and within the state-financed educational system to use the mother tongue in most official situations (including schools).[10]

Skutnabb-Kangas' Covenant does recognize the importance of instruction for all students in the official or dominant language of a nation. The Covenant would require nations to recognize and support instruction in minority languages while maintaining their official languages.

There is a problem in guaranteeing educational rights for minority languages when there are only a limited number of students speaking a particular language. This is a problem in a country with a high number of immigrants. Should the government be required to provide classes in a mother tongue that is spoken by only one or two students in a community? Some requirement must be added that this right can only be exercised when there are enough students speaking the same minority language to make it economically feasible to operate classrooms in that minority language. Considering the realistic problems associated with language rights, I would add the following to my proposed constitutional amendment:

1. Everyone has a right to an education using the medium of their mother tongue within a government-financed school system when the number of students requesting instruction in that mother tongue equals the average number of students in a classroom in that government-financed school system.
2. Everyone has the right to learn the dominant or official language of the nation. The government-financed school system will make every effort to ensure that all students are literate in the dominant or official language of the country.

Obviously, any proposed amendment to the U.S. Constitution would generate a great deal of debate that would change my initial proposal. However, it is time for the Constitution to guarantee the right to an education. Below is my proposal to amend the Constitution to ensure equality of educational opportunity, a public school system that fosters freedom of ideas and debate essential for the functioning of a democratic society, the right of parents to have the education of their children reflect their cultural and religious values, and protection of linguistic rights.

Proposed Education Amendment to the U.S. Constitution

1. Everyone has the right to receive an education.
2. Primary, secondary, and higher education shall be free.
3. Primary and secondary education shall be compulsory until the age of 16. The government will ensure through financial assistance, scholarships, or other means that no one is denied an education or access to an educational institution because of lack of financial resources including resources for food, shelter, and medical care.
4. Except in time of war, total government funds allocated for education should always exceed the total of government funds allocated for the military, weapons research, and other forms of defense spending.
5. Teachers in all government-operated schools will have the academic freedom to choose the methods of instruction and class materials to implement curriculum requirements.
6. Teachers in government-operated schools will protect their students' right of freedom of expression and the right to knowledge that does not threaten public safety.
7. The right to an education includes the right to a secular or religious education financed by the government. No student will be forced to receive a religious education.
8. The duty and right to an education includes the right of parents to choose a government-financed school based on their philosophical convictions and cultural values as long as that school does not advocate or teach anything that violates rights granted in the Universal Declaration of Human Rights. The exercise of this right is dependent on enough parents making the same choice based on philosophical convictions and/or cultural values to make it financially feasible for the government to operate the school.
9. The right of the parents to choose a government-financed school based on their philosophical convictions and/or cultural values includes the right for their philosophical convictions and/or cultural values to be reflected in the content and methods of instruction.
10. Everyone has a right to an education using the medium of their mother tongue within a government-financed school system when the number of students requesting instruction in that mother tongue equals the average number of students in a classroom in that government-financed school system.
11. Everyone has the right to learn the dominant or official language of the nation. The government-financed school system will make every

effort to ensure that all students are literate in the dominant or official language of the country.

Conclusion: Globalization and National Systems of Education

If current trends continue, then public schools will primarily serve the interests of business and the most active special interest groups influencing politicians; the curriculum will be narrowed and ideas will be restricted in the classroom by pressures from interest groups; and education will be in continual financial crisis. This is one reason why I am proposing an amendment to the U.S. Constitution.

One uncertain element is the future of national systems of education as the nation-state declines in the face of global trends. As I suggest in Chapter 8, the forces of globalization are resulting in the so-called reinvention of government which involves reducing government services and increasing government management of public sector activities. This is reflected in moves to privatize education while seeking to tighten controls through government standards and tests. Another factor is the role of a national system of education in forming citizens.

Schooling supports the political needs of the nation-state through educating and disciplining a loyal, patriotic citizenry imbued with nationalism and accepting the legitimacy of the state. A public school system strengthens a nation-state by culturally unifying sometimes multicultural and multilingual populations existing within its territorial boundaries. Citizens must be convinced of the validity of the state's territorial boundaries because they are politically constructed and might not reflect any meaningful geographical division. Also, a nation-state depends on citizens believing in the legitimacy of its government's organization and actions.

Consequently, public school systems serve the nation-state by creating a shared experience as students; developing a sense of nationhood and a common culture through teaching a national history and literature; instilling emotional loyalty to the nation-state through patriotic exercises, flag salutes, and nationalistic rhetoric and song; and educating a citizenry that accepts the legitimacy of the government and their own political role within the system. Also, the nation-state is built on a particular economic system which requires public schools to teach a commitment to maintaining that economic arrangement and training to fit into the economic infrastructure. In summary, the nation-state uses education to prepare disciplined citizens and workers.

Therefore, the citizenship education of national systems of schooling has severely restricted the free flow of ideas in the name of loyalty to the government. Most countries in the world restrict civic education to ideas and knowledge suitable for molding patriotic citizens. Will the decline of the nation-state and the reinvention of government support greater freedom of ideas in schools? Or will global standards and tests result in global uniformity and standardization of global school systems?

Notes

1 "Convention on the Rights of the Child," in *Basic Documents on Human Rights*, 3rd edn., edited by Ian Browne (Oxford: Oxford University Press, 1992), p. 187.
2 Ibid.
3 See Joel Spring, *The American School: A Global Context from the Puritans to the Obama Era*, 8th edn. (New York: McGraw-Hill, 2011), pp. 80–89.
4 Amy Gutmann, *Democratic Education* (Princeton: Princeton University Press, 1987), p. 76.
5 Ibid.
6 Spring, *The American School*, p. 362.
7 Joel Spring, *Globalization and Educational Rights: An Intercivilizational Analysis* (Mahwah, NJ: Lawrence Erlbaum, 2001).
8 "The Universal Declaration of Human Rights," in *Basic Documents on Human Rights*, 3rd edn., p. 25.
9 "European Convention on Human Rights and Its Five Protocols," in *Basic Documents on Human Rights*, 3rd edn., p. 342.
10 See Tove Skutnabb-Kangas, *Linguistic Genocide in Education or Worldwide Diversity and Human Rights?* (Mahwah, NJ: Lawrence Erlbaum, 2000), pp. 567–638.

Index

superintendents 68; in dominated
communities 72; in factional
communities 74; in inert
communities 75–76; in pluralistic
communities 75
supplementary education services
(SES) 5, 152, 172–174
Supreme Court 84, 118, 256
suspensions 38
Sweden 41
Switzerland 208
Sylvan Learning Centers 5, 150, 174,
175, 235, 236
Sylvan Learning Systems 237
symbolic analysts 209
syndical educational politics 58

Task Force on Teaching as a
Profession 97
taxation 186, 187, 190, 191, 194,
199, 202, 203, 209; abatements
204; amount needed for schools
12; concessions 204; law 84, 91,
95, 102
Taylor & Francis Group 237
teacher education programs 27
teachers: advanced degrees 5;
bilingual 2, 40, 44; deskilling 11;
evaluation 11, 26, 27, 33, 34, 88,
111, 112; freedom for 260; morale
38; political influence 60;
professionalism 254; quality 27;
reactions to financial crisis
197–198; recruitment 26, 66;
relationships with administrators
38; salaries 26, 30, 33, 34, 111,
145, 185, 195, 208; status 145;
training 66, 98, 134; views about
schools 30–35, 44
Teacher Working Condition Surveys
111
TEC Well Service 158
Technical and Vocational Education
and Training 78
teen pregnancies 92
TeloPhase 163
Templeton, John Jr. 101
Templeton Foundation 101
Tennessee 60
tertiary education 210
testing corporations xi, 5, 79, 150,
176, 243

Test of English as a Foreign Language
(TOEFL) 240
Test of English for Distance Education
(TEDE) 240
Test of English for International
Communication (TOEIC) 240
tests: alignment of curricula with 223;
and teacher evaluation 11, 26, 27,
33, 34, 88, 111, 112; global
216–219; high-stakes 5, 6, 43, 44,
67, 172, 177, 178; international 2,
12; mathematics 2, 52; media focus
on scores 20; science 2, 52;
standardized 2, 3, 32, 145, 191,
252
Texas: centralization in 60; rejection
of Race to the Top funding 65, 67;
social studies curriculum in 161;
textbook publishing in xi–xii, 154,
155–161
Texas Education Agency 155
Texas State Board of Education 154,
155, 158, 161, 165, 178
Texas State Textbook Committee
156
textbooks 153–161; government
expenditure on 4; mandated 11;
open-source 151, 153, 154
think tanks 78, 86, 87, 88; and
funding 88; and policy-making
102–108; and tax law 102;
conservative 102, 104;
distinguished from foundations 96;
influence 95, 96, 108; liberal 102,
103
Think Tanks, Public Policy, and the
Politics of Expertise 102
Thomas B. Fordham Institute 102,
123
Thomson (publishers) 237
thousand points of light speech 85,
86, 87
TIMSS, see Trends in International
Mathematics and Science Study
TOEFL, see Test of English as a
Foreign Language
TOEIC, see Test of English for
International Communication
Tor & Worth Publishers 237
Torreal S.A. 237
"town and gown" conflicts 74
trade associations 177

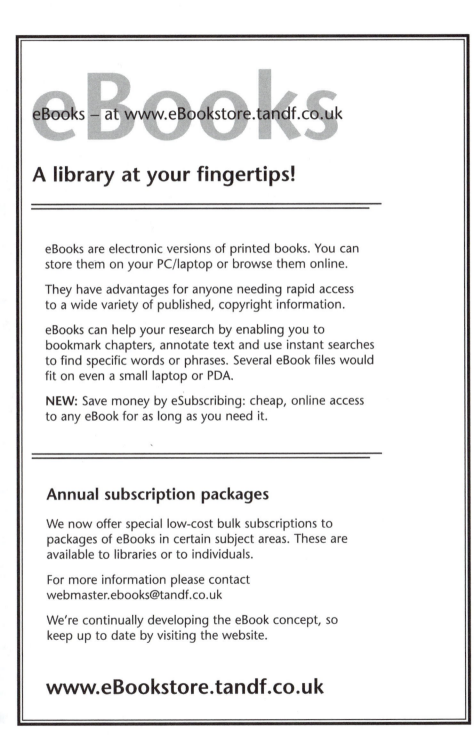